THE RUTHLESS GENE

SAM O'BRIEN

POOLBEG

Published 2021
by Poolbeg Press Ltd
123 Grange Hill, Baldoyle
Dublin 13, Ireland
E-mail: poolbeg@poolbeg.com
www.poolbeg.com

ISBN 978-1-78199-444-3

www.poolbeg.com

About the Author

Sam O'Brien grew up in Ireland surrounded by horses and has spent a working lifetime in thoroughbred racing and breeding.

At nineteen, Sam spent an almost malnourished year attempting to make it as an amateur jockey, before too much height and too little talent put an end to that dream.

Since then, Sam has worked on, or managed stud farms in Ireland, England, Turkey, America and Australia; trained racehorses in China; built a stud farm in Inner Mongolia and broken in wild horses in the sweltering Aussie outback.

Over the years, Sam has written analytical articles for several racing publications and loves nothing better than watching magnificent thoroughbred horses grow up to become tough, successful athletes.

The Ruthless Gene is Sam's third novel.

For Silla. In memory of Bill – the best mentor a teenager could have had.

Also by Sam O'Brien

A Sure Thing

The Mandarin Stakes

Chapter 1

Kildare Town
Ireland
2 October 2015

What lay in front of her on the desk could change her field of genetics forever. Fiona Buckley sat in her office, staring at her latest research results and the agreement from the development firm in America. She pondered the implications. Things would change for a lot of people. Owners, trainers, breeders, sales companies. Rich powerful people who might not appreciate such change. Johnny had always said to her that horse people tended to be set in their ways.

Johnny.

A flicker of sadness shadowed her eyes. She closed the files, stacked the discs and put the bundle beside her handbag. Exhausted, she stretched her willowy frame, picked up her things and turned out the light. As she walked down the narrow dark corridor, she saw the lights still on her secretary's office. Cocking her head round the door, she saw Maura putting documents and discs into the walk-in heatproof safe.

"It's far too late. You should be at home," said Fiona, leaning on the doorframe.

The trim woman looked up. "Just getting things squared away. That's the last of the back-ups inside." She swung the heavy door closed with a thud. Bolts clicked home.

"What would I do without you?" Fiona was lucky to have someone like Maura to deal with all the things that she neither liked nor had time for.

"I don't know at all," said Maura, a twinkle in her eyes. "You go on ahead, Doctor. I'll be out in a few minutes."

In the lobby, Fiona passed the elderly security guard. "Good evening, Ronan."

Ronan should have been retired years ago, but Fiona just couldn't bring herself to break it to him. Besides, it wasn't as if he had much to do during the long boring nights at Equigenes.

"How did your eldest grandson do in his rugby match?" she asked.

The ruddy-cheeked man lit up. "Played like a trooper. His coach thinks he's got potential."

"That's brilliant. Night, Ronan."

"Night, Doctor."

She shouldered the swinging door.

"Oh," he called, "mind how you go out there! The car-park light's not working."

"I'll be fine, thanks, Ronan."

She walked through the inky night to her car. As she placed the files on the back seat, her phone chimed. The screen said '**Private number**'.

"Hello?"

"Doctor Buckley," said a distorted voice.

"Who's this?"

"I know what the two of you have been up to and when I learn *how* it's being done – well, you will cease to be of any use to me or anyone else."

Fiona's face drained of colour. "Who *is* this? What're you on about?"

"No more games, Doctor Buckley."

The line went dead.

Fiona sat into her car and gripped the wheel to steady her hands. What on earth was that about?

She tried to put it out of her mind and focus on tomorrow's hospital visit. Sadness, regret and relief all tussled for dominance in her mind. Poor Johnny. No matter what had happened, he didn't deserve to die like this. Life had been unfair to him, maybe she had too. She had loved the man he used to be – a swaggering, optimistic terrier of a man. A genius on the back of a racehorse. Sure, he had a touch of hubris and a compulsive streak – what successful athlete didn't? She'd once thought she could soften that in him, and she probably would have. If it hadn't been for that fall. *That* ruined everything. She rubbed her reddening eyes and put the car in gear.

A few hours later, six shadowy forms slipped out of the research building into the moonless night. Each man lugged a canvas bag. They scanned the deserted industrial estate as they crossed the road and slid into a grey van.

The leader folded his muscular bulk into the passenger seat.

3

"Drive!" he barked.

The vehicle eased down the road and turned left into the darkness of the Curragh plains. In the rearview mirror, there was a single blinding flash. Then flames snaked high into the night sky.

The leader spoke into a burner phone. "We got the hard drives and emptied the safe."

"And covered your tracks?"

"It's burning as we speak."

There was a pause. "And the security guard?"

"Old fart got in the way, but the fire'll cover it up."

"I suppose these things can't be helped. Give everything to the tech people, then get out of the country. I'll contact you if I need you again."

"OK."

A few kilometres on, he tossed the phone out of the window.

Chapter 2

Johnny Buckley's pathetic frame was propped up with five pillows. He took laboured breaths and stared out the window at the overcast sky. His once muscled torso had shrivelled to match his useless legs. Forget lifting weights, he couldn't even sit in his wheelchair anymore. It didn't seem right that it would end like this. A hacking, guttural cough racked his whole body. His oxygen mask didn't help at all. It felt like a gag, but he was too weak to pull it away.

Johnny had realised a month ago that it was his own doing. Of all the stupid things he'd done over the years, this topped the lot. He tried to tell himself that he didn't regret a thing. Fuck it, he had to die sometime. Forty-three wasn't too young, not for a useless cripple. He fought to keep that notion shrouding his doubts but it wasn't working.

He turned his mind back to his father and the bees.

Dad, you were right, he thought, looking at the ceiling. *You knew there was something there before science copped on to it. And I proved you right.* "God help me," he mumbled. "God help us all. Maybe talk to you soon, Dad." His voice foundered and tears ran down his cheeks. Johnny had never been religious and he wasn't even sure that he was now, but he was desperate to believe that there was something to look forward to.

He recalled his riding days. Images and emotions of famous victories flashed through his brain, bringing a smile. All the magnificent horses he had partnered over the years. In his first life. Before paralysis and wheelchair bodybuilding. And the horsefeed company.

Down in the car park, Fiona wiped tears away and tried to apply a bit of make-up in the rearview mirror. Her hair was matted, her guts knotted and her eyes sunken and veined like roadmaps. She'd been up since three-thirty, dealing with police and firemen. Her lab was a smouldering ruin and poor old Ronan had perished in the blaze. The heatproof safe had been opened and the hard drives were gone.

And there had been that weird phone call. The voice had said *"the two of you"*. What on earth was she supposed to be up to with anyone else? She couldn't get her head around it. She had always published her results and given seminars about her findings. Her genetic tests and analyses were available to anyone who could pay the fees. Some of the biggest owners in racing were her major investors and they never stopped badgering her to create new tests. So why would anyone want to steal her hard drives and destroy her business, killing poor old Ronan in the process?

She glanced over her shoulder at the stack of files and discs on the back seat and felt very worried. No, it couldn't be. *Nobody* knew about that. She hadn't announced it yet. She hadn't even told Marcus about it.

On top of all this destruction, Johnny was dying of cancer. Part of her felt relieved: it would end the charade of their marriage and Johnny would be freed from his anger. But guilt needled her. She took a deep breath, got out, put the files and discs in the boot, locked the car and made for the clinic.

Inside, she was brought upstairs to meet the oncology consultant.

Dr. Frances Kinsella greeted her with a tight smile and serious eyes.

"Mrs. Buckley, please sit down. Coffee?"

Fiona declined the coffee. No medical doctor ever called Fiona *doctor* – it was as if she was not worthy because her field was equine genetics. Even an award acknowledging her achievements presented to her by the President of Ireland and the chief of the International Horse Genome Sequencing Project had done little to raise her profile. She clasped her hands on her knees and hoped this would be brief.

"I'm afraid we're at the end of the journey," said Dr. Kinsella. "The cancer is just too aggressive."

"How long?"

"As I said, we're at the end."

Fiona pursed her lips and stared at the floor. Fought

to keep her breathing slow and deep.

"Look, I wish there was something more we could do, but nobody here – or anyone I've consulted in Europe or America – has ever seen a case like it. In two months he went from being a healthy paraplegic – albeit one with abnormal muscle mass – to, well, as I said, we've *never* seen cancer dominate the body in this way, in this timeframe."

"I'll go and see him now," Fiona said, standing up. "Thank you for all you *did* do, Doctor."

The women shook hands.

Johnny dreamt of the year he won the Kentucky Derby on a horse of Pat McCormack's. Bronx Spirit had been the first foreign-trained horse to snatch the jewel of American racing – and he was Irish. Johnny remembered the winner's enclosure as he and Pat waved the tricolour at the television cameras.

The sound of the door snapped him back to reality.

Was that Fiona standing by the bed? Strange. Why had she bothered to come? He went to speak, but another hacking cough came out instead. He motioned towards the glass of water on the bedside locker. Fiona picked it up and guided the straw under his oxygen mask. He sucked the liquid into his aching mouth.

"Come to say your goodbyes?" he said, as she put the glass down.

Eyes down, she nodded.

Johnny looked at her. God, she was beautiful. What a firecracker! He loved her auburn hair and that mole on her cheek. Made her look like an old-fashioned movie star. When he'd been a champion jockey they'd been so happy together. Until the fall.

He looked at the door. "Is Marcus waiting outside?"

His wife went pale. "What?"

"*Relax*," he hissed. Then another cough. "I've known for years."

She looked dumbfounded.

"I just wanted to see if you'd have the guts to ..." he grimaced and grabbed at his temple like he wanted to reach inside his skull, "to leave a heroic cripple for the playboy trainer."

"Hero? You?" She exhaled sharply. "Obsessive-compulsive paranoid lunatic!"

Johnny ignored the jibe. After all, she was probably right. He squinted at her. She looked tired and haggard – he could swear her eyes were bloodshot.

"What's up? Don't tell me you've been crying over me?"

Shrugging, she chewed her lip. "My lab burned down this morning."

Johnny stared. "How? Was it an accident? Arson? Robbery?" His head pounded. He stared at the ceiling, tried to think through the haze of medication and realised he had to warn her. If her lab had been robbed, that meant they must be suspicious. He threw his eyes at the window for a second, wrestling with what to tell her. He didn't have the time or the energy to go into the details. She'd find *Endgame* eventually and she was easily smart enough to figure it all out. He returned his gaze to her.

"Listen, Fiona, you need to get to a safe place. The lab is only the beginning. They're going to come after

you and, believe me, they're capable of anything. They
–" Another hacking wet cough.

Fiona wobbled, grabbed the end of the bed. "What
did you say?"

Blood-spatters filled his mask and his head screamed
with pain. He pressed the call button in his right hand.
A nurse burst into the room.

Johnny pointed to his mask.

She removed it and wiped his face. "I'll get you a
new one."

"No," said Johnny, waving her away. "It's not like
it's going to change the result. I'm nearly at the line
now, and I just –" He coughed again. Spots of blood
stained the sheets.

"You need the oxygen," said the nurse.

"I need something for the pain. Please, I just want to
say goodbye to my wife."

The nurse left. Moments later a solemn doctor appeared
and fiddled with the morphine regulator on Johnny's drip.
He nodded to Fiona and left them alone.

Johnny began to float on a warm sea of delight. He
looked deep into Fiona's eyes and managed a goofy
smile. Her features softened a fraction.

He had to tell her more before he drifted into oblivion.
It was only fair.

"They're going to get you," he said.

Fiona rolled her eyes.

Johnny caught the look. Coughed. "Don't believe me
then."

Suddenly she looked ashen. "I had a threatening phone
call last night before the lab fire. Is that what you mean?"

Johnny's eyes rolled back briefly, he scratched his skeletal cheek. "You academics don't understand the real world, do you? Think you're a businesswoman – selling your tests and all, but – but – *buuu* ..." Everything was going dark. "Fiona, I ... was an asshole ..." His face twitched. "Not the first time, eh?" He rubbed his temple. "But, I was proved right ... and you could be right, you know that? So right, so, so ..." His eyes rolled up, showing her the whites. "Changed everything ... the fall ... " His eyes closed.

Fiona leaned over him. "*Right?* What about?" She took his hand in hers. Normally so tough and meaty, now it felt like her father's. "Johnny, *wake up!*"

The heart monitor slowed, then began speeding up.

Johnny's body convulsed, writhed and coughed. The monitors went wild, beeping and wailing. Fiona froze in shock and the nurse rushed in just as Johnny went still. She checked his pulse. Shook her head. Tight-lipped. Eyes down.

The tone of the flatlined heart-monitor cut the silence.

Chapter 3

Ten years earlier

Irish Derby Day 2005
The Curragh Racecourse

Johnny couldn't see her, even from his perch on the horse's back.

He told the groom to lead the horse on another lap of the parade ring. He frantically darted his eyes about, squinting in the sunshine. The crowd was a sea of colour, fancy hats and excited chatter. Where was she? Fiona always came racing at the weekends. Before big races she and Johnny had a ritual of making eye contact for luck as Johnny took his horse onto the track. Fiona teased him about his superstition, but she knew that all jockeys needed luck. That was why he always wore odd socks.

Then he saw her. Stunning in a simple silk dress. She pulled a strand of hair from her face. Johnny mouthed *Love you* and she winked at him: *Go for it, Johnny*. He promised himself that after the Derby he'd finally admit she was right – it was time to start a family.

Elegant Flaw's groom reached the gate to the track and calmly released the lead rope. Johnny collected up his reins and felt it straight away. The horse was like a coiled spring underneath him. Johnny willed his own muscles to relax and send calm vibes through his body as he eased the seething mass of raw energy underneath him into a jigging trot-canter. Tension strained the reins and his knuckles as the pair made their way across the Curragh plain to the starting stalls. Strange, because the horse had been calm and relaxed when he'd breezed him up the gallops last week.

By the time he got to the start, Johnny knew he'd have to use all his skill to keep the horse covered up in the race. If not, the beast would bolt for half a mile, fade out and struggle to get home in the first five. And that would make Johnny Buckley look foolish and inept. Out of the question. He knew he was on the best horse. He imagined he'd end up fighting out the finish with Equigene, Marcus Hamilton's steed. It would be good to see Equigene finish second and give Fiona's company a nice bit of publicity.

The starter called for the runners to be loaded. A helmeted stalls-handler beckoned Johnny. To his relief the horse loaded without a fuss. *Oh yes*. In a few seconds, he'd be on his way to another Irish Derby victory. It would be his first for Sheikh Abdul. If it all went to plan, the Sheikh would then want him to ride all his horses. Johnny wasn't going to sign a contract with the man, but riding the Sheikh's best horses would be a handy way out of his current predicament.

The stalls snapped open and fourteen runners erupted onto the turf. Elegant Flaw jumped into the race like his tail was on fire. Johnny fought hard to settle the colt, desperately trying to drop his hands and get the rippling mass of thoroughbred to relax, but the horse refused to comply and pulled hard. Johnny's arms strained as the colt careered ahead, broke out of the pack and loomed up on the pacemaker. Johnny looked at the lead horse's hindquarters and scowled. He couldn't believe his boss had expected him to ride *that* one-paced yoke after Fiscal Haven – winner of the Epsom Derby earlier in the month – pulled out of today's contest with a career-ending injury. Johnny Buckley didn't ride second strings and he hadn't ridden pacemaker duties since he was an apprentice. Now thirty-three, six times Irish champion, and winner of fifteen classics all over the world, he considered it insulting to ride a rank outsider just to save face for his boss. So when his agent called to tell him that he could have the ride on the second favourite, Johnny didn't hesitate.

In a final effort to control the wayward animal, Johnny clamped the reins down onto Elegant Flaw's withers, between the horse's neck and the saddle. With his reins bridged through his hands, the effect was like tying off a flapping rope on a sailboat. The more the horse pulled, the more it pulled against itself. Johnny's arms had a brief rest as his mount appeared to calm. Then the reins snapped back and the horse bolted. The broken bit dangled. Johnny lost his balance. Elegant Flaw crashed into the back of the pacemaker and Johnny's world blurred to black.

***

The crowd let out a collective gasp as the horse went down. Then the grandstands went eerily quiet as they watched twelve runners gallop over Johnny Buckley, crumpling him into the grass.

Up in his private viewing balcony, Pat McCormack leaned his bulk against the railing and watched the carnage through his binoculars. His own horse was lucky enough to be unaffected by Elegant Flaw crashing into its rear. It took the shunt and kept galloping along in the lead. The remaining runners turned into the long home straight, but Pat kept his eyes on Johnny's motionless body.

"Holy Mother of God. You just never know in this game, do you, Bill?" he said to his stud manager.

Bill's face was ashen.

The horses entered the final furlong, but the crowd stayed mute. Pat raised his binoculars and watched his horse hold on to the lead until the dying strides when Marcus Hamilton's homebred, Equigene, came from stone last to snatch victory.

Pat cursed and quietly drummed his meaty fingers on the railing. *Equigene.* Johnny Buckley's wife and Hamilton had set up a research company with that name two years before. Pat had thought it was just a vanity project so she could try to beat the American team and become the first to map the equine genome. So far, nobody had managed it, but last month Doctor Buckley had announced that she was on the verge of a major

15

breakthrough: the genome would soon be mapped and she would be able to predict whether a horse was more likely to be a precocious two-year-old or a late-maturing type. Pat and his trainer had laughed out loud at the news. Only idiots needed a test to figure that out. Hamilton had gone on record stating what a marvellous breakthrough it was – well, he would, wouldn't he? But now Pat wondered if that test would be the start of a revolution in breeding and selling racehorses.

He motioned for Bill to follow him inside.

"That bloody horse was by my stallion," said Pat, his accent veering between a soft Irish lilt and a dark New York growl, betraying his roots and his hard-scrabble days before he made his vast fortune. "I sent you to Hamilton's farm to look at his horses and offer him big money for anything you thought would be an athlete. Now he comes out of nowhere to take the Derby. Are you some kind of fuckin' eejit?"

"True, I looked at all his stock last year. They're like mountain goats. Thrown out in all weathers in massive paddocks." Bill shook his head, "I mean, he even leaves all the colts together in a herd right up till he breaks them in. They're covered in cuts and bruises. Snotty noses all over the place. How could I buy something like that for you?"

Pat growled.

"Your horses are looked after better than people. They're in immaculate condition."

"They'd better be." Pat blew out his cheeks. "My training facility is considered the best in Europe and so is my trainer. I invest a fortune. How the fuck is Marcus

Hamilton beating me with only a handful of nags and the remains of an old estate?"

Beads of sweat formed on Bill's brow.

"Call Fiona Buckley in the morning," said Pat. "Tell her I want to see her."

Bill glanced out at the ambulance on the track. "I'd say she's got other things on her mind at the moment."

Pat looked momentarily confused. "What?" He followed Bill's gaze. "Oh yes, well, better wait a day or two." His eyes narrowed and he clasped his meaty hands together, as if in prayer. "I'd say the Buckleys are going to need all the cash they can get in the coming months."

Two boxes further down, Sheikh Abdul Bin Omar Khaledam had to steady himself against the railing. In a state of deep shock he watched the paramedics gingerly roll Johnny onto a board, then transfer him to a stretcher as Elegant Flaw careered about the plains, dodging safety officers and having great fun. Equigene paraded in front of the grandstands. Despite the tragedy on the track, people seemed genuinely delighted to see Marcus Hamilton pull off an upset. All of a sudden, the crowd's polite clapping stopped as an image of Johnny being loaded into the ambulance was displayed on the big screen. As Abdul scanned the scene he found his eyes fixing on Pat McCormack's balcony.

Sheikh Abdul barked at his entourage in Arabic.

His assistant stood bolt-still, blank-faced and confused.

"Do you understand me?"

"Yes, sir, I'll get him here at once."

Chapter 4

Three weeks later

National Spinal Injuries Unit
Mater Hospital, Dublin

Johnny stared at the clock on the wall. It seemed to tick louder each day just to mock him. Go on, it said, come over here and tear me down. But he couldn't, he'd never walk again. If there was a positive, it was that he was off the ventilator and able to breathe for himself. His arms were still virtually useless, although the doctors had said he would eventually regain full feeling from the waist up.

It would take time, they'd said. *Time*. Johnny used to rush around like a lunatic from the gallops to the races all day, every day. He never had enough time, something Fiona had been getting tired of.

Now Johnny was at risk of developing bedsores and he'd need physiotherapy, but the registrar told him that the nurses were overstretched and his insurance policy only covered one physio session a week. He was going to need serious financial support.

Johnny glanced at the clock again. Ken, his agent, was to visit him this afternoon, hopefully with good news from the Irish Injured Jockeys Fund. Whenever a rider got injured, Johnny always assumed the money followed instantly, so what was the delay? He couldn't stand being in this overcrowded ward with only one TV. And no racing channels. He hadn't even been able to watch Elegant Flaw win at Sandown yesterday. Johnny was glad the colt had won. It wasn't the horse's fault he was paralysed.

Sometimes he wondered if he'd be better off in a box in the ground.

Fiona had come to see him this morning – with her father. She'd cried as she gripped his numb fingers. He caught her father looking at them in a way that said *I knew nothing good would come of this marriage*. Grouchy old bastard was an old-fashioned racing scribe and pedigree analyst who'd never accepted his only child marrying a jockey. He'd never understood how much Johnny adored Fiona.

The scraping of a chair on the linoleum dragged Johnny back to the present.

"How're ya, Johnny?" said Ken. He scratched at his shirt collar, avoided eye contact and drew the curtain around the bed. "Look, I called your wife and asked her to join us. I wanted to break the news to you both at the same time."

"What is it?"

"Not good, I'm afraid."

"Could it be any worse that this?" Johnny's eyes were dull and forlorn, devoid of the sparkle that had charmed women, made men laugh and seen strangers treat him like a rockstar. "Spit it out."

Ken looked at his watch. "I'd rather wait until –"

"Sorry I'm late," said a tired-looking Fiona, appearing through the curtain. "Traffic." She gave Johnny a peck on the cheek and stroked his hair.

Ken looked down at his shoes. "Right, so. The thing is: the Turf Club got on to me this morning." He chewed his lip. "They got the results of your pre-race urine sample."

Johnny rolled his eyes. "So what?"

"So you turned up positive for cocaine."

"Ah, would you fuck off, Ken! I'm not in the mood."

Fiona looked horrified.

Ken looked directly at his client. "I'm serious, Johnny. I've already contacted a lawyer. He'll be here in an hour."

Johnny couldn't believe his ears. "Ken, if I could get out of this bed, I'd go down to the Turf Club and kick them up their holes. There's *no way* I'd stick that shite in my body." He thought for a moment. "What about the B sample?"

Ken winced. "That's what I said. But it's gone missing."

"Then I'll sue for negligence."

"That's up to you and a lawyer, but there's a more immediate problem."

"You don't say?" said Fiona, rubbing Johnny's lifeless legs through the blanket.

"I was warned by the Turf Club that it'll hit the

20

papers tomorrow ... So the Irish Injured Jockeys Fund will refuse you financial support. They say it would set a bad example."

"Then how the hell am I supposed to pay for my recovery?"

"What about all your winnings over the years? You must have savings?"

"You'd be surprised how money goes when you're young and winning." Johnny stared at the sheets. "There's not enough left to build a new house and support myself for life as a cripple."

Ken looked at Fiona.

She blinked and wiped her cheeks. "We have a mortgage. I invested everything I have into my business. Johnny put all his savings into it too. So did Marcus Hamilton. All my equipment cost a fortune. We haven't the cash for the kind of care Johnny needs."

"That sample's been tampered with, I know it."

Ken gave Johnny a deadpan look. "You sound like a footballer. This is 2005 not 1985."

Johnny's gaze hardened. "Jesus, Ken. After all these years, you think I'd actually jeopardise my career by taking drugs?"

Ken's expression did not change.

"*Go fuck yourself!*" roared Johnny. "*And get the fuck out of here!*"

Ken stood up. "You're a talented jockey, probably the best we've seen in a generation, but you're an arrogant little shite. Nobody liked having to put up with your chopping and changing horses, your inability to ride to instructions. There'll be a right old throng waiting to see you take a fall from grace, regardless of your paralysis or how many winners you've ridden over the years."

"All the jockeys'll stand behind me."

"You sure about that? Half of them'll be trying to get your job with Pat Mac and none of them'll back you in public now you've been caught sniffing powder."

Fiona took Johnny's hand. "There's no need for that, Ken. I think you should leave now."

Ken shuffled towards the curtain. "Oh, and wait till Pat hears about it. Or your new buddy Sheikh Abdul, for that matter." He pushed the curtain aside with a flourish and left.

The other occupants of the ward were staring at Johnny. Fiona drew the curtains back around them and burst into tears.

Johnny felt numb, inside and out. He craned his neck as far as it would move, so he could look at her. "I can never ride again. Never be able to go running with you. Or make love to you. How am I supposed to get you pregnant now?"

She wiped her tears, put a hand on his face and ran her fingers over his lips. "We can see specialists. There's things they can do."

"Oh, yeah. More expense." Johnny stared at the mocking clock again.

Chapter 5

Trelawn Park Stud and Stables
Kildare
7 October 2015

Marcus Hamilton stood by the all-weather gallops and watched the horses canter up the hill. As they flashed past, he noted they were still moving like giddy teenagers. But they would shape up into nice athletes by next year's flat-racing season.

It started to rain. Marcus pulled a cap out of his pocket and turned to his head groom. "They're all ticking over nicely, Alfie. I'll leave you to get things squared away in the yards. Make sure you get a vet to take another blood from Oxygen Thief – I want to make sure he's spot on for Ascot next week."

"Grand job, Marcus," replied the weatherbeaten old horseman. "But I tell you, he's jumping out of his skin."

Marcus smiled. "Let's not count our chickens, Alfie." Then his smile slipped away. "Right. I'd better face into

Johnny's funeral."

"Give Mrs. Buckley my condolences, won't you now?"

"I will indeed."

The men exchanged tight-lipped smiles.

Marcus hopped into his Land Rover and set off down the lane as the tractor pulled a harrow up the oiled-sand gallop, smoothing out the hoofmarks. Marcus glanced left and right as he went, scanning the land, the grass training track and the pair of stableyards. He passed through the electric gate and on up the laneway through the stud farm. He glanced at the old mansion nestled in the trees on the far hill. This afternoon it would be packed with racing's great and good for Johnny's send-off. Marcus's father had sold the massive Trelawn House and its surrounding parkland to a luxury hotel chain twenty-five years ago. It was now one of Ireland's most prestigous golfing venues. Major Godfrey Hamilton's forethought had saved the family from ruin and allowed them to retain the stud land and training facilities.

Marcus grew up working with his father and had the reins flung at him suddenly in 2002 when Major Godfrey was killed by a fall from a horse. The Major, as everyone had called him, was the most successful gentleman owner-breeder-trainer in Ireland. Absolutely old school, he abhorred the new wave of commercialism sweeping through racing, and Marcus took pride in keeping his father's legacy thriving. It had taken him a few years to reorganise things but, from a small number of mares, he was now a regular producer of Classic and Group 1 horses. He knew that part of his advantage was the new feed produced at Winline and the deep knowledge he gleaned about his horses from the genetic testing at Equigenes. Investing in the company's start-up had been his smartest move ever. Initially, it all but broke him financially. Then he won the 2005 Derby with Equigene, the horse named after the company to promote Fiona and her work.

Marcus changed his clothes and drove to Johnny and Fiona's large modern bungalow at the other side of Kildare. Johnny's adapted minivan was still parked outside like a sentinel.

Fiona slammed the front door and jumped into the Land Rover. She gave Marcus a tired smile and a kiss. "How do I look?"

"Stunning as always."

She looked at her hands. Fiddled with her wedding band.

"You're sure you don't mind being seen with me in public? You know, so soon?" he said.

She touched his knee and looked him in the eye. "I'm sure everyone knew anyway. Turns out even Johnny knew," she sighed. "And I need someone to help me through today."

He pulled onto the road. "How are things going with the insurance company?"

Another sigh. "It's awful. Their investigators went through my finances – *'just to rule me out of the arson investigation'* – and still no talk of paying up. And," she looked at him, "poor old Ronan Lister ..."

Marcus sucked air between his teeth. "Must've been burnt to a crisp."

"Oh please, Marcus! The poor man!" She shook her

head. "His funeral was an ordeal. You know, he had five daughters and eleven grandchildren." She screwed up her eyes. "If I'd had the courage to retire him ... But the job meant so much to him. Kept him out of trouble, he used to say. How ironic is that?"

Marcus shot her a sideways glance. "Do they have any idea who it was yet?"

"One of them hinted to me that the fire looked like a professional job."

The car swerved a fraction. "What the hell does that mean?"

"I think it means that whoever did it was well organised and financed. And they didn't hesitate to kill poor old Ronan." She paused, looking like she was about to get sick. "And I still can't get that phone call or Johnny's words out of my head ... but all the cops say is '*Leave it to us*'." She sighed yet again. "And it's not like we can ask Johnny what he meant."

They drove in silence for a few minutes. Fiona looked pale and distracted.

"When Johnny told me '*They'll come after you*', he said it had all started with the fall."

"What did?"

"I don't know. I mean, sure, the accident changed our lives, but I don't get it. Unless ..." She put her hand to her mouth and then slapped the dashboard. "You know, he never would tell me where the money came from for the house and to put him through his Equine Science studies in UCD."

"Really? He kept that a secret all this time? I always figured it was backdoor, hush-hush money from the

Jockeys Fund to ease their consciences after his positive drug test."

Fiona shook her head. "I doubt it. Johnny hated them with a passion. Remember how everyone in racing politely ignored him after his drug test got leaked to the press? If the Jockeys Fund had backed him in secret, he'd have acted differently towards them. No, that money came from elsewhere. And I have my suspicions."

Another sideways glance from Marcus. "Who?"

"Never mind ... It's funny, Johnny always said it was none of my business. Told me to get on with my work and be glad I didn't have to mortgage the business again. I should have tried harder but he was so happy I suppose I didn't want to jinx it. Then, when he started to change, I couldn't get him to share anything at all. He'd bite my head off for almost anything. He was so bloody paranoid. So I just let it go – what did it matter?"

She looked out at the rain.

"I still have no idea what he meant when he said I could be '*right*' about something. Right about what? Maybe it was just his paranoia."

"Not Johnny's style to admit anyone else could be right."

"That's not fair, Marcus."

"Isn't it?"

Fiona stood by the grave, huddled under an umbrella. Heavy clouds threw rain down in stair-rods. It rattled on the lid of Johnny's coffin as six of his former colleagues lowered it into the ground. Every jockey in the country and most from Britain had turned out to give the legendary rider a proper send-off. In times of tragedy, jockeys tend to put away their differences and rally together. Ironic or hypocritical, Fiona couldn't decide. She saw faces who'd hated him during his riding days: jealousy and anger at being taken off fancied runners to make way for the precocious talent of Johnny Buckley. Where was the solidarity when Johnny was trying to fight his positive test and get money from the Jockeys Fund? She wondered how many of them looked at Johnny's coffin and counted their blessings. *There but for the grace of God* and all that.

The handshaking started. People filed past offering condolences before dashing to their cars and Trelawn House Hotel for the wake. Fiona was dreading it, but Johnny had recently altered his will to say he expected a send-off at the former Hamilton family pile. Piss-taking fucker always liked the last laugh.

Tony Carey, general manager of Winline Horse Feeds approached her. "I'm so sorry for your loss." Rain dripped off his nose. "Johnny was a gifted man, you know. In and out of the saddle. Some salesman too. Right from the moment he came to work for us, he changed the way we do business."

Fiona nodded mechanically. Her feet were soaked and frozen but the rain seemed as unreal as the funeral. She'd actually seen Johnny die, but still couldn't believe it.

"Look, *erm*, when you're in better shape," Carey continued, "I'd love to sit down with you and chat about Johnny's work. As a nutritionist he was on another level, but he wasn't the greatest at sharing information."

"Oh, OK. He was passionate about it alright," she mumbled.

Less than three months after the accident, Johnny had regained feeling in his arms and upper body. He swore it was due to intense physiotherapy and proper nutrition. Shortly after that, he signed up to study Equine Science at UCD in Dublin. From then on, he'd buzzed with a new urgency. While they were waiting for the builders to convert and adapt their house, they had rented a ground-floor flat near the campus – and for a while they'd been happy. Johnny had a new purpose and attacked his studies with the same intensity he had his riding career. Meanwhile Fiona's fledgling business was getting under way. Then Johnny began going to a gym in the evenings and got seriously into wheelchair bodybuilding. That was when he really started to change.

Out of the corner of her eye Fiona saw Pat McCormack in the queue. He shuffled towards her and stuck out a hand, softening his normally sharp eyes.

"Oh Lord, it's an awful tragedy. I know you've a lot on your plate, Fiona, but we must have a chat about the future of Equigenes. I have to say, I'm concerned on behalf of all your investors and shareholders."

Jesus, McCormack never stopped being a businessman. She wished she'd never taken his money all those years ago. He moved along and she looked after him. A shiver flickered through her. She really needed to find out for sure who financed Johnny's recovery and studies.

When everyone had gone, Fiona lingered at the graveside a while then slowly made her way to the cemetery gate where Marcus was waiting.

A white Rolls Royce cut through the rain and eased to a halt in front of them. A man in a black suit, with a military haircut and cold blue eyes got out of the passenger seat, readied an umbrella and opened the rear door. Sheikh Abdul Bin Omar Khaledam climbed out of the massive car. He was a tall, athletic man, who played polo when he wasn't overseeing his racing empire. He was also Minister of Culture and Procurement for the Emirate he would soon inherit from his ageing and infirmed father. He adjusted his tailored overcoat and offered his hand to Marcus.

"Mr. Hamilton, how are my horses?" he said slowly and deliberately.

The dark eyes of the bedouin bored into Marcus.

"Our horses are in great form, sir."

The Sheikh turned his attention to Fiona. "Mrs. Buckley," he said without extending his hand, "I am very sorry to hear of Johnny's passing. It is a great tragedy."

"Thank you, that's very kind."

"I also heard that your offices were burned down. What a terrible time for you."

At the mention of the fire, Fiona's mind swirled. She swayed, felt dizzy, almost dropped her umbrella. Marcus gripped her tight.

"Mrs. Buckley, if there is anything I can ever do for you, please do not hesitate to ask."

"You're ... very kind," she repeated.

The Sheikh gave her a tight smile and glanced at Marcus. "He knows how to reach my people." He got back in the car and his man closed the door.

Fiona watched the enormous vehicle disappear into the rain.

***

As his car sped up the motorway towards Weston Aerodrome, Sheikh Abdul stared out at the incessant rain. After a few minutes he lowered the glass divider and spoke to the driver and passenger.

"Ahmed, Vladimir. Turn around. Take me to Trelawn Park Stud. I want to drive around the farm while everyone is at the funeral."

Ahmed nosed the car off an exit ramp while Vladimir informed the pilot that their departure would be delayed.

When they pulled up at the security gates of the stud, Ahmed pressed the buzzer and announced that Sheikh Abdul was here.

No reply.

"Ahmed, pull forward. I will speak to them."

Ahmed did as he was told. The Sheikh lowered his window and pressed the button. He cursed in Arabic as rain soaked his shirt cuff.

"Who is it?" said the crackly voice.

Rain hammered on the metal intercom housing.

"This is Sheikh Abdul Khaledam. I've been at Mr. Buckley's funeral. Mr. Hamilton knows I am coming. I want to drive around the stud and look at the paddocks before I catch my plane."

No response.

"Can't you open the gates yourself?" the Sheikh barked at Vladimir.

The Russian shook his head. "Electric and too heavy."

The Sheikh pulled out his phone just as the gates slowly opened before them.

The Rolls Royce prowled up the drive.

"Turn left by the office and take me to the large paddocks," he said.

Ahmed saw a jeep approaching, but turned left at the junction as he had been told.

The jeep followed them and its driver leaned on the horn.

"Keep going," said the Sheikh.

He lowered his window and looked out over the large fields dotted with tall trees and ringed by thick hedgerows. Rain spat in on top of him. He saw twelve weanlings dashing across the lush grassland and stopping abruptly under a tree. Several reared up and wrestled, opening their jaws and grabbing at each other's manes. Young males playing like teenage boys.

The Sheikh noticed how contented they seemed, despite the weather. Abdul never put his horses out in the rain. He did turn them out in herds like that, but they never seemed to run around as much. They just ate the paddocks bare and stood about chewing the fences. Until he had electric fencing installed. Now they just stood about.

His reverie was disturbed by a flustered-looking man standing in the rain next to the car.

"Sheikh Abdul, I'm Alfie Connors. We met last June when you were here for the Derby."

The Sheikh couldn't remember him. "What do you do here?"

"Head man."

"I see."

"Marcus – Mr. Hamilton – never mentioned you'd be coming."

"That's not important. I'm just having a look. You may go now."

Alfie looked puzzled. "Oh, right. Well, see, it's usual to escort all visitors about and show them what they need to see."

"I know what I want to see." He pointed to the horses. "These are the colts, right?"

Alfie looked down the field. "That's right."

"Where are the fillies kept?"

"Behind barn two, on the right."

"Take me there, then leave us."

Alfie nodded, got in his jeep and led the way.

Sheikh Abdul was disappointed to see the fillies huddled in a corner, sheltering under a tall hedge. Their paddock was huge. He couldn't understand how Marcus raised such talented horses in those wild conditions. Was Marcus willfully neglecting his horses, or was there some other force at play here?

A man like Sheikh Abdul was not used to being kept in the dark. He needed to know *what* Hamilton was doing, and how he was doing it. He knew for a fact that Marcus only had forty mares and that he never bought yearlings at the sales either, so how was he consistantly breeding such superior athletes? Abdul lost count of his own mares but he knew he had nearly 500 horses in training in England. But still he found it difficult to breed a champion – unlike Marcus Hamilton, who seemed to have so much luck.

This conundrum bothered the Sheikh until Ahmed pulled off the motorway for the airfield. He lowered the glass again. "Vladimir, are the girls finished shopping?"

"Yes, boss. They're already on board."

The Sheikh smiled. He enjoyed the company of the young. It made him feel twenty-seven, not forty-seven.

Fiona and Marcus sat at a table in the packed bar. Jockeys, owners and trainers were scattered in groups around the mansion's former library. Bubbly chatter was punctuated by raucous laughter. Everyone recounted tales of Johnny and drank in his honour. Fiona wondered how many were genuinely nostalgic. She recalled Johnny's favourite saying: *In this game, you're only as good as your last ride, unless you're handing out free drinks.*

She turned to Marcus. "I'm surprised Sheikh Abdul had the neck to show his face after that steroid scandal during the summer."

"You know that wasn't his fault. His trainer took all the blame for that."

"And what was it with him speaking to you like that: *my* horses?"

Marcus picked up a beermat and began shredding it slowly. "Ah, you know what those guys are like."

She arched her brow.

He didn't look up. "Yeah, well. He buys a half-share in a few colts every year and thinks he owns me and the roof over my head."

"Still, he shouldn't speak to you like that. He should be singing your praises. You've won him five classics, creating as many stallions for him. That's more than he's done with his own homebreds. Hell, Marcus, he has hundreds of mares in Ireland alone – I know, he paid me to test them and their foals for stamina genes.

34

Some years he's lucky if he wins a handful of big races with his private trainers." She patted him on the knee. "You, on the other hand, are his golden goose."

"Yeah, I suppose. Anyway, what did Pat Mac say to you by the grave?"

"Can you believe he asked about my research? Basically wanted to know when I'd be up and running again."

"Well, I suppose I'm not surprised. He hasn't bred a decent horse in a while. A man as forceful as him, who spends that kind of money, expects results."

She downed her gin. "And what does he expect from me? Lightning in a bottle?"

"Bottle, injection, feed supplement – he's not fussy. After all, he made his millions in pharmaceuticals."

"*Huh*." She stood and went to the bar.

Marcus watched her order drinks. God, he loved her. He decided once things calmed down, he'd ask her to marry him. They were both nearly forty and he knew she wanted a child before it was too late.

His felt his phone vibrate in his pocket. He checked the screen and marched out to a quiet corner of the lobby.

"Hello?"

"Marcus, I have a question."

"Oh yes?"

"Fiona Buckley's new research – her unpublished results and proposed tests – was all that lost in the fire?"

"I don't know about any new results or tests."

"Did she have files at her home?"

"I'm not sure."

"I expect you to find these things out, Marcus."

"Yes, but –"

The line went dead.

Marcus bit his lip and looked out the window. His father would never have got himself into such a situation. He went into the bar and gave Fiona a peck on the cheek.

"Let's get out of here," he whispered in her ear.

"Good idea."

Fiona arranged for the bar to stay open for another hour and the bill to be sent to the executor of Johnny's will. She dozed as Marcus drove them back to her house.

Once inside the sparsely furnished bungalow, she kicked off her still-wet shoes. "Open a bottle of wine while I shower, will you?"

Marcus shivered. It was his first time over the threshold of the Buckley home and he felt like Johnny could wheel into view at any second. He placed the wine on the coffee table and saw the shiny laptop on the sofa.

"By the way," he called after her, "surely you had your work backed up on file here? I can't believe you'd have had it all at the lab."

"What's that?" she said, over the hiss of the shower.

Marcus opened the slim silver computer and it pinged into life.

"Never mind," he muttered, dragging a finger over the mousepad.

A box appeared onscreen: *username* and *password.* He closed the device, poured himself a glass of wine, sat back and looked at the bizarre set of steel rings set into the ceiling. They snaked around the open-plan space and looked like something found in a zoo or maybe an army gym.

Chapter 6

Winline Horse Feeds factory
Maynooth, County Kildare
November 2009

Johnny stretched his thick arms over his head. He brought them back to shoulder level and flexed his biceps until his shirt sleeves bulged. Next, he arranged the pens on his desk into a perfect line. He moved the notepad so that it was touching the last pen perfectly and straightened his laptop. Satisfied, he glanced around his office. He knew his obsessive tidiness had got worse, and that it had pushed Fiona further away, but he couldn't help it. The sense of organisation helped to keep him sane. That and lifting weights and his mission.

He was almost certain her business partnership with Marcus Hamilton had developed into something else. Not that he blamed her.

He spun his chair on the spot and focused on his new job. He was going to transform the place. Winline's owner and general manager, Tony Carey, had inherited the company from his father. Old man Carey had founded the business in the late 60s and had built it into one of Ireland's premier animal feed producers. However, the younger Carey was not the businessman his father had been. A few months ago, rumours flew about that Tony had accepted a generous offer for a controlling share of the ailing company. Nobody knew for sure what had happened, but Winline launched a policy of modernisation. A new nutritionist was needed and Johnny fit the bill perfectly. Tony nearly collapsed in squeamish shock the first time he'd seen Johnny's sculpted upper body in his light wheelchair. But he welcomed Johnny to the team, saying something about how his new image would help convince clients that he really knew about nutrition, exercise and maximising physical potential.

Not that it mattered what Tony thought.

Johnny's instructions were simple enough and he had no qualms about the deal. After his accident, he had been bailed out financially and had his life turned around. He would do anything to repay the debt. His current salary was a welcome top-up, but Johnny's benefactor had made it very clear that they were never to discuss the situation – even face to face. Deep cover. Like a secret agent. Johnny grinned.

So far, Tony had sent Johnny to a handful of small studs, and Johnny had persuaded them all to switch to Winline as soon as the new feeds came into production. Johnny spun himself around his desk and looked out the window at the factory floor. The brand-new machine was almost installed. Extrusion: the way forward, like giving a protein shake to an Olympic athlete.

Out on the production floor the supervisor was giving instructions and the staff were diligently going about their jobs. Nice people, but they were still making feed to last century's standards. Not that he could fault them; it was what most owners wanted. Including the company's biggest client: Pat McCormack's Balmain Stud.

Johnny had been to Balmain the week before. It was his first visit there since his riding days. It was a still a nice place alright, but nowadays the horses were as soft as butter. Mollycoddled, spoilt.

Johnny couldn't believe it when he saw the yearling colts standing forlornly in small separate paddocks. They hung their heads and looked bored.

"We don't want them kicking each other," the farm manager explained. "They're too valuable."

If Pat had been there, Johnny could've launched into his speech about digestible protein, strenuous exercise and athletic potential. Instead, he had tried to talk to Bill about it, but the man hadn't a clue. Johnny had made an appointment to go back the following week and talk to Pat in person.

After that visit, something else had occured to Johnny. At first he dismissed it, then he tried to discuss it with Fiona, but she too thought it was nothing.

That reminded him. He spun back to his desk and opened his laptop. His fingers tapped a word into the search engine and he scrolled through the results. He went to the site of an international news magazine and downloaded an article. Then another website caught his eye. There was an in-depth piece about honey bees and royal jelly. Johnny thought of his father, who had kept bees and had a thriving honey business before competition from the supermarkets forced him to quit and drive horse lorries for a local transport company. Literally driving himself into an early grave. He used to tell Johnny about bees as he put him to bed at night. How they all started out the same until they divided up into workers, drones and queens.

There was a knock at the door and Tony Carey let himself in, all red-faced and flustered.

"What's up, Tony?"

"Great news! First off, Marcus Hamilton has agreed to switch all his horses to the new extruded mix when the machine comes on-line."

Johnny nodded. "I thought he might. He had dinner with us last month. He's a sharp guy. He was the first to invest in Fiona's business and he knew nearly as much as me about horse nutrition."

"Yeah, yeah. Grand. More importantly, I just got off the phone with one of Sheikh Abdul Khaledam's people."

"Oh yeah?"

"Oh yes, indeed. I've an appointment for you to go to his stud in Tipperary and do your thing."

"When?"

"Next Tuesday."

"I'm going to Balmain that morning, but the afternoon's free."

Johnny hauled himself out of bed at five the following Tuesday. Fiona lay sleeping. He pulled spongy, sock-like boots over his feet, knelt in his modified chair and, using padded canvas straps, bound his shins to his thighs and put kneepads on. Ready, Johnny wheeled himself through the bedroom door and snatched the rope hanging from the ceiling. Hand over hand, he pulled himself up until he was close enough to the ceiling to grip the first ring. Letting go of the rope, he grabbed the second ring and hung like an Olympic gymnast, looking down at his empty chair. He stretched his back muscles and flexed his deltoids. When he could feel the blood pumping, he lunged from ring to ring like an ape until he reached the back door. He nudged the spring-loaded door and ducked under the frame into his sanctuary. The door closed itself behind him and he hung for a second on the final ring before snatching the rope beside it and lowering himself to the ground hand-over-hand.

The garage was now a fully equipped gym with machines and weights that had been adjusted for Johnny's physical limitations. There also was a treadmill in the corner for Fiona which she used nearly every day but never when Johnny was training. He had made that clear to her. This was his alone time. It helped him channel his pain into something useful. He unlocked his supplement cabinet and took his morning pills and powders with a bottle of water.

He spend five minutes stretching before hauling himself onto the bench. He set the weights and began pressing the bar away from his body. He squeezed his chest at the top of each repetition and exhaled sharply. As he exercised, he considered the information he had read on the internet over the last few days. Despite

Fiona's doubts on the subject, he knew there was something to it. It just made so much sense. Most people in racing gambled on genetic luck – now *there* was a contradiction in terms – rich breeders spent so much money on horses with the 'right' pedigrees. Wouldn't it be funny if it turned out they'd wasted their money?

He exhaled and put more weight on the bar.

Afterwards, his muscles were drained but his mind was fresh. He growled as he flexed his pectorals and felt the ecstasy of muscle burn. He sucked in lungfuls of air and gazed at the thick novel sitting on a chair in the corner, almost like a shrine. He knew he should let go and give *the book* away, but he couldn't. The worn paperback was the first thing he had read when he regained feeling in his arms. It had helped him through the darkness, its central message being *patience and hope.* Now Johnny was done waiting and he was beginning to hope.

Three hours later, he steered his adapted minivan through the Kilkenny hills, arrived at the security gates of Balmain Stud and lowered the window.

"Jesus, Johnny, how's things?" said the gateman. He glanced over each shoulder and leaned on the car door. "Any tips, Johnny?"

"Yeah," he said with a lopsided grin. "Eat right and exercise."

The man looked puzzled. "Oh, right you are, Johnny. On you go, so." He waved him up the winding, treelined avenue.

Johnny passed an immaculate stone stable barn where workers were turning out heavily pregnant mares into a paddock. He stopped his vehicle and watched the staff. They dumped the mares in the paddock and ran straight back to the barn. Heads down, no banter or chat.

Next he passed the poor yearlings in their solitary-confinement paddocks and the same idea nagged at his mind again.

He drove on to the huge offices and braced himself for his meeting. He remembered his riding days for McCormack. He knew what a formidable negotiator the man was. That wasn't all he knew about Pat.

An only child, Pat McCormack was born in upstate New York to Irish immigrant parents. His mother had died giving birth to him in a home delivery and his father, a general practicioner, never got over her death. So his practice suffered as his drinking escalated. Pat left home as soon as he finished school, disgusted by his father and the squalor he had grown up in. He moved to New York City and worked every spare hour to put himself through university, majoring in chemistry. Soon after graduation, he went into partnership with a talented scientist and they patented a drug that reduced cholesterol. Tragically, his business partner died in a car crash just as they got US FDA approval for the drug and sales exploded.

Twenty years ago, Pat returned to Ireland, bought a large tract of land in the Nore valley and turned it into a state-of-the-art stud farm and training centre. Pat was a force of nature. His staff called him 'The Whirlwind'. A teetotaller with a Japanese wife and two grown sons, people loved to gossip that he had New York mafia or Tokyo yakuza connections. Or both. He spent millions on horses and had been rewarded handsomely over the years. He stood four stallions at the Irish National Stud and had been champion owner in Ireland five times and twice in Britain. Johnny had won him the English, Irish, French and Kentucky derbies.

Johnny was shown into a cavernous office by a tired-looking secretary.

Pat was at his desk poring over the *Thoroughbred Daily News* and the *Racing Post*.

"Pat! How's things? Long time no see."

Pat looked up and examined Johnny intently. He narrowed his eyes. "You popping steroids or what?"

Johnny forced his smile to remain and cocked a finger at Pat. "Nutrition and exercise. That's the key."

"Ah, you were always a funny little fucker. Right, so tell me – what's new at Winline Feeds? I lost four horses to colic last year and I'm blaming your feed for that."

Johnny raised his hands. A horse's intestines were complicated, like a canal network made by committee. During his equine science studies, Johnny became convinced that modern feed practices were going against how the horse's gut worked. Prolonged periods in stables were combined with large quantities of oats and other raw grains. It wasn't natural. Wasn't conducive to performance either. His lecturer had applauded him.

Johnny took a deep breath. "Actually, I'm here to tell you the price will go up slightly, but the product will change radically and for the better."

"Another price hike? Forget it."

Johnny kept smiling. "How much does a colic case cost you?"

The remark caught Pat by surprise. He opened his mouth.

Johnny cut him off. "Five to seven grand, assuming all goes well."

"About that."

"And if you lose the horse, then the financial blow to your stud is considerable. With the pedigrees you've got here, we could be talking seven figures."

"I insure all my horses against such things."

"So then the policies get a hike and the older mares are uninsurable."

A pause. "OK, what's your point?"

Gotcha. "My point is, that with our new feed you'll never need to give raw, uncooked grains to your stock again and you'll kiss goodbye to colic." He arched his brow. "Now, *that's* worth a few extra pennies."

"And Winline'll still test the grass and soil, tailor the product to complement our land?"

"Absolutely. Just like before."

Pat leaned back in his chair. Stared at Johnny. Eventually he smiled. "Tell you what I'll do – leave me all the information and give a copy to Bill on your way out. Get your team to make up a trial batch."

Johnny winked at him. "Pleasure talking to you, Pat. The brochures are already with your receptionist."

Pat stood and shook his hand. "Still sure of yourself, anyway."

Johnny cocked his head to one side. "In a previous life, I used to know what made a horse tick and how to get it to run. Now I know what makes them grow and achieve full genetic potential. Just ask Fiona. I'm sure she'd agree." He spun his chair around and made for the door.

That afternoon, he found himself being driven around Sheikh Abdul's Tipperary estate by the general manager, Alan De Courtney. Tall, young, affable and polite, Alan was one of a new breed of stud managers, long on marketing theory and university degrees, but short on practical hands-on experience. In a blazer, tie and slacks, he looked more like a stockbroker than a farm manager. The estate was once the property of an old couple who had bred several famous National Hunt steeplechasers in the 70s and 80s. Declining health and disinterested children had led them to sell to Sheikh Abdul, who'd spent a fortune refurbishing the property over the last ten years. He preferred to race in England and most of his animals were in training there, but he believed that Ireland was the best place to breed racehorses. Although he had yet to win the Epsom Derby, he had taken several European classics and had an unquenchable thirst for horseracing.

Alan stopped the SUV in the stallion yard. "I've told the lads to walk the horse past the car – save you getting out."

"Thanks." Johnny only wanted to catch up with one horse here.

When Elegant Flaw appeared, Johnny broke into a smile. The stallion was marched in an oval on the gravel, then his handler stood him stock-still near Johnny's window.

"You've probably heard he's hardly had a winner in his first two crops," said Alan.

"*Mmmm ...*"

"The Sheikh's very disappointed. Wants to sell him, quicksmart."

"You're only as good as your last winner in this game." You and me both, old horse, thought Johnny. "Thanks, Alan, I've seen enough."

"Do you want to see Equigene? He's flying! Sired a Classic winner this year. I'm delighted we bought him from Hamilton after that Derby win." Alan winked. "Another smart move by the Sheikh."

"No, you're grand. I don't need to see him."

Johnny hid his misgivings as he was driven about the farm. The fields were packed with horses and in places the pasture looked tired, the grass worn out.

"You've plenty of stock anyway," he said.

"What can I say, the Sheikh loves his horses."

That nagging thought kept returning to Johnny.

"Anyway," said Alan, "I've been instructed by the boss to give you full control of our nutritional program. We've been a bit short of winners this year and the boss feels it's time to change the feed."

"Well, you tell him not to worry," said Johnny. "It's all under control." He launched into his speech and wondered if Alan was listening to a single word.

Chapter 7

8 October 2015

Fiona woke with a start and reached across but Marcus was gone. She rubbed her eyes and checked the time. Almost six. Moments later, an alarm on her phone went off. She read the reminder and swore silently. She'd forgotten all about the seminar which had been organised several months ago by the Irish Thoroughbred Breeders Association. And to top it all off, her slides and presentation files had been lost in the fire. All she had was the stuff on her personal laptop. Still, it would give her a distraction, something else to think about. As keynote speaker, she didn't want to let the country's small breeders down. Even if most were simply preoccupied with selling their produce as opposed to trying to create better racehorses. She'd print off a few pages of notes and ad-lib the rest from memory. There'd be no visual aids but it would have to do.

That bizarre phone call the night of the fire and Johnny's weird remarks nagged at her. She decided against mentioning the forthcoming tests in her talk and she couldn't risk leaving the only remaining files and discs concerning her work in her car either. She would put them in the safest place she knew of, even if that meant enduring the cutting remarks.

Fiona dressed, made breakfast and called her secretary.

"Good morning, Doctor Buckley," said Maura. "I hope the funeral wasn't too hard?"

"Would it be awful of me to say it was a relief?"

"Oh God, it wouldn't. Not after all you've been through. How're you bearing up?"

"I, well, I'm OK. Not looking forward to this seminar, though."

"I'll ring the Breeders Association and cancel."

"No, no. It'll probably do me good to get up there and talk. Did you speak to the phone company?"

"I did indeed. They've arranged for our office numbers to be forwarded to my home landline and I'll work from here until we can set up somewhere else. I told Cathy and Denise to take holidays until we get another lab set up. I also got on to the insurance people again. I've to meet them at the site this morning and I've a mind to give them an earful, I tell you."

"You're fantastic, Maura."

"Oh, sure I know," she said with a chuckle. "Mind yourself, Doctor."

"I will."

Fiona tossed the phone on the counter, sipped her coffee and stared across the room at the laptop on the sofa. She'd take that with her and work on it while she waited for her turn to speak. Surely it contained some answers.

Dawn broke over the Kilkenny hills, clearing the mist as the sun rose. McCormack stood on the hilltop observation platform with his trainer Joe Nolan. A white railing snaked down the hill before them, flanking the gallops. Horses came thundering up the hill. Pat and Joe grinned in unison as the first pair cruised past effortlessly on the high-tech artificial surface, held on tight reins by their riders.

"They look in top form," said Pat.

"That they are. Atavistic'll take his chances in the Queen Elizabeth II stakes on British Champions Day next week. He's a good each-way shot."

"Each way? He'd better bloody win. My homebreds haven't given me a group one winner for three years. People are starting to talk."

"Ah now, in fairness to Atavistic, he's had more than his share of setbacks. He deserves a big win and I'm sure he'd have been champion two-year-old last year if he hadn't had that chip in his fetlock. Not to mention that massive infection he had over the winter. He deserves a big win."

"Plenty of horses – and people – deserve good things, Joe. But usually all they get is shite on top of shite. I need this horse to win that race. I'm starting to look like a flash in the pan in this business. People are saying I spent too much. They're even saying that the only reason the early years were so good was because I invented some secret wonder drug in my American labs."

"Don't mind the gossip. People are assholes when they're jealous. Your homebreds are just going through a slump, is all. We've been unlucky. It'll pass. It always does."

Pat glared. Joe turned his attention to the next batch of horses.

Forty freshly broken-in yearlings cantered slowly up the gallops in single file. As none of them had been named, Joe recited their pedigrees as they passed. In a month he would know their personalities and foibles better than his own children's.

"What do you think of the latest crop?" demanded Pat.

"Ah, they're a bit soft and babyish, but they're coming along nicely." Joe sucked air between his teeth. "It's early days yet, of course, but that colt by Fiscal Haven out of Shine On is useless. His action is awful."

"Jesus. I paid five million dollars for his mother. She's had three foals: the first broke down, the next had a wind problem and chips in his hocks, and now you're tellin' me this one's useless? You've only had him in training a month! And it's not the stallion's fault – he's flying. Best sire they have up at the National Stud."

Joe shrugged. "Shine On's a bad producer."

Pat swore.

"I'd say it's time to cut your losses on that mare," said Joe.

Pat weighed the options. "Get that colt to win a

couple of races next season as a two-year-old. Any kind of races. Anywhere. Anything to get a win on her pedigree page. Then I'll consider selling the mare. OK?"

It was not really a question. Joe nodded.

Pat looked at his watch. "Where's Bill?"

An SUV appeared at the bottom of the hill and splashed its way up the sodden roadway.

Bill lowered the window as he pulled up alongside the platform. "Morning, boss – morning, Joe."

"About time. We need to talk," said Pat, getting into the vehicle. "See you tomorrow, Joe."

Pat scanned the trees and paddocks as they made their way from the training grounds to the stud land. "It's meant to piss with rain this afternoon. Make sure the mares are in early."

Bill pursed his lips and nodded. After sixteen years working for Pat, he'd lost the will to argue.

"Joe reckons the latest colt out of Shine On is useless."

Bill grimaced. Prepared for the onslaught.

"Jesus, Bill, have you nothing to say? I mean, that mare's not the only one. What the fuck is happening on my farm? If it's not sickness and infection, it's tendon strains and breakdowns. I mean, other people are breeding winners by my stallions, but my families are going through the biggest drought I've ever known." He shook his head. "A dozen years ago we were virtually unbeatable,we even won the Kentucky Derby. First time a European horse had ever done it."

"The good old days. I remember alright. They were Johnny Buckley's glory days too."

"You think a jockey was the key to my success?

Fuck!" He wagged a finger. "Now you go and check every weanling. I want X-rays on all of them every two months. I want every animal kept in pristine condition until they go into training in a year's time. Not a scratch or blemish. Understand?"

Bill nodded.

Pat sighed. "Looks like I'll have to buy a few yearlings at the sales just to keep the whole show on the road. By the way, what's the news on young Cathal Regan?"

"Not good, I'm afraid. I spoke to his mother last night. They found a lump in his throat. The big C."

Pat went pale and blessed himself. "Oh Lord, that's tragic. He's still a kid."

"Twenty-one."

"How long's he been working here?"

"Three years."

"Good kid?"

"Dedicated."

Pat stared out the window. "I'll have to do something for him. Make sure he gets the best treatment possible. Have Catriona put his parents' number on my desk, will you?"

"I will indeed."

Pat's acts of kindness were the reason that Bill put up with all the shouting, demands and abuse. He knew that should anything happen to any of them, Pat would look after them as if they were family.

They drove on in silence.

"And as for that Buckley woman, I want results." Pat tapped at his phone and put it on speaker.

"Good morning. Equigenes."

"Hello, Maura, how're you? Pat McCormack here. Are you up and running again?"

"In the process," she said hesitantly.

"Can you put me through to Doctor Buckley, please?"

"I'm afraid not. She's on her way to speak at this afternoon's Breeders seminar."

Pat's mind whirred. "Really? Where's it on?"

"Duggan's Hotel, Kilkenny town."

"Ah, that's only down the road. Thank you, Maura." He hung up.

Bill pulled up at the office.

Pat looked at his watch as he got out. "I'm off to Mass. Make sure that number's on my desk when I get back."

The young man's fingers clattered on the keyboard. He paused, blinked, wiped his clammy palms on his jeans. Popped another can of Red Bull and stared at the seductive glow of the monitor – the only light in the gloomy room.

The mobile phone on his desk rang.

"You again," he muttered, looking at the number.

He took another long swallow of Red Bull and swiped at the device. "Hello?"

"When I had that phone delivered to you, I expected you to answer it promptly," said the distorted voice.

He rolled his eyes.

"You should be finished by now. I want everything emailed to me within the hour and there'll be someone at your door to collect the hard drives within ninety minutes."

"I cracked the access codes and copied everything onto disc. I'm now combing the drives for hidden files, but I doubt I'll find any. This isn't exactly a US military encryption on these things, but there is a lot of information here. Anyway, it should be ready to go in an hour."

"It had better be."

"Yeah, no sweat, man. So, like what's so interesting about horse genetics anyway?"

"Count your money and don't get curious."

The caller hung up.

Chapter 8

Fiona sat with the other speakers on the stage of the hotel ballroom. Billed as the final speaker at the Irish Thoroughbred Breeders Association seminar on raising commercial horses, she wasn't sure if that made her subject the most important, or the least. For the last two hours, she had listened to stud masters, vets and horse traders drone on about how to minimise cost and maximise the financial return on the horses one bred. Marcus always said that if you bred honestly, with the aim of producing a tough athlete, then the rewards would be self-evident. She was inclined to agree with him. That was one of the few things she and Johnny had agreed upon, too. It took the accident to make him see it that way, though. Before the fall, he was always too busy trying to find the next big thing to ride, so he never stopped to look at the big picture. *The big picture*. That was always Marcus's forte. He had a gift for stepping back, seeing which way the wind was going to blow and being ready when it did.

Fiona heard her name as the Breeders Association chairman introduced her. She stood and went to the lectern. The crowd gave her a polite applause. She smiled awkwardly and stared out at the two hundred people crammed into the function room.

"Good afternoon, ladies and gentlemen. In late 2003, I set up a company called Equigenes. My goal was to help thoroughbred racehorse breeders understand more about the genetics of their horses. Unfortunately, as some of you will have heard, we had a fire in the Equigenes building which will briefly set us back in our research. Everyone at Equigenes is devastated that our security guard Ronan Lister lost his life in the blaze."

The room went utterly still for a moment.

Fiona cleared her throat. "First, a little background on the field of genetics. The equine genome consists of thirty-two pairs of chromosomes. Horse DNA is made up of strings of the letters G, A, T, C, which are arranged in blocks as particular genes. The horse has over twenty-five thousand genes, consisting of three billion letters and each one contains instructions for the body to make a specific protein. And I try to decipher this for you owners and breeders."

She paused for breath. The room was quiet, she seemed to have their attention.

"In some cases, a single gene makes a particular trait: like eye colour. However, in most cases it is a complicated picture with multiple genes contributing to a trait. And like a jigsaw puzzle, these pieces need to be arranged in a particular order to be influential. And further complicating matters, we know that DNA can be categorised as either 'somatic' – not passed on to offspring – or 'germline' – passed on. We now believe that some traits are influenced by the environment on a long-term basis: what you may call evolution. Furthermore, we know that certain equine genes contribute to athletic ability, just as we know this in humans. The full equine genome was mapped in 2007 by the team of scientists at Massachusetts Institute of Technology and Harvard. However, back in 2004 under the collaborative banner of the International Horse Genome Sequencing Project, my team and I were able to get involved – with initial funding from private individuals, along with co-operation from Trelawn Park Stud and other major breeding operations, who let me take DNA samples from their horses. We picked up on research already done in Boston and were able to compile a DNA database."

She was in her rhythm now and she continued for another forty minutes, exploring the genetics of muscle mass, growth rates and preferred racing distances.

"Sharing our information with the team in Boston," she said, nearing the end of her talk, "we were able to confirm our findings on a global scale. As you may know, we have been able to develop a reliable way to test thoroughbred racehorses to ascertain their precocity, stamina and therefore each individual's ideal running distance."

She was getting close to her conclusions and the reason she set up her business.

A hand shot up in the second row. Fiona made eye contact and was about to suggest that questions wait until afterwards, when the elderly redfaced man stood and began roaring.

"That's all very fine now, Mrs. Buckley, but anyone in this business could tell you those things by reading a pedigree and looking at the horse in front of them!"

Fiona nodded slowly, fought to keep her expression neutral. No matter where in the world the seminar, she always had to answer this same question and she was so tired of it.

"Well, if you look at a young foal, you can't tell how it's going to develop –"

"Oh, but you can!" he interrupted.

"But if you have the animal tested you can have a definitive answer *before* you see it develop."

"Yeah, you would say that. You're the one selling the tests!" He broke into a grin and a few people chuckled. "But what's the point?"

This guy was persistent, she had to give him that. "Well, the point is that it removes the guesswork and allows you to better plan your matings and manipulate your pedigrees by weeding out the genetic traits you do not want."

The man sat down, apparently out of steam.

Fiona had opened her mouth to continue when another man stood up the front row and launched into a question. Fiona recognised the well-dressed man as Alan De Courtney, Sheikh Abdul Khaledam's stud manager. He looked as if he was reading from a card cradled in his palm.

"Doctor Buckley, do you have any plans to announce new tests for equine athletic breathing deficiencies, racing ability, or the developmental bone condition Osteochondritis Dissecans?"

Fiona's brows shot up. She coughed and reached for a glass of water. She didn't want to get into this. Not right now.

"Well, ability is a complicated picture involving many genes," she said, "but we are narrowing this list and are close to announcing a reliable test. But again, any new tests will tie in with previous tests."

De Courtney smiled, nodded and sat.

A voice heckled from the back. "*Oh yeah, so we'll have to shell out for all the tests at once, is that it?*"

Fiona scanned the crowd, to no avail. "Well, er, Marcus Hamilton has found my tests to be most useful and look at his success rates."

"*Oh, I'd say he has!*" said the voice, full of innuendo.

Sniggers from the back of the room.

"*What about the the gene for cheating on your husband? How do you test for that?*"

Out of the corner of her eye, Fiona saw the chairman of the Breeders Association stand and approach the lectern. She composed herself and motioned for him to sit.

"Obviously the genetic tests we offer are not absolute guarantees, because how you feed, raise and train your horses is so important. Now, any further questions must wait. You may ask me them directly, after the lecture, in the lounge."

Fiona continued speaking for another five minutes.

"To finish up," she said eventually, aware that her audience was flagging, "I want to highlight the importance of equine genetic research as part of a broader perspective." She took another drink. "In America, the fifteen-million-dollar Horse Genome Project was partially funded by the National Human Genome Research Institute, as horses share over ninety hereditary diseases similar to those found in humans. To that end, I ..." Her mind suddenly filled with images of Johnny in his last moments. Oh, Johnny. What were you doing? "Well, I've run over time – I had better leave it at that."

The chairman stood again and suggested a round of applause for their keynote speaker. Fiona thanked the audience and sat in her chair. She desperately needed to go through that laptop.

Later, as the speakers mingled with the audience over canapés and wine in the lounge, Fiona nodded, smiled and answered the usual questions.

A man wearing a Winline Feeds jacket took a break from pitching sales and dishing out leaflets to offer Fiona his condolences. "Johnny was a great fella," he said, before moving on to collar another prospective client.

She glanced at her watch – it was definitely time to slip away.

A young man came up to her just then, offering a handshake and a keen smile.

"Doctor Buckley," he said. "I found your talk most interesting."

"Thank you very much."

"It's the second time I've listened to you speak. You

came to the National Stud to lecture us last April when I was doing the stud management course there."

"Oh yes, I remember. The stud chairman invited me to speak. Did you enjoy the course?"

"Oh yes. In fact, I won the silver medal and they let me stay on to prepare yearlings for the sales. I finished up last week and I'll be off to work at Balmain Stud in the new year."

"Will you indeed?" said Fiona, checking her watch.

"Anyway, I'm very interested in genetics. It's the future, as far as I'm concerned."

"I couldn't agree more."

"So, I wanted to ask you why you don't ever refer to epigenetics in your lectures? Do you study the concept in the lab at all?"

Fiona blinked, taken aback. "Well, that's not the usual question from a National Stud alumnus. Epigenetics is a fledgling science, still in the research stage. I'm still inclined to believe these sorts of things are very slow-moving. Similar to evolution. I'm sure we'll know more in years to come."

He eyed her intently, nodding all the time. Thanked her and moved on.

On her way through reception, she couldn't help but think about Johnny's father and his bees. She stopped and considered the laptop under her arm. It would have to wait until she got back home. It was already dark and she hated driving at night.

Her phone rang. "Hiya, Marcus. How was your day?"

"Not bad. Horses ticking along nicely. How did your lecture go?"

"OK, except for a heckler making snide remarks."

"Oh no. God, I'm sorry."

"What for?"

"Well, you know."

She smiled. "Thanks, Marcus."

"Tell you what, I'll go straight to your place and by the time you get home I'll have a bottle open and dinner ready."

"You're spoiling me, Mr. Hamilton."

"It's what you deserve. Now that you're no longer Mrs. Buckley I'm free to spoil you as I see fit."

"There's a spare key hidden under the seat of my bicycle. You'll find it parked behind the oil tank. Keep the key, it's yours now. I'll see you in half an hour."

Outside, the wind whipped at her cheeks and drove the rain sideways. Fiona huddled round her bag and the laptop as she headed for her car. She kept her eyes on the ground as she walked carefully over the sodden leaves stuck to the wheelchair ramp and made her way across the car park, wishing the amber lighting was more efficient.

Suddenly a car alarm whooped and blared. She broke into a run and rounded the tall hedge, skidding and nearly falling over. Then she saw the black shape in the back seat. She froze, unsure what to do. Her heart pounded.

The man in her car looked at her.

The noise was deafening and the flashing lights distorted him into a grotesque form. He climbed out and ran at her.

Fiona remembered the old mace spray Johnny had

bought her, way back when they lived in Dublin. Clutching the laptop under her arm, she fumbled in her bag. Her fingers closed around the small canister. She pulled it out, flipped the cap and pressed as the man charged at her. And missed his face. The man ducked and hit her in the side with his shoulder, knocking her backwards. She landed with a squelch on wet leaves, dropping the laptop.

"*Help!*" she yelled. "*Help!*"

The man looked up at the hotel then down at the laptop on the ground. He hesitated, unsure whether to take it or flee. Fiona aimed the spray at him and pressed again. Nothing. "*Help!*"

He glanced over his shoulder and bent down to grab the laptop. She jabbed at him with the useless canister, hitting his wrist. He backhanded her on the cheek.

She heard footsteps and someone shouting, "*Hey, you! Stop! Somebody call the guards!*"

Her attacker jumped through the bushes and vanished into the night. Another man bent over her. He was young and looked concerned. She heard somebody else come running. The wailing alarm scored the scene.

"Doctor Buckley, are you alright?"

Fiona picked herself up and brushed leaves off her suit. She checked her lecture notes and the laptop, found her key fob and disarmed the alarm. The silence was welcome. "Thank God for that," she said, massaging her cheek. "I'm fine, I think. Thanks, lads. I just want to get home."

"Don't you want to report this to the guards?"

"I've enough on my plate," she muttered. "I'll talk to the cops when I get home."

She thanked the two men and got in her car. Two miles later she stopped in a lay-by and let her body shake and the tears flow for a few minutes. Then she pulled herself together and looked at the laptop on the seat beside her. "Oh Johnny, what have you done?"

Her phone rang and made her jump. The screen said '**Private number**'. Fiona stared at the device a moment, cleared her throat and swiped at the screen.

"Dr. Buckley," said a distorted voice. "Things will be easier for you if you cooperate and provide me with the information I need."

"Whoever you are, I don't know what you're talking about. If it's my latest research you're after, you don't have to resort to threats – it'll be in the public domain soon enough."

"Don't try to be clever, Dr. Buckley. You know *exactly* what I am talking about."

"Right, that's it. I'm going to the police about this. They'll trace your number."

"The police cannot help you or stop me," replied the metallic voice. "I know that you two did something to my horses. You will tell me how you did it and then you'd better pray that you can rectify it. This is your last chance, Dr. Buckley. I try to avoid unpleasantness, but sometimes I have little choice."

The line went dead.

Chapter 9

Winline Horse Feeds
January 2010

Johnny sat at the window staring out at the extrusion machine. It had been running for nearly a month now. He had succeeded in convincing half of Winline's existing customers to switch to the new formula and with new clients the rate was eighty per cent. Still, it bothered him that some had simply refused to listen or give the new feed a chance, even when he pointed out the advantages. Fear of the unknown made people reluctant to embrace change. Johnny could sympathise with that. He'd had change forced on him and had no choice but to adapt. Other people rarely had that kind of catalyst. Still, he wasn't sure whether he envied them or pitied them.

An alarm on his watch went off. He opened the sack on the back of his chair and pulled out the large pillbox. He opened it on the table beside a bottle of water and placed his midday regime in a neat line on his notepad. Twelve pills. Muscle, protein and metabolic supplements, bowel regulators and bladder-control medications.

He swallowed his cocktail and ate a grilled vegetable sandwich he'd prepared at home that morning.

Then his guts cramped. Regular as clockwork. He wheeled himself to the bathroom, ripped off his disposable pull-up pants and dried his skin. Despite the constant redness, he preferred to deal with intermittent incontinence and rare infection – as opposed to catheterisation and constant infections. Johnny hauled himself onto the toilet and did what he needed to do. Using the toilet was his least favourite part of being paralysed. Shortly after his injury, he had asked the doctors if he could be fed with a drip and injections so he could forego bowel movements altogether. That was before he read *the book*, strengthened his mind and resolved not to let his condition dominate his life. He became a new person after that.

Afterwards, he washed his hands, pulled up his sleeve and checked his tattoo in the mirror. Fiona hated it but he didn't care. When he started bodybuilding, he and his training partner had gone to a Temple Bar parlour to get ink done. He had L5 etched onto his bicep in blood red. *Lumbar Five*. The official name for his condition. Johnny knew he was lucky: lumbar five was the last vertebra. It attached to the pelvis and meant that he had feeling on most of his upper body. But his penis no longer worked, not sexually anyway.

Johnny heard the buzzer, signalling the end of the working day. He wheeled himself back to the window. The machines would shut down in a minute. When everyone had left the factory he would test his agility. One by one, Johnny folded his legs under him, strapped his shins to his thighs and put on his kneepads. Stretched his arms and waited.

The extrusion machine was a kind of pressure cooker. When cooked feed exited the extruder through the tiny nozzle at the end of the barrel, the trapped steam dissipated rapidly and the soft pellets expanded like miniature, fresh-baked cookies. The pellets then were passed through a dryer. When the finished product emerged at the other end, it went directly into sealed bags, guaranteeing freshness. The raw ingredients for the following morning's batch were ready in the mixing hopper, so production could begin first thing and the feed would be on the road in the afternoon.

Johnny picked up the phone and asked security if the floor was clear. He was told it was. "Fine," he said. "I'm just going to work a bit longer. No need to make a round of the plant until I've gone."

Johnny went out to the factory floor and pulled on fingerless climber's gloves with padded knuckles. Running his eyes over the extruder, he figured out the best route up to the walkway. He had considered going up the stairway, but it was narrow and steep. This method would be quicker *and* a good workout. Johnny had considered doing it when everyone was around, claiming that he wanted to check the machine, but he knew the health and safety officer would never allow it. He spun his wheels a moment before gliding over to the supports which held up the gantry and the machinery. He glanced about, saw nobody. In one swift movement, he grabbed the support, pulled himself out of his chair and swung his bulk up to the first crossbeam. From there he powered from beam to beam like a legless ape, taking care not to let his strapped-up legs hit off anything. Back in his early bodybuilding days he'd once dropped a weight on his thigh and, unbeknownst to him, bruised the bone, which almost caused a serious infection. He'd been more careful after that and padded his knees whenever he worked out or hung from his rings at home.

He heaved and pulled until, with a final pivot, he was sitting on his ass on the raised walkway fifteen metres up. Looking around, he had a view of the whole production floor, including the microniser and the older machines used for making the traditional muesli-style feeds.

He padded along the walkway on his knuckles, dragging his protected knees behind him, until he reached the dryer and examined the flexible pipe connected to the air intake. A huge fan drew air from outside, heated it over a coil and forced it into the drying unit. An extractor fan at the other end pulled the used air into a chimney.

Satisfied, he flung himself back down again and was slightly out of breath when he got back to his chair. He stretched his arms. With daily practice it would get easier until it became second nature.

Back in his office he got out the local yellow pages, jotted down numbers and made lists.

When he got home that evening, the bungalow was deserted. Fiona was still at work, or somewhere else with Hamilton. Johnny was glad to have the place to himself. He pulled out the adapted hoover and did some dusting and cleaning, then he prepared a roast chicken, steamed vegetables and baked potatoes. He served himself and made sure there was enough left for Fiona. If she didn't come back for dinner, he'd eat it at work tomorrow. He attached his laptop to the printer and ran off an article about 1940s wartime Holland and a scientist who had gone through the historical records and formed conclusions about babies born to women who were pregnant during the Nazi occupation. It made enthralling reading as he swallowed more pills and munched his dinner.

After that, he scanned a news magazine. He read a piece about micro-particles of plastic. There was also an article about the inventions of the year: a retail saliva DNA test kit for people featured prominently. He'd show that to Fiona, if she hadn't already seen it.

Chapter 10

8 October 2015

Fiona pulled up outside her house in the damp darkness and knew something wasn't right. The lights were on, but the front door was ajar, blowing to and fro in the howling wind. Johnny's minivan was standing there, plastered with wet leaves, but she couldn't see Marcus's Land Rover anywhere.

Remaining in the car, she clicked the lock button and called the Garda Sergeant she'd dealt with after the fire. He told her to wait for the squad car.

She backed up the short driveway as far as the gate, but she was determined to keep watching the house until the police showed up. Wind rocked the car as she waited. She kept the engine running, stared at the dash clock and drummed her fingers on the wheel.

Eventually, flashing lights appeared in her mirror.

"Finally," she muttered, but her watch told her only fourteen minutes had passed.

A garda knocked on her window.

"Evening, ma'am," said the fresh-faced young officer. "If you could let our car pass, we'll check the house for you."

Fiona edged onto the grass verge.

The guards parked by the front door and cautiously went inside, talking into their radios all the time. A few minutes later the young guard emerged and told her the house was empty.

Inside, the place was a mess. Every drawer had been pulled out and emptied, every book tossed off the shelves and even the sofa and cushions were ripped open. Fibre and feathers dusted the wooden floor like a light snowfall. The kitchen area was a mess, but the oven was on and smells of a chicken casserole wafted through the open-plan space.

"Were you expecting company?" said Sergeant O'Dowd.

"My friend, Marcus Hamilton, was supposed to be here cooking dinner."

"The horse trainer?"

She nodded.

O'Dowd scribbled notes.

In the bedroom, the strongbox in the wardrobe had been opened. It looked undamaged, unforced but that was impossible. She kept the only key in her handbag. She was glad she had dropped the files and discs to her father's house.

The gym looked strangely untouched. As if Johnny's ghost had rearranged everything with military precision.

There was no sign of Marcus anywhere.

"Is anything missing, ma'am?" asked the young officer.

O'Dowd shot him an incredulous look.

Fiona threw her eyes over the mess. "Not at first glance, but it could take some time to give you a proper answer."

She was about to dial Marcus when she heard his Land Rover crunch to a halt outside on the gravel.

O'Dowd hauled his bulky frame to the door and barred a startled-looking Marcus from entering.

"What on earth's going on? Fiona? Are you OK?"

She nodded mechanically and sat on a stool, her eyes fixed on the torn cushions.

"Mr. Hamilton, were you here earlier this evening?" asked O'Dowd, letting Marcus step over the threshold and out of the wind.

"I was. Fiona had a tiring afternoon, so I said I'd meet her here and have dinner ready."

"So where were you when we arrived?"

"I'd forgotten to buy a decent bottle of wine. So after I put the casserole on, I dashed out to get one." He waved the bottle in his left hand.

"Where did you purchase it?"

"Excuse me?"

"The wine. Where did you buy it, sir?"

Marcus moistened his lips. "In the, *er*, off-licence in town."

"Kildare town?"

"Look, what the hell is this?"

Sergeant O'Dowd checked his watch and jotted in

his notebook. His cheap ballpoint scratched the paper as he wrote.

Fiona noticed Marcus clench his jaw.

"Will that be all, officer?" he said.

O'Dowd eyed him up and down. "For now. We know where to find you if there's anything else." He turned to Fiona. "Are you alright, Dr. Buckley?"

Another mechanical nod.

O'Dowd stepped out to use his radio and returned a minute later.

"Right so. We'll be off now, but in light of today's developments and because we haven't ruled out an organised crime connection to the lab fire, we'll be leaving a couple of officers outside for the night."

"Oh, that's hardly necessary," said Marcus. "I'll stay with her."

He crossed the room, set the bottle on the table and wrapped an arm around Fiona. He rubbed her shoulder and she leaned into him.

O'Dowd eyeballed Marcus. "We have our orders, Mr. Hamilton." His features softened as he addressed Fiona. "Dr. Buckley, I'll be back in the morning with the Super. We'll go over things again. Let us know if you discover anything missing."

"Thank you," she said in a near-whisper.

They let themselves out.

Minutes later, another squad car arrived and reversed up to the front door. A garda rang the bell and introduced himself and his partner. Fiona thanked them and offered tea. They declined.

Marcus checked the food, poured the wine and set

about cleaning up the mess.

Fiona took a long swallow from her glass. "I'll help you," she said, half-heartedly.

"No, you won't," he repiled softly. He got a blanket from the bedroom. Threw it over the ripped sofa cushions. "Here, sit down and relax."

Fiona flopped down, nearly spilling her wine. She stared at a painting of Johnny winning the Kentucky Derby and shut out Marcus's frantic sweeping and hoovering, just like she used to shut out Johnny's obsessive tidying, cleaning and organising.

She screwed up her eyes and let out a breath: the laptop was still in her car with her own briefcase and the stuff she'd had at the seminar. She fetched it while Marcus was busy stuffing feathers into a bin bag. Making straight for the bedroom, she glanced at the open strongbox and hesitated briefly before stuffing the slim computer under her mattress. She couldn't bring herself to turn it on right now.

A hot shower freshened her up and helped her remain positive. Marcus had the worst of the mess bagged, swept and cleaned. The table was set and dinner smelled inviting. He offered her a full glass, a kiss and a warm smile. The stress-induced cortisol left her system: she was exhausted and famished.

Over dinner, Marcus grumbled: "Bloody cop. I can't believe he gave me the third degree like that."

"He's only doing his job."

"*Hmm.* Oh, by the way; you should really get rid of Johnny's old van."

Fiona nodded.

"I mean, it's only a reminder, having it sitting there gathering leaves and grime."

She dropped her fork. "This *house* is a reminder of him. The business I work in is a reminder. The whole bloody mess I've been in since he died is a reminder. It's like he's watching me all the time. Trouble is, I'm not sure if he's laughing or crying. I have to confront it, Marcus." She stopped, apparently out of steam. Her features went blank. She drained her glass and motioned for more.

Marcus filled it up without a word. She took another hungry gulp.

"And, don't worry, that van's going to the Irish Wheelchair Association. It was in his will. I'll get round to it when I can."

"I'm sorry, I didn't know."

She smiled and took his hand. "I know. I'm sorry too. It's all starting to get to me." She pushed her plate away and went to the sofa. "Open another bottle, please. There's one in the rack," she said, flopping down.

A few glasses later, the events in the hotel car park seemed foggy and unimportant. Fiona was happy to push them to the back of her mind. She'd deal with all that in the morning.

She wished she could be back in her lab. Safe. In a controlled environment. If she was being honest, she'd craved controlled environments all her life. She'd once thought Johnny's obsessive personality was impressive, disciplined. Cute, even. Marcus was the same in many ways. *The devil's in the details*, he'd said to her the day they first met at Trelawn, when she was taking DNA samples from his horses. He had flashed her his dazzling

76

grin and winked. Like a knight in shining armour he'd invested in Equigenes. He'd make a good dad one day. Sooner rather than later, her body kept telling her.

She watched him dry his hands and crash down beside her. They kissed. She yawned. Marcus led her into the bedroom. Helped her into bed. Jumped in beside her and pulled her close.

"Have you thought about what they were searching for?" said Marcus, looking at the strongbox in the open wardrobe.

Fiona wore a pained expression. "I'm pretty sure I know," she said. "I caught someone going through my car at Duggan's this evening."

Marcus's eyes went wide. "You bloody what? Why didn't you mention that to the guards?"

"I told Sergeant O'Dowd when I phoned to get them here tonight. Seemed like he couldn't really see what the fuss was all about." She shrugged. "I suppose people in the wider world don't give a shit about horses or their genetics."

Marcus looked impatient. "So, whoever went through this place – was looking for what?"

"Well ... do you really want to know?"

He lit up. "Of course I do."

"I made a breakthrough last week. It'll be a game-changer, the racehorse business will never be the same, and I won't need to take blood or hair-root samples for testing anymore either."

"Tell me more."

"Thing is, nobody outside the lab knew what we were looking into, but seems like somebody knows – or at least thinks they know."

She had ruled out Cathy and Denise. They were young girls, keen and devoted to raising their academic profiles. Plus, they were devastated after the fire and worried about their jobs. As for Maura. No, she wouldn't. Maura was a vault.

"I just don't get it. I was going to publish the results and announce the tests in a few months anyway."

"Results of what?"

"It's a long story, but it'll change things and it'll piss off anyone who's breeding commercially – the sales companies too, for that matter. I've been liasing with a guy in America that makes analysis units. Anyway, I'm glad I took all the data home with me the night the lab burned." She yawned.

"You did? My God, Fiona. Where is it now?"

"It's somewhere safe and out of the way." Another yawn. "Marcus, I'm knackered." She rolled over and nestled into him. "Tell you in the morning."

The man sat at his desk sifting through the information. There was nothing in here he didn't already know. Raiding the laboratory had been a waste of time. The wily Buckley had stashed everything somewhere else. He sat back and sighed. This was getting out of hand. The gloves would have to come off.

They did something to the horses, he was sure of it. Something effective. Something very subtle. He'd had blood samples tested in America, England and Australia, and nobody could find any kind of substance, residue, or metabolite of a substance, but he knew something was wrong. It was the only explanation. Now the important question was: how would this get played out and who would suffer first? In moments of rage, he felt like torturing them all. Slow agonising deaths. But, with calm, rational thought, he knew he needed their knowledge and expertise. Once he had what he wanted he could arrange their disappearances.

He put his hands on the desk, palms down, and ran over scenarios in his head until his phone rang, rudely breaking his train of thought.

"I've been waiting for your call," he said, answering.

The man on the other end was audibly upset.

Chapter 11

Fiona woke and for a brief minute felt fresh and happy. Until her eyes settled on the open strongbox in the wardrobe. Marcus's side of the bed was empty and cold.

She dragged herself upright and stretched her muscles before hitting the treadmill in the gym. After a few minutes, when her heart began to pound and her blood flowed, she smiled. It was Johnny who'd introduced her to the therapeutic benefits of exercise. She never could get into weights like him – the treadmill was her thing. It freshened her thoughts.

She forced her mind past denial and anger. Now she needed to find out what was going on. Johnny was right, she didn't really understand the real world, mostly because she didn't want to be a part of it. Not full-time anyway. But it was time to face up.

She powered the machine down and did her cooling-off stretches. Johnny's book caught her eye. Dusty faded old thing. She couldn't believe the almost religious importance he'd attached to it.

After a shower and breakfast, she took tea and toast to the guards outside. She was told that Sergeant O'Dowd and the Superintendent would be there in an hour.

Inside, she retrieved the laptop from under her mattress, plugged it in and opened it on her knees.

"Johnny, Johnny, Johnny, what secrets have you got in here?"

Funny how he seemed more a part of her life since his death. She wouldn't put it past him to have planned it like this.

The computer booted up and demanded *username* and *password*.

She typed **Johnny** into the first box and then her fingers hesitated. She knew Johnny wouldn't use a date or number password. He was never that good with figures. It would be something personal. Remembering his awful tattoo, she tried **L5**. No access. Then **Lumbar 5** and **Lumbar Five.** Not those either. Tried them without the space. No access.

She chewed her lip. Her gaze wandered to the painting of him winning the Kentucky Derby on Bronx Spirit. She scrutinised the likeness: Johnny crouched on the regal beast, driving it over the line to win by a nostril. She remembered that weekend with fondness. Pat McCormack had flown them to America and the day before racing they'd toured the flagship stud farms of the Bluegrass. Then, when the horse had won, it'd been like a second honeymoon.

"What's your code, Johnny?" she asked the painting. "It'd be a horse, wouldn't it?"

Her fingers typed **Bronx Spirit**. No joy. Tried it without the space. No.

She went to the bookshelf in the corner and pulled out the unauthorised biography of Johnny's life up to his accident. Unimaginatively titled *Elegantly Flawed*, it was part homage, part character assassination by a well-known English racing journalist. Johnny had devoured the book when it was published while Fiona watched him get angrier with each page. She had told him not to torture himself, but he'd stopped listening to her months before that. She winced; he probably knew about Marcus even then. A year after the book was released, the author had gone public with his alcoholism and sought treatment. She remembered Johnny laughing as he read the newspaper confession. "*Not such a judgemental fucker now, are you?*"

She opened the book at the list of all Johnny's Group One and Classic winners. There were a lot of names. She tried a few. None worked. She drummed her fingers. It was a horse missing from the list that popped into her head. God, he loved that horse, despite what it did to him. "*Not the horse's fault,*" he used to say. "*Neither of us lived up to our potential,*" he said years later, when Sheikh Abdul sold the failed stallion to Korea. Horseracing's a fickle business.

She typed **Elegant Flaw** and the computer whirred into life. The desktop image was an ultra close-up of a honey bee pollenating a flower.

The desktop was almost bare. No random files

scattered over the image. An icon appeared informing Johnny that an overdue automatic desktop clean-up would proceed. Fiona rolled her eyes. Even a tidiness freak on his computer.

She went into **Johnny's documents** and scrolled through the contents. Clicked on the folder entitled **Bodybuilding.** There were dozens of articles about paraplegic bodybuilders and a diary / calender with thorough details of Johnny's every training session for the last four years. It listed every weight lifted and every rep performed. There was a side column listing all his meals, with breakdowns of every gram of protein, carbohydrate and fat he ate. It stopped abruptly a couple of months ago. She pursed her lips. The cancer had hit him like a steamroller. Didn't seem fair.

Scanning the diary file again, Fiona let out a whistle. She was impressed by the attention to detail. She had no idea Johnny went to all this trouble to get in shape. Like everything else, she mused, serious bodybuilding wasn't as easy as it looked. Even for able-bodied people. She fingered the touchpad and was about to back out of the folder when she saw a strangely named file. She stared at it a moment. Part of her didn't want to open the bloody thing. It was in pdf format and was called **Juice.** She had a bad feeling as she clicked on the icon.

It was a list of anabolic steroids: their dosage rates, effects, side-effects and tissue withdrawal times. All the information was given for both horses and humans.

"Oh, Johnny. Not that. Please tell me you didn't do that."

Needing a break, she made herself a coffee and

drank it staring out the window at Johnny's minivan and the police car.

Installing herself at the laptop again, she opened a folder named **Research.** It was a collection of files and downloaded articles from all kinds of websites.

She began trawling.

She read about Nazi-occupied Holland and how the local population were basically starved by their oppressors. A prominant historian described the horrors faced by the Dutch, but declared it was nothing compared to what the Russians endured during the seige of Leningrad. There was another piece from a news magazine about an analysis of Dutch children born to women pregnant during the occupation.

"Jesus, Johnny, genes passed from parent to child – you never let that one go, did you?" She closed her eyes, bit her lip. Unsure if she was mocking her dead husband or admiring him.

There was a similar piece about a study of historical information from remote villages in northern Sweden in the 1860s. Fiona read through statistics of farmers' life expectancies. She had to concede, there were some bizarre occurences. She digested the information with another coffee. There *might* be something here. However, she wasn't sure it had anything to do with horses.

Fiona skimmed through a long piece about the Defence Advanced Research Projects Agency funding research into vitamins and DNA defects in humans in America. A team of researchers in California at Berkley were looking into whether certain ailments could be cured simply by ingesting the correct combination of vitamins.

There was a piece about the life of celebrated American Olympic champion Florence Griffith Joyner. Fiona remembered Johnny talking about her with admiration.

The next article was a boring analysis of plastic micro-particles. Some researchers indicated that in normal daily life, people were at risk of ingesting molecules that migrate from the packaging to the food, particularly when the packaging is subjected to high temperatures. Direct sunlight and microwave ovens were considered to be the most widespread cataylsts for the migration.

Fiona rubbed her eyes. "Jesus, Johnny, what were you into? You're one weird puppy."

Deciding she'd had enough of reading all this doom and gloom, she closed the folder and opened another entitled **Notes and questions**. It contained a single document. Pasted at the top was an extract from Fiona's usual introductory speech on genetics.

Specifically, her blurb about the child of two Soviet weightlifters having abnormal, highly defined muscle mass, even as a toddler.

Fiona read comments that Johnny had typed below her speech and her jaw dropped open.

Why did this happen? A freak genetic occurrence? Or was it because the Soviets had a habit of slipping all kinds of substances to their athletes. Many were given performance-enhancing drugs without their knowledge. Fuck sake, there are even arcane stories of hermaphrodites being made to live as women and having cocktails of hormones and steroids fed to them.

What the fuck for? To win medals and prove a point in the Cold War?

Fiona's so bloody naive. She can't see the relevance. Doesn't believe me. Typical. Nobody listens to Johnny Buckley anymore, but they will.

Beads of sweat formed on her hairline. She had simply accepted that the children had naturally inherited this gene mutation. There was no why. It was just a given fact, a parameter of her research and rationale.

There was nothing else written in the file. Strange. Not like Johnny to let it go. Fiona had the feeling he'd either stopped in mid-sentence or had continued his theory in another file. She scoured the laptop, searching every file, folder and document. When she was done, she was struck by how little real information there was on it.

She was about to power down the device when she clicked her fingers. "Stupid, Fiona," she muttered, opening Johnny's email. The inbox was empty. Fiona shook her head. More paranoid cleaning. Her finger hovered over the mousepad as yesterday's events flashed through her mind: maybe *she* wasn't paranoid enough?

Eventually, she clicked refresh and waited. A single mail appeared. It was from someone called Brendan Tynan, reminding Johnny that next year's rent was due in December.

What the hell would Johnny be renting?

Fiona tapped out a reply, explaining that she was Johnny's widow. She shuddered as she typed the word, not sure if she deserved to be called that. She wondered if, during the last few years, Johnny still thought of himself as her husband.

Fiona asked for information on the rental item, offering to send next year's money from her bank account tomorrow, just to ensure a reply. She gave the landline number and her mobile and said she could be contacted at any time.

She hit send, stared at the screen and waited.

The landline rang.

Fiona jumped, sending the laptop tumbling to the floor. She picked it up and answered the phone.

"Morning, Dr. Buckley."

"Morning, Maura. How did it go with the insurers?"

"Oh, not too bad. They'll return again in a week. They'll expect to see you next time."

"Yeah, I know," she said in a distant voice, staring at the laptop. "Look, I've got something I need to figure out before I concentrate on getting the business running again."

"*Em*, look, I know you've a lot on your plate, but we need to get up and running soon. Wages need to be paid. Cathy and Denise are devoted, you know that, but Christmas is only a couple of months away and they need to know if their jobs are safe."

"What? Oh, of course they have jobs. Look, I'll meet the insurance company next week and try to fast-track a payout. In the meantime, we'll have to rent a building and order new equipment."

"OK then, I'll pass that on. Oh, by the way, Tony Carey from Winline called me an hour ago. He's in a bit of a tizzy. Says he needs to talk to you about Johnny. Something to do with the factory."

Fiona winced. "I'll give him a shout," she said without conviction.

Chapter 12

February 2010

Under an overcast sky, Johnny parked outside his lair. He undid his chair from its mounting, wheeled backwards slightly from the driving position, slid the side door open and pressed the lift button. Part of the floor moved on hydraulics, pushing Johnny and his chair out of the modified minivan, before gently lowering him to the ground. The mechanism was inspired by a forklift truck and had cost a fortune to install, but along with the system of levers on the dashboard, it gave Johnny complete independence to drive alone.

He glanced at his watch and right on cue a white van bearing the livery of a courrier company appeared round the corner. Johnny waved at the driver.

While the truck positioned itself, Johnny unlocked the shutter of his lair and pushed it up with a dramatic thrust of his thick arms.

The driver stared, jaw agape. "*Er*, delivery for a Mr. Buckley?" he said eventually.

"That's me."

Three boxes were signed for and unloaded.

Johnny shut himself into his lair and began unpacking. He put the machines on the aluminium table and admired his new workstation. He'd have to do the final preparation by hand, of course, because the smallest finishing equipment he sourced on the internet was capable of handling five tons per day. Quite a bit more than his needs.

Next, he retrieved his briefcase from the car and began taping his research notes, inspirations and conclusions to the wall over a desk he'd positioned opposite the table. He pulled a video camera and tripod out of the pouch on his chair, set it up by the desk and connected it to a monitor. Pulled a diary from the pouch. Set it beside the monitor. He'd need to chart his progress in case he ever decided to go public. When the time came, he'd also film himself giving the message and put it onto a disc, ready for delivery.

Johnny let himself out of the unit. Checking nobody was around, he popped the boot of his van and removed several large plastic bags. One at a time he balanced them on his knees and wheeled them inside. The last one smelled like a butcher's shop. He made a mental note to purchase air freshener.

His phone alarm beeped. Time for lunch and meds. After that he might as well begin. The sooner he started, the sooner he'd have results. Excitement bubbled inside him. If this worked – *when* it worked – it would change everything. And his guinea pigs wouldn't feel a thing. Wouldn't suffer. Wouldn't even notice the change. But their owner would.

The next morning Johnny called Tony and asked for a meeting. The manager parked his bulk in Johnny's office. "Look, it'll have to be quick. I've a conference call with China in half an hour."

"Thinking of global domination, are we?"

"That's right, Johnny. I'm working with a couple of our politicians on this one. There's a trade mission going out there next year and if we can get in as the official feed supplier to the new Equine Cultural City, we'll be laughing. We can build a factory out there an' all."

Johnny didn't give a shit about China. It had nothing to do with his mission.

"Yeah, right. Look, Tony, seeing as this extrusion thing is my baby, I'm going to take control of production from now on. I'll set the manufacturing schedules, delivery dates and times for all batches. I'll personally take a small sample from each batch – which we'll keep for a year, under lock and key." He gestured to the large steel cupboard in the corner.

Tony craned his flabby neck, straining his collar. "Oh, when did you have that installed?"

"Yesterday. I'll supervise the loading of the silos and hoppers each evening, so we can run off a batch first thing in the mornings and get them straight out to the clients."

Tony shrugged. "Fine by me."

"This'll be a game changer, Tony – horse feed will never be the same again."

"Yeah, yeah. Whatever. As long as it sells and the customers are happy."

"Don't worry, Tony. It'll be worth it."

"Better be."

Johnny clenched his jaw and flexed his shoulders. He saw fear in Tony's eyes.

"Er, look, Buckley," said Tony, hauling himself to his feet, "you're a gifted salesman and you know your stuff, I'll give you that. But, if this fails, you'll be out on your ear. The new owners want results not expensive failures."

Johnny knew he wouldn't be fired anytime soon. He winked at Tony. "Don't worry."

The manager hurried out.

Johnny clapped his hands together and smiled with his whole face for the first time in, well, he couldn't remember how long.

Chapter 13

9 October, 2015

Fiona gritted her teeth and made the call.

Tony picked up on the first ring. "You're a difficult woman to get hold of," he blurted out.

Fiona cut the phone a sideways glance. "What is it you want?"

"Look, not over the phone. Can you come to the factory?"

"I suppose. When?"

"Anytime after lunch."

The doorbell rang, she hung up and let Sergeant O'Dowd and his Superintendent in.

They went over the sequence of events several times.

As the Superintendent closed his notepad, Fiona rubbed her temples and ran her hands through her hair.

"I'm afraid we still have no leads on the arsonists,"

he said. "The only cameras in the vicinity were on your laboratory and, unsurprisingly, we have yet to find a witness. Taking the follow-up events into consideration, it certainly appears as if well-financed persons unknown are willing to go great lengths to obtain the results of your latest research, Dr. Buckley. Due to the serious and professional nature of the crimes, I'm afraid I have to insist that you hand over the information relating to your latest discoveries."

His speech had sounded prepared.

Fiona had been expecting this. She responded in a similar tone. "I don't wish to reveal that at this point."

The Superintendent's features hardened. "Madam, I hope I don't have to remind you that your refusal to hand over the documents could easily be considered as witholding evidence pertaining to a murder and arson investigation."

Fiona chewed her lip and fiddled with her phone. Those files and discs were all she had left of her life's work. She really didn't want to see them lost in the Garda holding vaults while all this was sorted out. If they caught the culprits, the evidence would surely be held until after their trial. She needed to get her business up and running as soon as possible.

"Look, I'm sorry, but those files are all I have left of my livelihood. I'm not trying to be difficult, but now I'm starting to think that the best way forward is to get back to work, finalise everything and make it all public."

The Super pursed his lips. Stared at her like an irritated schoolteacher. "Might I further point out that we could always get a warrant and force you to hand them over."

She looked at the table.

The Superintendent cleared his throat. "However, in light of the trauma you have undergone during the past week, I don't wish to go down that road. Yet. But, perhaps you should bear in mind that your life would be safer if these documents were in Garda custody."

He had a point, but still something nagged at her, telling her not to hand over the goods. If she got back to work and went public, it would surely remove the danger. What would be the point in more theft and arson if the information was already out there? She stared at the painting of Bronx Spirit. *Time to kick on and get the whip out,* Johnny used to say whenever he wanted to get something done.

"Please give me some more time to think about it. I'm really grateful for all you're doing, but I need a couple of weeks to get my life back in order."

The Super frowned and stared at his notepad.

Fiona could feel her palms becoming clammy.

Eventually, he nodded. "Very well, I'll give you some leeway." He cleared his throat and pointed to his colleague. "Sergeant O'Dowd will be in charge of your security team. We'll have officers stationed outside this house during the hours of darkness. You'll be required to check in with us regularly during the day. You'll contact Sergeant O'Dowd directly on his mobile. I would recommend that you advise him of all your movements."

Both men stood. O'Dowd produced a business card and placed it on the table.

"Keep in touch now," he said, a goofy smile on his moonface. "And don't worry, we'll keep you updated on the investigation." Then he paused, looking puzzled. "I have to say, despite being stationed in Kildare the past two years, I had no idea people even did genetic research on racehorses. It's amazing the lengths rich people will go to, just to win a horse race."

Fiona was about to reply when her phone rang in her hand. "I should take this."

The men nodded and made for the door.

"Hiya, Marcus."

The Super froze with his hand on the doorknob, ears flapping.

"Hang on a sec, Marcus," she said.

She walked to the door and quickly ushered the guards out.

Flopping onto the sofa, she said into the phone, "Oh, that's better. I've had the cops here."

"Really? What do they think? Any leads?"

She told him what the Superintendent had said. "They kept on about my hidden data, but I'm buggered if I'm giving the remnants of my livelihood to the cops. I'd never see it again."

Silence.

"Marcus?"

"Couldn't you just have copies made?"

She frowned. "Why would I want to spend all that time copying it out and burning more discs? No, thanks."

"Oh, so you've stuff on disc too? How much material are we talking about here?"

"Look, it doesn't matter. Anyway, I've decided: I'm going to get back to work."

"That's great. Good for you. When?"

"Soon as possible."

"By the way, you never got round to telling me the full story last night. Where is all this precious info? And, more importantly, what's it all about?"

"Not over the phone." God, she thought, I'm getting like Johnny. Maybe that's a good thing. "I'll tell you tonight. You coming over?"

"If you'll have me," he said with a chuckle.

She smiled. "Of course. You're all that's keeping me sane at the moment."

A pause. Then, "I'll see you later."

"OK. Hey, wish me luck – I have to meet Tony Carey at Winline this afternoon. He says it's urgent."

On the way out, she checked Johnny's email. Still nothing from Brendan Tynan.

On the way to Maynooth through the murky drizzle, Fiona noticed a grey hatchback in her mirror. It stayed behind her for several miles and at times seemed to fade into the weather. But it didn't turn off. Johnny's warning scratched at her mind. The hairs on her neck rippled. Approaching Maynooth, she turned onto a backroad. The car followed. Her heart pounding, she decided to slow down, hoping it would pass her. Instead, it got very close. She could see two occupants wearing hoodies. The driver had a phone clutched to his ear.

Panicking, she indicated and pulled over. The car almost rear-ended her. The driver leaned on his horn. She stared at the men and dialled a number as they shot past.

"Sergeant O'Dowd, I'm being followed."

"Are you sure?"

"Yes, I think so. Oh, I don't know. I'm not used to this. But they came so close they nearly rear-ended me."

"Where are you now? Is the car still behind you?"

"No – I pulled over and they passed."

"What make of car?"

"I don't know. Grey. A hatchback. A rear spoiler."

"I don't suppose you got the number?"

"No. I ..."

A discontented pause. Then, "I'll make a note of this, but that sounds like two roadhog young fellas. Calm down and go about your day."

She turned the car, continued to Maynooth and eventually found Winline Feeds at the far end of an industrial estate. She'd never been to Johnny's place of work before.

The pretty receptionist sprang into action when Fiona gave her name. She led Fiona out of reception, across the production floor and into an office. Fiona saw the immaculately arranged desk missing a chair behind it. A cold shiver rippled up her spine and over her scalp. There was a large storage cupboard against one wall. Its doors were open and the shelves were empty.

"Yeah. So, Mr. Carey wanted to meet you in here," said the receptionist, her eyes down. "He'll be with you in a minute."

Fiona nodded.

The young woman hovered in the doorway. "Dr. Buckley, I'm Niamh Redmond. My father Malachy breeds jumpers over in Galway. He got some tests done from your lab a year ago."

Fiona plastered on a grin while she searched her

mind. "Oh, that's right. I hope the results were helpful."

"They were." A pained expression spread over her features. "I'd like to say how sorry we all are about Johnny's passing."

"Thanks very much."

"He was some worker. Usually first in and always last to leave. In just a few years he changed opinions on horse feed for a lot of people. My father included – and that's no mean feat."

The women smiled at each other, but Fiona felt slightly embarrassed. She knew little of Johnny's work during the last few years, bar the glowing reports Marcus had given her about the feed – he swore by it.

Niamh checked over her shoulder, then leaned close to Fiona. "They're lost here without him. Mr. Carey doesn't know what to do. Between you and me, it was all down to Johnny." Her eyes dulled and her tone changed. "He was an inspiration. After all that happened to him, it just –"

Tony Carey bustled into the office. "Thanks, Niamh, that'll be all."

She left hurriedly and he closed the door behind her.

"Welcome, Mrs. Buckley. Please sit down. Tea? Coffee?"

He removed his jacket and plonked himself on one of the chairs in front of the desk. His neck spilled over his shirt and there were dark patches seeping out from his underarms.

"Neither, thanks. And it's Dr. Buckley."

"Oh. Sorry. Anyway, I've asked you here in the hope you can shed a bit of light on something."

"I'm happy to help in any way I can but, as you may

know, Johnny and I weren't close the last few years and I knew little of his actual work."

Carey looked flummoxed. Beads of sweat had formed at his hairline. "I'll get straight to it, so. We've heard a few rumours lately, that the extruded feed products aren't what they should be."

"What do you mean?"

"Ah, well, that is, people are saying that the product is not what it says on the bags. Rumours are a killer in this business. Most people know so little about feeding horses that they happily believe any old gossip and change suppliers. Yesterday, our sales guy at the breeders' seminar said he was inundated with questions and one of our major clients has been making unhappy rumblings for the last month or so."

"Surely you or your clients can have the feed tested?"

He raised a finger. "That's the problem. Johnny kept a small sample from every batch here under lock and key." He cocked his thumb at the open cupboard. "The extruded feed has a shelf-life of five months printed on the bag, but Johnny always said that the feed would be good for a year, due to the decreased moisture content. So he kept each sample for a year. We went through everything in the cupboard last week and ran off the results in our own lab." Carey fingered his tie and wore an expression that could have been constipation or confusion.

"And?" said Fiona.

"Well, basically everything checked out. Except for one thing: the vitamin and mineral levels on the feed for our extruded clients were all exactly the same."

"Sorry, I don't follow."

"Our large clients – and any small ones that want to pay for the service – get feeds that are directly tailored to their needs. This includes soil and pasture analysis of the land, so we can make sure the trace-mineral levels are perfect for each client."

Fiona nodded. She'd heard Johnny enthusing about this at some stage.

"So, for example, Pat McCormack's Balmain Stud is in Kilkenny, Sheikh Abdul's place is in Tipperary and Trelawn Park is in Kildare. And we've many small clients scattered all over the country. There's just no way the land is exactly the same in each place."

"That seems logical. Are you sure your people didn't mix up the samples?"

"Positive. Johnny was so organised, he had everything clearly labelled. They tested exactly what came out of each bag."

"All the same, you should probably run the tests again."

Carey looked agitated. "They're doing that as we speak. What I need from you is any work-related stuff that Johnny may have kept at home and, if his laptop is at home, I'd appreciate it if you returned it. It's company property, and there may be stuff on it that can help clear up all this mess."

Fiona looked past Carey, through the huge window onto the production floor. She was most definitely not handing over Johnny's laptop to Tony Carey. She needed it more than him. Anyway, she was never going to let anyone read his training diaries or the **Juice** file. Whatever had happened between them, she didn't want a posthumous steroid scandal to taint his name all over again. True or untrue, it would convince people that he really had taken cocaine before the Irish Derby all those years ago. And Fiona was sure that he hadn't done *that*. He'd always maintained his sample had been tampered with. Johnny might not have been an angel, but not cocaine. Never.

"Dr. Buckley?"

"What? Oh sorry. I was just racking my brains. Look, I know he never kept any work papers or files at home. I'll let you know about the laptop."

Carey frowned. "Haven't you seen it around the house?"

Fiona hated lying. "I suppose it must be somewhere but we, that is, *I* was burgled last night and the place is still a mess."

Carey's jaw dropped open. "Holy mackerel! I'm sorry, I had no idea. I know you're having a difficult time of it lately, but I'm under a lot of pressure as well." He hesitated and screwed up his face. "I suppose you know I don't own the company anymore?"

"I had no idea."

He blew out his cheeks. "I had to sell the majority when the economy went belly-up. It was either that or shut down. Anyway, I was basically forced to take Johnny on and get into this whole extruded feed rigmarole. So, if it turns out he's been fiddling the product, I'll lose what little I have left."

"Who did you sell to?"

"*Huh*. Would you believe it, I don't even know." He chuckled in self-mockery. "Some businessman, eh? I've only met a couple of suits. Hedge-fund fellas. They fly over from London every quarter and invade my office." He pulled at his collar. "If they get wind of this ..."

Fiona wanted to feel sorry for Carey but, as they say, if you lie down with dogs you might be prone to fleas. What was Johnny's part in all this?

"Tony, I'll have another look through the place at home and let you know," she said, standing up.

"Grand, so. And please, Dr. Buckley, don't breathe a word of this to anyone until I've had a chance to get to the bottom of it. Apart from the hedge-fund lads, if Pat Mac heard about this he'd take us to the cleaner's."

Fiona arched her brow. Maybe working in the feed business made you paranoid. "Wouldn't dream of it." She shook his clammy palm and walked out, thinking that all roads led back to Johnny.

Back at home, she parked outside the house and stared at Johnny's van. That thing needed to get off the place. She went inside and called the Wheelchair Association. They would be delighted to receive it, but could Fiona arrange delivery? She said she could.

Afterwards, Fiona checked in with O'Dowd. She heard him scribbling notes as he said the night shift would be there at six.

Then she opened both Johnny's and her own laptops and set them up side by side on the table. With a heavy sigh, she began replying to emails and looking for suitable places to station her business until the money came through to rebuild the lab.

She refreshed Johnny's inbox every five minutes, but

only a bodybuilding newsletter appeared.

She scribbled a list of equipment she'd need to get her results properly compiled. She was about to phone Maura to discuss the way forward when she heard a ping.

There it was: new message. Brendan Tynan.

She hesitated a second before she clicked it open.

Dear Dr. Buckley,

Mr. Buckley paid me a retainer to ensure a special level of privacy. I'm afraid that I cannot enter into any discussion or disclose any information about the arrangement I had with him without receiving proof of his passing. An obituary or death notice is not sufficient. I need to see a colour scan of the original death certificate. I am sorry if this seems unhelpful or callous under the circumstances, but I have been deceived in the past by a married couple who became estranged. One party misled me in order to obtain information and access. I was subsequently threatened with legal action.

Yours sincerely, Brendan Tynan.

Bloody hell – more paranoia.

She picked up the phone.

"Hi, Maura. I want to get up and running ASAP. All we need is an office and computers. Find a quiet premises with good security and tell Cathy and Denise to order the following equipment. Got a pen?"

"Fire away."

Fiona read the list to her secretary. "Right now, all I want is to get my ducks in a row and announce the new tests. It'll take the pressure off the company and give people something to talk about while we rebuild."

"I've been waiting to hear that, Doctor – well done yourself!"

"Thanks. And Maura?"

"Yes?"

"Keep all this under your hat. I don't want anyone to find out what I'm doing, or where I'm doing it."

"Right you are. Leave it with me."

"Oh, by the way, where would I go to get Johnny's death cert?"

"Sure you can do all that online now. It might take a few days, so don't you trouble yourself. I'll handle it."

"What would I do without you, Maura?"

The older woman chuckled. "I don't know!"

That evening, Marcus arrived just before seven and cooked dinner. Afterwards Fiona snuggled into him on the sofa as they watched mindless TV.

He stroked her hair and asked her about her meeting with Carey.

"Now that Johnny's gone, he's in a bit of a pickle."

"Will it affect the feed?"

"I'm sure there are other nutritionists in the world. You've always loved that extruded feed that Johnny came up with, right?"

"I tell everyone that'll listen: it's the way forward. No need to feed raw grains with it." He looked at her. "So no digestive upsets: in the last five years, not a single case of colic at Trelawn."

"That's impressive alright. You've never had *any*

problems with the product?"

"No. Why? What did Tony say?"

She felt his torso stiffen next to her.

"He asked me not to repeat it. He's investigating something. You know he doesn't own the place anymore?"

"I'd heard rumours a few years ago, but they fizzled out."

They sat in silence for a minute, but she could tell Marcus's mind was turning.

"You never did tell me what you'd discovered just before the fire. What breakthrough did you make?" he asked.

She kissed him and looked into his eyes with a mischievous grin. "Are you asking as an investor, a trainer or my lover?"

"All of the above, naturally," he said in a dry tone.

There was a glint in her eye. "Well, I'm going to disappoint you on all counts, Mr. Hamilton."

"And what can I do to change your mind?"

"Absolutely nothing." She kissed him again.

He pulled away and for a split-second looked angry.

"Look, Marcus, I decided today that the best way to stop all this shit getting any worse is to get back to work again and announce the findings ASAP. As soon as Maura finds us a nice secluded place to work and we get some equipment, I'll go to my dad's place and get all the files from him. I should have a full report ready for you, and everyone else, a month after that."

"So that's where you put everything," he laughed. "Good choice!"

"What are you trying to say?"

"Your father's a grizzly bear. I bet even Johnny was shit-scared of him."

"He's not that bad."

"But, seriously, you're not going to tell me about the breakthrough?"

"No, but I'll whet your appetite."

He looked at her eagerly.

Perhaps a little too eagerly.

Fiona had a strange feeling.

"Let's just say I won't have to bother taking blood to test for anything pretty soon. Saliva is the future. And there's a company in America which is already developing hand-held analysis units for humans. But you'll have to wait for the gene news. I was thinking about a Christmas announcement." She smirked. "That'll give the sales companies something to panic about."

"*Hmm*." Marcus stared at his shoes.

Fiona eyed him, her brow knitted. "What's up?"

"I'll be up to my neck in it next week. You might not see much of me. Big races at Ascot. So the Sheikh might appear at Trelawn to look at the horses during the week."

She nodded. "I understand."

"But, how would you like to come to Ascot next weekend? It's Champions Day and I'm running Oxygen Thief. We could stay the night in London?"

"*Um, wow!* That sounds great, but I'd really rather dive into work. Sooner it's done, sooner it's out in the open."

He put his arm around her. "You can take a weekend off, surely? I want to finally walk into a parade ring with you – as a couple."

She gazed into his eyes. "You're a wonderful man and I love you. Thanks for the invitation, but I've got to get on with things here. Just make sure you come back with a winner." She kissed him again. "Let's go to bed."

The stocky, hooded men prowled through the field and silently crouched behind the hedgerow. They were both soaked from the long grass and sodden earth. Pieter Koster and Wikus Heyns hated rain. Being South African, they preferred to ply their trade in sunnier parts of the world, but a job was a job and the client had apparently not yet found what he was looking for, so they were stuck with this gig. Pieter pulled night-vision goggles over his eyes and adjusted the settings. He cursed when he saw the police car.

"She's got protection," he said.

"*Ag*, I can see that," said Wikus. "It's a moonlit night, you don't need those things. That's it then. There's no point in staying out here all night. Let's go."

"Oh, fok it, Wikus, it's only a pair of Paddy cops. Let's do them, get the goods and get out of here. They'll be as easy as that old security guard."

Wikus wagged a finger. "We're not shooting black fellas in the bush back home, *oke*. If we kill a cop, all hell'll break loose. We have our orders: low-key for the moment, my mad friend. But, don't worry, you'll get action soon."

Pieter grunted. A lopsided smile distorted his scarred face.

They slunk back the way they came and slid into their car.

While Pieter took off his goggles, Wikus said, "Tomorrow, I'm driving. And thanks to your overzealousness today, we'll have to change the car too."

"OK, whatever."

"Now, give me your weapon."

A small black shape was handed over. Wikus paired it with his own and stashed them under the dashboard next to the fuse panel.

Pieter started the engine and they drove off.

Marcus lay in bed staring at the ceiling. Fiona slept soundly with her head under his shoulder and an arm over his chest. Marcus had an obligation to fulfill, but he knew he shouldn't go through with it. Deep down he knew he should tell the fucker where to go, but if he did that ... No, it would be too much to bear. Marcus raised Fiona's arm and carefully slipped out of the bed. Crept out to the kitchen and paced barefoot on the tiles. He saw the pair of laptops on the coffee table and considered opening them, then decided against it.

"*Shit, shit, shit*," he muttered. Then, he flung on his coat and, opening the door very quietly, stepped outside. The cold stone doorstep cut into his feet and he shifted from one foot to the other as he opened his phone and made a call.

When he'd finished he turned around and saw the gardaí sitting in their car. Staring. He forced himself to wave before dashing to his Land Rover and pretending to look for something. Then he hurried back inside.

Chapter 14

Eight days later

17 October 2015

Fiona didn't know whether to rent an office in Dublin or a small bungalow in the Wicklow Mountains. She was unsure which would be safer. O'Dowd urged her to go for the Dublin option. Fiona decided to pospone her choice until the computers and equipment were to be delivered. A few more days' breathing room.

Maura had ordered the death certificate, but the postal service had yet to drop the document through Fiona's letterbox.

That week, she rose each morning, called O'Dowd and made her way to her father's house. Thomas Riley lived on the outskirts of Naas in the modest detached house Fiona had grown up in. Alone since his wife died of a heart attack twelve years before, he worked from home churning out reams of pedigree analyses for private clients and racing publications. Whenever Fiona visited, she brought bags of shopping and stocked his fridge with food that wasn't processed and packaged. Not that she'd ever told him it was an idea of Johnny's. He'd refuse to eat the food if she said that.

She made tea and spread her files out on the dining table.

Thomas Riley sat opposite his daughter and chewed nicotine gum.

"I'm glad you gave up," said Fiona. "Stick at it, you'll feel better."

"I feel tetchy, is what I feel."

"More than usual?"

He cut her a sideways glance.

She inserted a disc into her laptop and opened a file.

Thomas ran his eyes over her work. "I don't mind holding onto this stuff for you, but I wish you'd get it done and out there. You've been here a week already, and I don't like the idea of a bunch of lunatics coming after you for it."

"Oh, and you think I do?" She sighed. "Sorry, Dad. Don't worry, I'll be out of your hair soon."

"Oh, it's not that." He cast a sullen glance at his wife's photograph. "It's nice having you here every day." He picked up a file and scanned through it. "So you really think you'll be able to come up with a handheld unit that can analyse saliva and give instant results?"

"That's the plan. Well, part of it anyway."

He shook his head. "Sure, that'll put you out of business."

"No, it won't. If anything, it'll expand it." She took a

sip of tea. "Look, you used to go to horse sales and give people pedigree advice and analysis, right?"

"Not for a while now, but yes."

"And you helped people to make a more informed decision?"

"I did my best."

"OK. Well, my service is the next step on from that."

"I don't follow."

"Imagine, buyers can purchase a DNA test unit. They can swab saliva from a prospective purchase and bring the unit to me – I'll have offices at all the major sales – then I can print and analyse the results and give them certain genetic information about the horse."

"And you're sure your jiggery-pokery is accurate?"

"Look, Dad, I know you've always preached that pedigree is God, but I get inside that, underneath it. Down to the building blocks of life. It's dead certain. Besides, I'll be announcing new findings which will give people information on things we've never touched on before."

"Jesus. That'll piss off every commercial breeder in world. Not to mention the sales companies. No wonder they're breaking into your house and burning down your lab." He stood abruptly and left the room, returning a minute later with a shotgun and cleaning rods.

"Dad, what the hell are you doing?"

He set the weapon gently on the table and began disassembling it. "I may be a grumpy auld bastard, but I'll not let a shower of cunts burst in here and take your hard work."

"Put that away now. Or I'm leaving."

He carried on cleaning the weapon. "I haven't shot a

pheasant in years. I only kept the licence up because I thought I'd have to take this to yer man one day."

Fiona rolled her eyes. "You're never going to say his name, are you?"

"He was a selfish, arrogant little bollix." Thomas smirked. "Still, it's funny the way life works out. You're happier with Marcus – it's written all over you. He's a decent man. Honest. And perhaps the other fella got what was coming to him."

"That's enough." She stood and began stacking files.

Her father raised his palms. "I'm sorry, Fiona. Really. Sit, carry on. Please. It's so nice having you here." He put the gun back together and took it out of the room.

A couple of hours later, Fiona looked at her watch. "God, is that the time? I've got to go. I want to watch Ascot at home."

The old man furrowed his brow. "Ah, watch it here with me, go on." He spread the *Racing Post* out on the table and scanned the runners and riders.

But Fiona wanted to hit the treadmill, then sprawl on the sofa with a bottle of wine and cheer on Marcus's horse. She didn't want to listen to her father berating her for drinking during the day. Maybe he was right, but she needed to unwind.

"Sorry, Dad – I've got things to do at home while I watch the races." She closed her laptop, stuffed it in her bag and stacked the files and discs.

"Leave them," said Thomas, flapping his hand. "I'll lock them away."

She kissed him on the cheek and dashed to her car. Backed onto the road and drove off.

She said a little prayer that Marcus would win this afternoon. She had a feeling which she tried to ignore, but it keep pecking at her.

At home on the treadmill, it occurred to Fiona that her dead husband might have known more about genetics than she gave him credit for. She did her warm-down stretches and Johnny's book caught her eye. She picked it up and suddenly her heart turned upside-down.

Feeling light-headed, she sat and stared at the thick tome. Was that what it was all about? Was *that* his motivation? So who was the target, and why? She needed to know what he'd been renting. Where was that bloody death cert?

She opened Johnny's laptop and went over things again. Still unable to see the big picture, she closed the device and turned on the TV to watch the Ascot races.

In the Dorchester Hotel on London's Park Lane, the occupant of the top-floor Terrace suite was pacing the master bedroom. Pondering scenarios and options. One way or another, this afternoon would be crunch time. The outcome of today's races would decide his plan of action. And that, in turn, would determine the futures of a few people. He was tired of waiting. He smiled, checked his tie and joined his companions in the living room.

Chapter 15

March 2010

Johnny paid the shop assistant for three large tubs of bodybuilding protein supplements. The pretty girl smiled as she handed him the bag. Johnny gave her a bitter look. Back in the day, he'd have flashed her a grin that climbed to his sparkling eyes and she would've melted. Not that he ever cheated on Fiona, he just enjoyed flirting with women and cajoling men to do his bidding. Nowadays, he couldn't be bothered with that shite. It all seemed such a waste of time and, anyway, he was no longer interested in connecting with people. He had more important things to think about.

He left the sports nutrition shop with the bag on his knees and wheeled himself through the suburban shopping centre. The place was alive with Saturday-morning shoppers of all ages. Spinning down the brightly lit passageway, he noticed two shops had closed, their windows papered over. Sign of the times. He turned the corner and saw a woman putting the finishing touches to a window display. *Jasmine's Food Eden* was promoting a new line of Irish-made natural bee products. Johnny gripped the handrim, stopping his chair suddenly so he could read the advertising. If only his father had kept his bees! He was ahead of his time, talking about this stuff decades ago, but nobody in Ireland would listen to him. The bank thought he was mad when he had the guts to ask them for a start-up loan.

There were three products on display. Bee-pollen capsules which promised to boost circulation and blood function, bee amino powder that promised to increase immune defences and the all-conquering royal jelly tablets which promised everything bar eternal life and had a price tag to match. Just because this stuff was essential for bees, it didn't mean it would deliver for humans. That's what his dad used to say, but he knew that wouldn't stop people queuing up to buy it. Johnny's mouth formed a sad smile. His dad could have made a decent living out of this stuff without having to sit behind the wheel of a truck all hours.

He wheeled into the shop and saw a taut woman in a finely tailored trousersuit placing ten boxes of royal jelly on the counter. Her fingers glittered as she handed her credit card to the orange-tinted sales girl. When the woman turned around, Johnny grinned at her. She hastily donned oversized sunglasses and waltzed out, carrying her booty in a flashy bag. Another one trying to make herself a queen. It wouldn't change her of course, not in the way she hoped – too late for that, his father would say. But Johnny wondered what would happen if she'd been raised on it from birth. Or if she was actually a bee and not a wasp in fine clothing.

Johnny picked up a leaflet and left. On his way out, he passed the food court where the smell of fried trans-fats thickened the air. He stopped in his tracks to watch a man and his young son stuff burgers into their mouths. The man had a pasty complexion and sat in a floppy way, probably the result of too many hours in a cubicle with a computer. The child looked about six or seven – Johnny was never really sure how old kids were – and already had the complexion of his father. In Johnny's day, kids were lean and tough They walked everywhere and nobody had money for burgers and chips. That shit'll kill you, he wanted to say to them. He wanted to tell the man not to condition his child's taste buds to crave that food, but he told himself not to judge. Perhaps today's meal was a rarity, a one-off. He hoped so for the kid's sake.

The place was filling up for lunch. Johnny dodged his way past hungry shoppers gawping at shiny, illustrated menus and wheeled out to his van.

In the car park, he noticed three Goth teenage girls. They skulked between two minivans. Smoking, complaining, swiping at their phones. They threw paranoid glances at Johnny as he wheeled by. Johnny thought they looked about thirteen or fourteen. He watched them inhale deeply on the thin white sticks and wondered how that would affect their children.

He drove to his lair and went to work.

Chapter 16

Ascot Racecourse
Berkshire, England
17 October 2015

It was a long-shadowed autumn afternoon, leaves clung to trees with dying breaths. The massive modern grandstand loomed over the track while the parade ring behind it was bathed in a warm glow. People milled about, chattering. The atmosphere crackled as the crowd swapped tips and opinions for the day's races.

The highlight of the afternoon was the Queen Elizabeth II stakes. The TV pundits agreed there was little to separate the pair of Irish raiders. Atavistic, representing the once all-conquering Pat McCormack stable, was a supremely talented individual who had been plagued with injury. Trainer Joe Nolan was quoted as saying the horse was in top form and would relish the good ground.

Marcus Hamilton's runner, Oxygen Thief, had been a backward sort who'd taken time to come to hand, never racing as a two-year-old. After a string of close seconds earlier this season, including the Irish 2000 guineas, Oxygen Thief had won France's top mile race under the humid August sun at Deauville. He had not been seen on the track since, and was rumoured to be in rude health. Worth a bet, the pundits said.

Marcus had butterflies since he stepped off the plane at Gatwick with his horse and grooms. Now it was half an hour to post time and the pressure was intense. This win would solve a lot of problems. He leaned against a stall door in the saddling-up paddock, watching his groom lead Oxygen Thief in circles with the other runners.

He checked his watch. He'd give the horse a few more minutes' relaxation before tacking him up and fixing the girth tight around the animal's ribcage. Marcus didn't care if the horse was last into the spotlight of the parade ring – though Sheikh Abdul might be a bit upset. That was *his* problem though. Marcus had laid it out firmly in the beginning when the Sheikh wanted to secretly buy into horses at Trelawn: no interference in the raising or training of the athletes would be tolerated. It was even in the contract. Although several other things weren't.

Those were the things that kept Marcus awake at night. He'd even started smoking again a few days ago and, as a result, he found himself avoiding Fiona. She never approved of smoking and was the one who'd got him to quit two years ago. He'd enjoy a few more today – help him deal with the stress and his guilty conscience. Then he'd have his last cigarette tonight. He missed her too much to stay away from her any longer.

Out of the corner of his eye, he saw Pat McCormack slip into the paddock and disappear into the stable where Joe Nolan was saddling Atavistic. Marcus admired Joe. He knew how difficult it was to bring a horse back from injury, but if Joe had the talented steed right, he'd pose the biggest threat to Oxygen Thief.

Inside Job, Sheikh Abdul's official runner in the race, walked past Marcus and he assessed the animal. Bloody thing looked overdone and worn out. A vanity runner if ever there was one. Marcus tut-tutted. Horses were not fancy cars to be trotted out for parties to impress people. There was no point in having a runner just to give people the impression your stable was doing well. But then the general public didn't know the Sheikh owned shares in Marcus's horses, although Marcus supposed many in racing knew, or at least suspected when a Hamilton champion ended up as a stallion on the Sheikh's stud.

The runners were saddled and sent to the fishbowl of the parade ring. Marcus nodded to his groom and followed his horse. "Talk to him, Conor," he said to the groom. "Try and keep his mind off the crowds."

Marcus spotted the Sheikh flanked by three burly, earpieced men in tailored suits, a pudgy dark-skinned youth fingering a tablet and a statuesque young woman with creamy skin.

As if just in passing, Marcus stopped a moment and shook the Sheikh's hand.

"He's in the form of his life. He'll run a big race," he said, barely moving his lips.

"I expect nothing less."

"You could stick a few quid on him," said Marcus, glancing at the girl.

She looked away.

The Sheikh's dark eyes darted from Marcus to the girl to the grandstand. He screwed his face into a half smile.

The Sheikh rarely smiled in public. Marcus couldn't tell if he was happy or displeased. He found an empty patch of lawn to wait for his jockey.

A moment later, the riders filed out of the weighroom and dispersed to their various owners and trainers. Inside Job's trainer and jockey sidled up to the Sheikh.

Christy Ryan trotted up to Marcus, his withered features a picture of stern concentration.

"Break fast and make all," said Marcus to the rider. "Manipulate the pace from the front. Keep it at even twelve-second furlongs and you'll have enough in the tank to quicken for the finish. Atavistic'll aim to give you a fight, but you're on the toughest horse."

The veteran jockey grunted acknowledgment as Marcus legged him onto the horse. His dessicated complexion twisted into a grimace. "I won't get into a fight for the early lead. If anything else goes off at a crazy lick, I'll stay at an even pace. Derek Jones can do what he likes on Atavistic, I'll be in front when it counts."

Marcus nodded. He knew Christy had a clock in his head. "Just don't let Inside Job get in your way."

The runners walked a lap of the parade ring, before passing under the grandstand and out onto the racetrack. The Sheikh swept towards a lift, his burly guards holding the doors for him.

Marcus made for a ground-floor bar and installed himself in front of a TV screen, preferring to be alone in moments like this.

Christy was last to be loaded into the stalls. He was drawn one, against the grandstand rail. He glanced down the line of horses. He saw goggled faces drawn tight with concentration and hunger. That little shit Derek Jones was in the next stall, perched on Atavistic. Why did McCormack always pick arrogant jockeys?

The starter raised his flag. Christy faced forward and braced himself.

The gates flicked open with a clatter. Nine runners erupted onto the hallowed turf. A mile between them and victory. Oxygen Thief broke well and took his place snugly against the rail. Inside Job surged up beside him under the young Australian Craig Simpson, with another runner on his outside.

Running three abreast, Christy had to work to settle his mount's rhythm. *"Lads, I'm making the pace here, so take a pull or fuck off!"* he roared at the others.

They made no reply, but Christy could see Craig gently tug on Inside Job's mouth. In a few strides, Oxygen Thief was half a length ahead and travelling smoothly. Ducking his head, Christy glanced between his legs and saw Atavistic directly behind him, nicely boxed in by Inside Job. He was going nowhere.

The runners cruised along, passing the halfway stage as a tightly packed group. Parallel to the rails, an ambulance followed the runners along with a veterinary vehicle, preceded by a jeep-mounted TV camera capturing the thrill of the race up-close. Like slow-rolling thunder, the sound of horse's hooves hitting the manicured turf resonated from televisions at the venue and throughout the country.

With three furlongs to go, Christy felt his mount pull against the bit. The jockey flicked a glance over his shoulder. Behind him, Inside Job had moved out and gone half a length up, allowing Atavistic to move off the rail. Derek Jones positioned Atavistic beside Oxygen Thief's hindquarters. Atavistic's head was level with Christy's boot, its flaring nostril inches from his whip.

With that, the young jockey changed his hands on the reins and squeezed Atavistic as they approached the final furlong. The effect was dramatic: Atavistic surged past Oxygen Thief. The crowd bellowed.

Christy checked behind him: Inside Job faltered and veered towards the rail. The horse was cooked already. Christy gave a little on the reins and let his mount's stride lengthen. As they flashed past the final furlong marker, Oxygen Thief was nearly back level with Atavistic. Derek Jones twirled his whip, giving Atavistic a sound crack. The horse strained to give more, but couldn't.

Christy squeezed again and tapped Oxygen Thief on the shoulder as they drew level with Atavistic. The grandstand rattled with emotion. Everyone loved a battle. Christy drove with all his might and yards from the line he gave Oxygen Thief one slap of the whip. The gallant horse lengthened his stride again.

Jones hammered Atavistic three, four times. Atavistic kept on, the two warriors neck and neck.

Christy gritted his teeth. *"Go on, my son!"* he screamed, driving Oxygen Thief on with steely determination.

But Atavistic wouldn't quit. The two horses seemed to move in unison, their heads bobbing as their feet dug into the turf.

Behind them, running on empty, Inside Job gave chase. One of the other six runners made his move and threatened to overtake Inside Job but, desperate to stay in third place, Craig flailed his arms, legs and whip.

Up in the roaring stands, Sheikh Abdul stood on his balcony. Inside Job was staying on for third, but was he capable of winning this race? Perhaps he wasn't fit enough? Perhaps it was something else?

On the other hand, Oxygen Thief was providing the crowds with an emotional battle as he got to the line locked together with that horse of McCormack's.

Pat McCormack leaned over the railings with his wife and eldest son. He knew Jones had been trying to unsettle that yoke of Hamilton's, but he thought his jockey had still gone for the line too early. "You'd better not fuck this up," he muttered.

As the horses galloped through the final furlong, he waved his racecard and joined in the shouting. "*Go on, Jones, tan the arse off him! Go on! Go on!*" He clenched his fist as the line approached, banging it off the railing.

His wife shot him a disapproving look while keeping a thin smile on her face. Their son Alex jumped up and down, red-faced, breathless. Lost in the moment.

Christy knew it was going to be on the nod of a head. Pure luck, if you like, but the winning jockey would be hailed as a genius, while the loser would be labelled a fool with no sense of pace or timing.

Then, right on the finish line, Atavistic's front legs buckled, cartwheeling him. His tail and hind legs spun in the air, flinging Derek Jones into the ground with a dull thud. Atavistic landed on top of his rider. Behind the carnage, Craig Simpson yanked on his reins, trying to swerve Inside Job around the stricken horse and jockey, but he was too close. He had too much momentum. The crowd went silent. Craig was flung through the air as Inside Job half-jumped, half-fell over Atavistic. Both horses rolled onto their flanks and lay winded. Nostrils flaring. Eyes bulging. Sucking in massive gulps of air. Craig rolled himself into a tight ball, hoping another horse wouldn't crash into him. Beside him, Derek Jones lay motionless, his right arm at an unnatural angle. The other runners were far enough back to avoid the carnage. They veered towards the opposite rail and eased down to a canter, their riders throwing glances at the fallers.

Christy pulled up and doubled back, hoping to see horses and riders getting to their feet, but all he saw was the ambulance stopping at the line and stewards hurriedly erecting screens.

The remaining riders took their mounts through the tunnel under the muted grandstand and back to the paddock. They unsaddled as sombre-faced owners and trainers arrived to get race reports.

Christy dismounted and instructed the groom to circle the horse between the first and second position markers. The whole racecourse held its breath while the medical teams worked behind the screen and the judge and stewards pored over the photo-finish to see if Atavistic had won before he collapsed.

Marcus appeared beside Christy as he slid his saddle off the heaving, sweating horse. "What happened? Did he knock into you, or did you knock into him?"

"We didn't touch each other," he said breathlessly. "Coming to the line I thought I had him, but he stayed on. Then all of a sudden we're at the line and the poor beast goes down. Any word on young Jones or Simpson?"

"No."

Christy shook his head. "Horrible fall." He walked towards the weighroom wondering if he should retire on his forty-fifth birthday next year. Before his luck ran out.

The tannoy system crackled. The announcer cleared his throat. You could hear a pin drop.

Fiona stared at the TV. For a moment, she thought that Oxygen Thief had gone down, but then the picture switched to Christy, pulling up with the other horses.

The jockeys exchanged sickened glances while the TV commentators reassured viewers that vets and paramedics were already on the scene.

Fiona rushed to the toilet. Memories of the 2005 Irish Derby made her vomit.

Afterwards, she flushed the toilet, wiped her mouth, brushed her teeth and stepped outside for a breath of fresh air. That's when she saw him.

She dashed back in, locked the door and dialled O'Dowd.

"There's a man outside," she blurted. "On the driveway."

"Lock yourself in the house and I'll be right over. Can you describe him to me?"

She looked out the window. The man turned and walked away and she lost sight of him behind the hedgerow. "He's – he's – I can't see him now. He's wearing a hoodie. A green one. He looks well built. You know, strong."

"I'm on my way. Stay on the phone. I'll put you on hands-free while I'm driving."

Fiona stared at the TV and kept the line open. The racing had gone to a commercial break.

"The winner is Number Four, Oxygen Thief," the judge declared over the tannoy in plummy, theatrical tones. *"Steward's enquiry,"* he continued.

The atmosphere in the parade ring thickened. People murmured.

Sheikh Abdul had a face like thunder. Phone stuck to his ear. Lips moving rapidly, he looked at his watch.

Moments later, the tannoy crackled again. The plummy voice announced that Number Seven, Atavistic, was second: his jockey had not hit the ground until after the line. The voice then announced that Atavistic's jockey was injured. In such cases, a jockey was not required to weigh-in so the result would stand.

Sheikh Abdul pocketed his phone and broke into a grin. His entourage discreetly congratulated him and ignored Marcus.

Marcus dismissed his groom who led his charge back to the racecourse stables. The crowd was strangely quiet as Oxygen Thief left the parade ring. None of the usual polite applause granted to a winner.

***

Pat McCormack stood pale-faced on his balcony, staring at the green canvas screen being erected on the track.

His wife carefully wiped a tear without smudging her mascara. "Please, Pat. Go down there. See if that poor boy is alright."

He whipped his head around and stared at his wife blankly.

She put her hand on his. Pat looked at it. Then he spun on his heel and made for the door. "*Poor boy?*" he muttered. "*I'll give him poor boy!*"

In the lift, he called his trainer.

"Joe, I'm on the way down. Where are you?"

"I'm on the track. We have decisions to make."

Pat ended the call and swore. An elderly lady in the lift cut him a disapproving glance.

On the ground floor, Pat crossed the huge betting hall and emerged onto the front lawn. At the railings, he flashed his badge to the bowler-hatted attendant and told the man his name. A small gate was opened and Pat was admitted to the turf. He saw Inside Job being led away from the scene by a relieved groom. The horse looked sound, if a little stressed. Pat strode his bulk towards the screen and slipped in between the ambulances and the screen.

Craig Simpson was standing, helmet in his hands, staring. The paramedics carefully encased Derek's arm in a splint and rolled his body onto an immobility mattress. Then they moulded it around him, sucked the air out of it and, when it was rigid, gently lifted him onto a stretcher.

Not far from the stretcher lay Atavistic. Prone. Calm. There was an inflatable splint the entire length of his left front leg. A vet, a thin young woman, was crouched over the animal with a stethoscope pressed to his ribcage.

Pat pointed to Derek and barked at the paramedic. "Did he break his back?"

The man shook his head. "We've had some response to stimulus. I'd say he's just badly concussed with a broken arm, but we're not taking any chances." The man nodded to his colleague and they eased the stretcher into the ambulance.

"What hospital will he go to?" asked Pat.

"Heatherwood. It's just across the road. They'll decide from there."

Pat flicked his right hand across his chest, blessing himself. He glared at Atavistic's front leg. "Show me the damage."

The vet looked puzzled. "I can't, sir," she said. "The pastern is fractured. It's not compound, but I can palpate loose pieces. The patient is sedated and I've requested another horse ambulance with a winch. It's on its way from the racecourse stables."

Pat glared at Joe Nolan. "Jesus Christ! Now the whole fucking world'll see this horse get put on the truck like some kind of cripple. I thought you said he was in the form of his life? Now look at him. How the fuck am I supposed to make a stallion out of him now?"

Joe opened his mouth, but no words came out.

Pat turned his ire on the vet. "Listen, pet," he began.

Her face turned to thunder.

"If you get him to surgery straight away, can he be saved for a stud career?"

She pursed her lips, her eyes darted between Atavistic and his owner. "It's impossible to say for sure until radiographs are taken, but these kinds of things are usually fixable."

"Can he travel to Newmarket?"

She shook her head. "It's a long way. And with Saturday evening traffic I wouldn't recommend it."

"Where's the nearest clinic?"

"Berkshire Vet Hospital," she said. "It's where I work."

Pat swiped a finger at his phone. Scrolled till he found the number. He looked at his horse as he made the call.

"James," he said. "Pat McCormack. I assume you've been watching the racing?

"Indeed I have. I'm so terribly sorry."

"Right, thanks. Look, I'll send a chopper to Newmarket immediately. I need you down here to operate on Atavistic at Berkshire vet clinic."

"You'll need to clear it with their surgeons and pay their fees in addition to mine."

"Consider it done."

"Then I'll clear my schedule and await your helicopter."

"Thanks a million, James. See you in a bit."

Then he called a helicopter charter service and issued orders. After that, he addressed the vet again.

"OK. Call your employers and tell them the best orthopaedic surgeon in Newmarket will be leading the surgical team."

Her eyes went wide. "James Whiting?"

Pat nodded.

The vet made the call. Pat listened, ready to snatch the phone if the clinic owners made trouble.

When she had arranged everything, Pat relaxed his shoulders and said; "Right. Thank you." He stared at the horse for a minute. "If you want, I can get an industrial winch truck here within . . ." he checked his watch, "twenty minutes."

The vet arched her brow in surprise. "*Um,* that won't be necessary. The ambulance has a powerful winch and padded floor mats which slide out. We'll just load the patient onto the mats and he'll slide right in."

Pat nodded. He handed the vet his card. "These are my numbers. Do you need a down payment before surgery can begin?"

The vet looked embarrassed. "That is usually required, sir."

Pat called his personal assistant. "Catriona."

"Mr. McCormack. I'm so sorry. How are the horse and rider?"

"The horse needs surgery. I need you to call Berkshire vet clinic and arrange payment. And Derek Jones is on his way to Heatherwood Hospital. Doesn't seem too serious, but call his parents anyway. Tell them everything'll be taken care of. And call the hospital too. That's all, Catriona."

"Consider it all done."

"Thank you."

Pat thanked the vet again. "Joe, you stay with the horse tonight. Keep me updated."

His trainer nodded.

Pat left them to it. He crossed the track, darted through the gawpers on the lawn and made for the nearest elevator. There were seven people already waiting, so he exited the back of the grandstand and found another lift. He pressed the call button and stared at the tarmac, considering possible scenarios for action.

The doors slid open and Pat advanced without looking up. He bumped into a muscular man with a military haircut and an earpiece, who said; "Move back, sir," in an unusual accent, while sweeping Pat aside with a thick arm.

"What the hell –" he began, before his eyes settled on the man behind the bodyguard.

Sheikh Abdul emerged with a young man, a tall girl and another bodyguard.

The Sheikh fixed his dark eyes on Pat. "I am so sorry for your misfortune, Mr. McCormack. I do hope your horse and jockey will recover."

Pat's cheeks flushed red. "Oh right. Thanks, thanks." He forced the words from his reluctant lips. Then couldn't resist adding, "Pity about Inside Job. Still, at least Hamilton conjured up another win for the pair of you."

The Sheikh's eyes hardened. "Don't worry about Inside Job – he'll live to fight another day. In fact, I'll probably take him to the Breeders Cup."

"Grand job, so," said Pat, dashing for the sanctuary of the lift. As he ascended to the fifth floor, he muttered. "Wanker."

Sergeant O'Dowd sipped tea at Fiona's kitchen table. His high-visibility jacket rustled as he moved his arm.

"I'll stay here until a squad car turns up. The night shift will be along to relieve them in a few hours. Furthermore, it's my duty to inform you that you need to consider handing over your research to us or, at the very least, setting up offices at a place of my choosing."

Perhaps he was right. Her nerves were frayed,and she'd never forgive herself if anything happened to her dad. Sooner or later, somebody was bound to connect the dots.

"Let me sleep on it," she said. "I'll let you know tomorrow."

O'Dowd waved a finger at her. "It's one or the other, Dr. Buckley. You cannot continue as you have been. Understood? It's clear that the pressure is mounting on whoever wants your research."

"How do you figure that?"

"Because their presence is becoming more obvious. Now, if they were amateurs, that might not mean much, but we're clearly dealing with organised professionals here. That means they want you to panic. No doubt they hope you will lead them to the information unwittingly."

Fiona thought of her father again. No, that was impossible – she'd taken a different route there every day and made sure she was not followed.

They heard the squad car pull up outside.

O'Dowd headed for the door. "We'll talk in the morning."

Fiona tried to call Marcus. Got voicemail. That was strange – he always used to say that a trainer could never switch off his phone. Then she remembered he was probably on the plane back to Dublin with his horse.

Chapter 17

He sat alone in the master bedroom of the top-floor Terrace suite at the Dorchester Hotel. Staring out the window at London's flickering sea of lights, he sipped sweet iced tea from a large tumbler. On television the Racing Channel blared with a panel of experts analysing the dramatic events of Champions Day. Marcus Hamilton was mentioned.

He hurled his glass at the wall. It bounced stupidly off the thick wallpaper. The man shot it a dark look. *I can't even break a glass properly.*

On the plus side, today had been interesting. Hamilton had won and confirmed the man's suspicions: he was up to something with that Buckley. There was no doubt anymore. How could Hamilton make his own horses so successful while at the same time getting at other people's? The only logical conclusion was Buckley but so far he'd drawn a blank on that front. It was time for drastic action before any more face was lost and any more horses were got at. It wasn't supposed to turn out this way. Losing was for little people.

The man went out to the balcony and barked into his phone. The voice on the other end answered in succinct, military tones.

"What?" said the man, leaning against the balcony railing. "Are you sure?"

The voice responded.

"What am I paying seven of you for?" the man said. "Split yourselves into teams. As they say, kill two birds with one stone. And let me know when it's done."

He ended the call, changed his clothes and went down to the dining room to join his companions.

Wikus Heyns placed his phone on the table. He pushed aside the empty pizza boxes and formed a plan in his mind.

"What's the deal, man?" asked Pieter Koster.

Wikus frowned, his train of thought broken. "Shut up for a second, and bring the others in."

Pieter stood. Cigarette smoke wafted in as he opened the door. "Put those filthy things out and get in here," he said to the five tall men waiting in the darkness.

When they were all seated round the table, Wikus began. "Right, plan's altered. We have two missions tonight. I'm off to the airport with Danie and Oscar. When we're done, we'll go with the prize."

Danie nodded and cracked his tattooed knuckles. Oscar sat stony-faced.

"Pieter, you and Felix do the other thing. Vaughn, you and Mike stay here with the van. You'll be contingency, just in case."

Pieter grinned. Felix shrugged. Vaughn and Mike sighed.

"What happens if he gives us shit?" asked Pieter.

Wikus gave him a hard stare. "Do what you have to *but*," he jabbed a finger at Pieter, "*try* not to make a foken mess."

Pieter nodded.

Wikus looked at his watch. "Right, grab your bags and off you go."

Chapter 18

The Boeing 737 freighter eased to a halt at the cargo terminal and the ground crew went to work. A skystair was parked at the forward door and a customs inspector armed with a clipboard and manifest trotted up into the plane. A few minutes later, Marcus descended the skystair and went to the rear, where a ramp was being positioned. Oxygen Thief ambled down the ramp like a frequent flyer.

"He drank a lot on the flight," said the groom. "Race was hard on him."

"He'll be OK. He's done enough for the season. I'll give him a break for the winter."

The horse's aluminium-shod hooves clacked rhythmically on the tarmac. Marcus squinted under the floodlights, could just make out the silhouette of his lorry parked by the hangar.

"Great bloody win, Marcus." said the driver.

"Had a few quid on him, did we, Dave?"

"I took a price last week, when he was still four-to-one," said Dave, winking.

They loaded the horse and Dave climbed into his cab. "You comin' back with me?"

"No. My car's at the other side. I'll get a lift over with security or ground crew."

Dave started the lorry and trundled away from the hangar. Marcus watched them pass through security and head out onto the Dublin road.

He punched the air in delight. Once again, he'd shown them all. He couldn't wait for the morning papers.

As he walked back towards the hangar, he dialled Fiona. No reply. He was about to leave a message when the whine of a jet engine flooded his senses. A private jet had just landed and was taxi-ing to the cargo hangar. He'd try her later, or maybe just surprise her. It'd be nice to see her tonight. He'd missed her this last week.

Thomas Riley lay in bed, engrossed in a book about the racehorses of the English monarchs. Riley loved pedigrees. *Class will out,* was his maxim. Some of the Queen's mares descended from horses bought by her great-grandfather. He was proud of what his daughter was trying to achieve, but he felt it took the thought and even the fun out of breeding racehorses.

There was a dull thud outside. Maybe it was the wind, or next door's cat dropping off the wall. He put down the book and strained his ears. There it was again.

Then glass shattered. Sounded like the kitchen door. He reached past the nightstand, grabbed his shotgun and lay it on the duvet beside him. Hoped the briefcase on the floor wasn't too obvious. Too late to move it now. He turned out the light and picked up the phone.

Fiona was asleep on the sofa. Dreamt that her phone was ringing. The musical tones soothed her. Eventually it stopped and she drifted again. Then more ringing. This time she yawned and wiped saliva from the corner of her mouth. Her phone was ringing alright, shuffling about on the table beside the empty bottle of wine. Her head throbbed as she picked it up.

Thomas sat up in bed. Gun in his hands under the duvet. He could hear them creep about downstairs. It was only a matter of time before they drew a blank and made their way up to challenge him. Still, the longer it took them the better. He was ready to shoot but he hoped he didn't have to. He'd threatened that little jockey shite with it once, just before the wedding, but he'd never actually used it on anything other than a pheasant. For all his talk, he didn't really know what would happen if they called his bluff.

Pieter opened the curtains, letting in the amber glow from the streetlight. He told Felix to watch the stairs as he turned the sitting room over. Nothing looking like genetic research. He went into another room and his heart sank. Walls lined with stuffed bookshelves. A desk piled with papers and folders towering around an old laptop. A coffee table and two chairs all stacked piled high with books, papers and ring-binders. He went to the desk, picked up a sheet of paper and held it up to the window. It was about horses alright. Something about genetic breeding crosses. He picked up a folder and flicked through the pages. More horse stuff.

Pieter ran his hand over his shaved head. "Shit," he muttered.

He dropped the file, touched the weapon under his jacket and moved over to Felix.

Outside, another man crouched in the overgrown shrubs by the gate. Waiting for the right moment. He scanned the house and flicked glances up and down the road. In a downstairs room, curtains had been thrown apart, bathing the intruder's face in streetlight amber. The man outside pulled his woolly hat down over his ears and dropped his knees onto the wet soil. These clowns might just do the job for him. Save him the bother of having to go inside.

"We'll have to get the old fucker out of bed," Pieter whispered to Felix. "I need to know which stuff is his daughter's. Otherwise, we'll need a truck to get all this shit out of the house."

Felix followed Pieter as they prowled up the stairs.

There were three doors leading off the top corridor. Two were ajar. Pieter could see a toilet and basin to his left. Slowly, he eased the opposite door further open. Cocked his head round and saw an empty bed.

Moving on, he crept towards the third door and

closed his hand on the knob. Felix followed, pushing the hem of his jacket up to expose the gun nestled in the small of his back.

Pieter eased the knob round and let the door swing open. He slid into the room. Caught sight of the old man sitting up in the bed.

He stopped in mid-step, flicking his eyes around the room. He noticed a briefcase on the floor before he settled a hard gaze on the old man.

The two men stared at each other in the darkness. Pieter slid a hand behind his back and beckoned Felix into the room.

The old man raised his hands under the duvet and a long shape rose from the bed.

"Don't move, the pair of you," said the old man.

"Easy there, old man," said Pieter. "Put your walking stick down. We only want to ask you a question."

"No questions. The cops are on their way. You stand very still." He wiggled the long shape and the duvet fell away.

Pieter found himself staring at the business end of a side-by-side shotgun. A grin cracked his face. "Listen, old *oke*, I hate to ruin your buzz, but this isn't the first time I've had a gun pointed at me."

"Well, pal, if you don't fuck off and leave me and my daughter alone, it'll be the last."

In the darkness, Felix slipped his hand to the small of his back and closed his fingers around cold steel. "*Ag*, Pieter," he said. "Leave it. Let's go."

Pieter weighed his options and cast another glance at the briefcase on the floor. Had this old fucker really called the cops? There was no way he was going to end up in an Irish jail. Wikus's words echoed in his mind. *Try not to make a mess.*

He shook his head. "I tell you what, old oke," he said, slowly crouching down. "I'll just take this briefcase here and we'll leave you in peace."

"Not a chance, pal." The gun shook slightly.

Pieter reached out and took the case. Felix gripped his pistol.

"Drop it, I'm fucking warning you!" shouted the old man, a quiver in his voice.

Pieter froze in his crouch and said, *"Vuur."*

In a lightning movement, Felix whipped his right hand from behind him and aimed.

The watcher outside had waited for an eternal five minutes before he heard the sounds. Gunshots. A small crack and a baritone boom. He could distinguish them in the same way a musician could separate a ride cymbal from a high hat, no matter how frenetic the drummer.

The man swore. Now he'd have to abort. He brushed the dirt off his knees, stepped out of cover and walked calmly onto the road. He went two houses down before ducking into a garden. Then he dashed behind the house, vaulted over the rear wall, climbed through a border fence and fled through the grassy field behind the housing estate. The cattle residing there watched a strange figure momentarily invade their night.

Chapter 19

September 2011

The evening sun blazed through the windows as Johnny swung from bar to bar. He threw himself along, thrusting his way from the hoist rope by the bedroom door, to the kitchen, then back to the garage door. It was a triangular course. He completed six laps before his muscles screamed for mercy.

He slid down the rope onto his chair and stretched his arms and chest. Lactic acid burned. Endorphins pumped. The feeling was close to ecstasy. A times like these, Johnny forgot all about his useless penis. Arnold Schwarzenegger was right: it was possible to achieve orgasmic feelings from working out. Johnny watched the famous Austrian's film *Pumping Iron* at least twice a year. It was an inspiration. Arnie's ruthless discipline was absolutely awesome.

From there, Johnny wheeled himself into the gym and slid himself onto the bench. He pressed 140kgs in four sets of ten repetitions. When he'd finished he roared, sat up and stretched again, relishing the burn. His eye was drawn to *the book*. He gave silent thanks to his lucky stars that he'd taken the time to read it back then.

After his workout, Johnny hauled himself in to the shower seat and washed off the sweat. Feeling fresh and alive, he wheeled to the kitchen to prepare dinner. He checked the clock: nearly seven. He guessed Fiona would call soon, telling him she'd too much work on or some other excuse and not to wait up for her. She was a terrible liar. Sometimes Johnny wished she'd drop the charade and come clean about Hamilton. A couple of months ago, he'd even considered telling her that he knew and asking for a divorce, but he didn't want to make it too easy for her. She was free to go any time but she had to have the guts to tell him straight. So Johnny waited and got on with his mission. One side of his mouth curled into a grin. Patience: he was getting good at it. Johnny turned up the music so he wouldn't hear the phone and started preparing brown rice, spinach and avocados.

After dinner, he opened his laptop, read through his research articles again and entered his workout into the diary.

The next morning he woke at five to find Fiona beside him, her body rigid on the edge of the mattress. Johnny had a quick workout before driving to his lair. It was a glorious Saturday morning, so he decided he would drive up to the Wicklow Mountains after he finished. On days like this, he didn't miss the constant slog of a jockey's life. Working a five-day week was so much more liberating.

He let himself into his lair and locked the door. He pulled the plastic poncho over his head and spread it over his chair. Then he fixed the mask over his mouth and nose before pulling on latex gloves. Most of what he worked with was harmless in itself, but he still didn't want to get any of it in his mouth. Not if his theory was correct.

An hour or so later, he finished work and washed his hands and face. Used baby wipes to clean every last speck off his chair. Then he washed and disinfected his hands again. Satisfied, he wheeled to the desk and wrote in his journal. It was a habit he'd formed when he started working out. A gym friend of his had said that serious bodybuilders kept track of every weight lifted and every calorie eaten. Of course, in his lair diaries he omitted all names. Just in case he was discovered before it was time.

Another hour or so later, he parked in a forestry clearing up in the mountains and wheeled himself along the track. He loved the smell of the wood and heather. The wind whipped his cheeks and he checked his thermal leg bag was tight around him. He'd heard horror stories of paraplegics in Canada getting frostbite without realising it. A blustery autumn afternoon in Ireland was a far cry from the Canadian winter, but he wasn't taking any chances, hating the cold as much as the thought of amputation.

144

The mountain track opened out onto a vantage point. He stopped by the railing and applied the brake. Shielding his eyes from the sun, he stared out at the valley below. A vibrant sea of green which seemed to ripple as the wind drove small clouds across the sky, casting racing shadows on the land. Ireland was beautiful when it got the weather.

Johnny took a sad breath. Dark nostalgia washed over him. He wasn't sure what had changed him the most. Getting bailed out, or getting rejected. Maybe it was the intense training and, oh yes, the steriods. All in all, he wished he'd never taken them. Bloody roids, but they were so good at first. So empowering. So enabling. And it wasn't his fault. After he started training, he'd gone for a check-up to a physio that a friend recommended. This guy had given him two shots to strengthen his shoulders to support his weight better. Said his body needed all the help it could get. Johnny loved the results. Apart from growing muscle, for the first time since his fall he had felt exhilarated. Almost invincible. He became convinced that they helped to hone his hatred into a refined plan. When he stopped to think rationally he knew it was wrong to pollute his body like that and several months later he'd stopped doing it after the mood swings became too much to bear. One night, Fiona had come home after a soirée with Marcus, and Johnny had felt like pinning her to the bed with a barbell and beating her until she ... Well, that's when he realised it was the 'roid rage' and not him.

Fiona, Fiona. She just needed to be stronger. She needed to get out of the lab more often, confront life and him. But she'd always found it easier to face a petri dish or a microscope than problems in the real world. If she told him she was leaving, it'd be better for both of them. He'd stopped thinking of her as his wife nearly a year ago. Apart from the Marcus thing, he knew that once he'd read *the book* and made a plan, he had mentally divorced Fiona and joined himself to working out, Winline and His Plan. *That* was a marriage he was willing to sacrifice everything else for. It would be worth it. He blinked. Wiped something from his eye and his cheek. Spun round and wheeled back to his van.

By next racing season, his work should produce results. He had already drawn some conclusions from studying two-year-old racing form this year. It could be coincidence, of course. Next season would reveal all. He hoped the effects would be dramatic, but he would settle for subtle. Oh yes. Subtle would do the job just as efficiently.

Chapter 20

County Kilkenny
18 October 2015

Pat blessed himself when Father Hanlon finished reading from the Gospel of Saint John. Then he got off his knees and sat back for the sermon. Not that he ever listened to the priest's words. No, Pat liked to use the time to consider his own affairs. He only really came to Mass to hedge his bets. Praying was an inexpensive way to attempt influence over the few things in his life he couldn't directly control.

During the priest's sermon, Pat clasped his hands and silently recited a decade of the Rosary. He prayed that Atavistic would make it through the next few months and be able to start his new life as a stallion next year. The horse had badly fractured two of the pastern bones in his left front leg.

James Whiting had inserted six screws to stabilise

the bones and the horse recovered well from surgery, sporting a cast over the whole leg, complete with two steel braces under the knee, bypassing the fetlock and joining onto a carbon-fibre footpad. Antibiotics would be given as would medicines to promote blood flow and dull the pain. Whiting had explained that the big worry in these cases was the patient developing laminitis in the opposite foot due to the pain and stress.

Pat sighed. He knew all about laminitis, he'd lost a horse to it a few years back. The walls of a horse's hoof are held onto the bones inside them by thousands of tiny attachments, fed by tiny blood vessels. If the blood supply is disrupted due to stress, toxicity, or obesity, the bone falls away from the hoof. The condition can occur in a matter of hours and, in the worst cases, the bone would rotate through the sole of the foot, resulting in euthanasia on humane grounds.

Pat decided on another decade of the rosary and moved the beads through his fingers. It was imperative the horse remained calm and unstressed during convalescence. For highly strung thoroughbreds, six months' rest in a stable was not a natural state. Pat felt that the matter required serious prayer.

He prayed Derek Jones would recover quickly. That reminded him – he'd have to tell Joe to find another jockey. Derek's broken humerus, shattered clavicle and fractured skull would certainly rule him out for the rest of the season. Pat wondered if the wily Christy Ryan had done something during the race. The head-on cameras showed no interference during the final furlong, but how else would Atavistic just fall? And with all the feed supplements the horse had been raised on, a pastern shouldn't just snap like that.

When Mass ended he blessed himself and stepped into the aisle. His son Alex followed. His wife never came to Mass. She preferred to meditate and practise a mixture of Shinto and Japanese Buddhism in the privacy of their home. Pat was just glad she wasn't a drinker or a depressive, like so many wealthy wives.

Pat liked to sit at the front of the church, but not to earn him Brownie points with the parish priest and the Lord. It was so he could be the last to leave, watching everyone else as they filed out. He noticed Cathal Regan and his parents. Cathal looked pale, his parents frail with worry. It just didn't seem right, let alone possible, that someone so young could get cancer.

Outside, Pat tapped his son on the arm. "Run ahead, now. Don't let Cathal's parents drive off."

The teenager hurried off in the direction of a green hatchback.

Pat walked after him, avoiding eye contact with several eager villagers who wanted to be seen talking to him outside the church so they could bullshit about it later in the pub and bask in the reflected glory of a conversation with the great Pat McCormack.

Cathal was in the back seat with his mother. His father Eddie stood by the driver's door, wearing a black coat and a pained smile. He stuck a hand out. Pat shook it heartily.

"Like I said on the phone, it's a terrible blow," said Pat, genuine concern furrowing his brow. "But they can do so much for cancer nowadays."

149

"We went up to Blackrock yesterday to get the test results. His throat's riddled. Lymph nodes too. He's to go up next week and start treatment." Eddie's voice started to crack. "We're all stratching our heads – sure, he's not even twenty-two. I dunno." He looked at the ground. "The wife's taking it worse than Cathal – sure the young think they're bulletproof, don't they?"

Pat's stomach churned. "They do, they do. Look," he wagged a finger at Eddie, "whatever he needs, it's on me. Understand? It'll be taken care of. And if he needs to go to America for treatment, I'll make sure my plane is free for you."

A tear formed in the corner of the man's eye. "Oh Pat, you're very good."

"I know people in America. Influential medical people. If there's anything you need, just let me know. I can have him flown to New York tomorrow on my plane."

The man nodded, wiped his cheek. "Do you really mean it?"

Pat smiled warmly, his eyes softened. "I do, of course."

Eddie hesitated a moment. "Well, d'you know what? I'd love to have a second opinion from one of those American specialists. Would that be possible?"

Pat took Eddie's hand and clasped it between his meaty palms. "Don't you worry about a thing. I'll get it organised."

Eddie's tears welled up again.

Pat smiled. "Leave it to me." He turned on his heel and crossed the road.

His son had the car running. Pat got in and the black

Mercedes slipped away. As they wound through the backroads, Pat looked into the fields and wondered about aggresive cancer. He hoped Cathal wouldn't end up like Johnny Buckley.

Pat made a call. "Catriona, has the plane left New York yet?"

"It's in the air as we speak."

"As soon as it touches down, get it checked and refuelled. It's going back with Cathal Regan. I want you to accompany them."

"I'll let you know when we have a wheels-up slot."

Pat looked at his son behind the wheel. He couldn't imagine such a young man getting cancer. How on earth did it happen to Buckley and Cathal? I mean, they were both active; Cathal worked all hours God sent on the farm. He was dedicated to the horses. Buckley looked like a gorilla from all those weights he lifted. How could they just get cancer like that?

They got to Balmain and waited for the electric gates to open. Passing the security guard onto the farm, they drove slowly up the avenue.

Pat turned to his son. "Take a tour of the place. I want to see the yearlings."

They stopped outside the yearling barn. Pat got out and walked down the aisleway, glancing into each stable as he went. They'd just had their breakfast and were now munching hay, waiting for the staff to return and let them out to their paddocks. He hoped this bunch contained a future champion. He was getting fed up with disappointment on the track. He needed a big winner from his homebreds. Buying decent yearlings at the sales was so expensive and anyway, nothing compared to the satisfaction of seeing a horse he'd raised here win a big race. Bronx Spirit flashed through his mind, making him smile briefly. Still, if it hadn't been for sales purchases, he wouldn't have had a Group One winner for four seasons.

Yet Marcus Hamilton managed it, year in, year out.

He checked all the horses one more time and left the barn. Pat told his son to take the car home. He felt like walking back to the mansion. He needed a bit of sunshine on his back – and in his life.

Sheikh Abdul drummed his fingers on the mahogany desk as he waited for the video link to open on his laptop. He frowned. The connection was taking longer than it should.

The door opened and a liveried waitress set a silver tray on the desk.

"Thank you," said Abdul, without smiling. He watched the girl's legs as they carried her out of the room as he stirred four lumps of sugar into his tea.

His computer screen relayed a *fault* message. Abdul swore, swiped at his phone and held it to his ear. He barked orders into the device and tossed it onto the shiny desk.

He sipped and drummed his fingers. A minute later, a video link image opened on the screen and he saw his stud manager Alan De Courtney sitting, suited as usual, in the conference room of the stud farm offices in Tipperary.

Abdul put down the tea and leaned close to the screen. He stared at Alan's image as if he were trying to thrust his gaze through the device into Alan's mind.

"Good morning, Alan."

"Oh, good morning sir." He twitched, fiddled with his tie.

"Alan. I was not pleased by the loss yesterday."

"*Erm*, what?" Alan's face screwed into a knot. "I thought it was a great victory for you and Marcus Hamilton."

"I'm not talking about that. I don't get recognition for that. Inside Job was a total disappointment."

"Oh, that was awful luck. At least the horse and rider are in one piece. Pat McCormack wasn't so lucky."

"*Inside Job*," Abdul repeated, each syllable heavy and deliberate. He paused, sipped tea. "Inside Job was the latest in a long line of underperforming horses that I have bred on my stud. The stud that you manage for me."

"But he ran a stormer. Atavistic going down in front of him was pure chance. As they say: that's racing."

Abdul slammed his fist on the table. Onscreen, Alan actually flinched.

"*I'm not fucking talking about that, you idiot!*" He bared his teeth as he spoke. "That horse has underperformed his whole career and so have far too many of my expensive racehorses. I want to know why! Can you tell me why, Alan?"

Alan shuffled papers on his desk and appeared to be searching for something to say. He swallowed and looked at notes as he spoke. "Well, as I've said to you many times before: I blame the feed. I mean, *no oats* in their diets? It's unbelievable. And as for that fancy extrusion thingy that Winline use to process the feed – I reckon it's a step backwards. I mean, whatever happened to traditional feeds?" He scratched his chin. "I'm not sure if you've heard, but there's rumours flying around that Winline's extruded range is defective – a con job. People are saying it's not what it says on the bag. Tony Carey's in an awful panic," Alan arched his brow. "Just goes to show you. What would an ex-jockey know about feeding horses anyway?"

The Sheikh's dark eyes bored into Alan. "I'm starting to ask myself what my stud manager knows about breeding horses."

Alan's eyes flickered. "Well, I've a feeling that the land's getting a bit clapped out. The grass is not what it used to be when we bought the farm. I don't know, maybe we should get rid of a few horses?"

A stony gaze gave him his answer.

"Alan, I want you to look into this. I don't care how much money you have to spend or which specialists you have to hire, but you *will* investigate the matter from your end. Immediately. And I will not be selling any horses."

Alan nodded, his voice stuck in his throat.

"In addition, I am taking matters into my own hands. It is going to be interesting to see whether our ... different research methods will bring us identical results."

Alan's face screwed into a knot.

"You can consider this a test of your suitability to carry out your job."

"Oh, don't wo–"

Abdul hit cancel and the connection shut down. He sat back in his chair and wondered if he had made a mistake all those years ago. He reached for his phone.

"Get me Winline Horse Feeds manager on the phone. Immediately. And send Vladimir in."

Chapter 21

Fiona sat by her father's bed, watching the heart monitor. Guilt thumping through her, churning her insides. What had she been playing at?

The events of last night replayed in her mind like a looped video. When he had called her to tell her to run and hide, he'd said that they wouldn't get her files – no matter what. She'd said she would call the guards and come straight over. "No way, Fiona," her father said. "Stay away. Hide." It was probably the only time her father's advice would have concurred with Johnny's. She still couldn't bring herself to heed it, even if part of her just wanted to be shut away in a controlled environment, poring over genetic information.

She chewed her lip and squeezed her father's hand.

When she'd arrived to her father's house last night,

two squad cars were blocking the road. Flashing blue lights cut through the darkness. An ambulance was backed into the driveway. A garda was running crime-scene tape around the house. Her stomach turned. She parked and told the guard who she was. He radioed Sergeant O'Dowd, who emerged and led her into the house.

In her father's room, three paramedics were at work. She felt bile rise in her throat. They'd cut his pyjamas open and put a large dressing over the left side of his ribcage. The skin around the dressing was stained with blood residue and the sheets were red. A paramedic asked him how much pain he was in. He flapped a hand dismissively. They gently lifted him into the immobilising mattress they'd placed beside him on the bed. Two folded it around him while the third extracted the air with a pump, forming a rigid cocoon around the old man.

Fiona watched in stunned silence.

They gently lifted the cocoon by the carry straps and began the delicate procedure of getting him out of the room and down the narrow stairs to the ambulance.

On the way out, a wicked smile cracked Thomas Riley's face. "I got one of the little fuckers," he whispered to his daughter. "The other one made off with – with –" he gasped for air.

On the carpet, the corpse's chest was blown open. Blood and flesh mixed with the cotton fabric of his hoodie. She put her hand to her mouth.

"Your father took a bullet from that pistol." O'Dowd pointed to the compact handgun on the floor near the body. "But *his* weapon was considerably more powerful at this range. He says that the other man grabbed a briefcase full of papers and bolted. Your father couldn't get off another shot because of his injury."

"Oh my God," she said through her hand. She couldn't believe her father had done this. Actually she could. She knew he'd do anything to protect her and that realisation made her feel dizzy. Part of her wanted to go to bed and sleep until this all went away.

A police photographer came and began taking shots of the body on the floor. It was like a scene from a movie, not her dad's house. Her mouth was dry.

"I'll go to the hospital," she mumbled.

O'Dowd nodded. "I'll be sending officers. We'll keep the pair of you under twenty-four-hour surveillance. But before you go," he motioned to the body, "is this the man you saw this afternoon?"

She willed herself calm and concentrated on the guy's face. She couldn't. Her throat was thick with emotion, her eyes cloudy with tears.

She nodded. Then shook her head. "The hoodie was a different colour."

Now, sitting by a hospital bed on a Sunday afternoon, waiting for her father to wake up, her world was unravelling. Why would anyone go to such lengths to steal her research? How was this connected to Johnny?

Right now she wished that she'd asked him for a divorce years ago and married Marcus. However much it would've hurt him, it would've been better in the long run. Likewise, if she'd let Ronan Lister go and hired a younger man, well ...

Fiona released her father's hand and checked her

phone. Still no word from Marcus. She stepped into the corridor and tapped the screen. Voicemail again. That was unlike him. She wondered if he'd been shown some London hospitality by the Sheikh and was now nursing the mother of all hangovers in a hotel suite. She half-smiled. He deserved to celebrate after that win.

Pulling the chair closer to the bed, she took her father's hand again, lay her head on the blanket and was instantly asleep.

She awoke to the gentle prodding of a nurse. She rubbed her eyes and wiped saliva from the corner of her mouth.

"How're you doing?" the nurse asked her.

"Oh, I'm fine." Fiona yawned, looked at her father. "Any progress?"

Just then, the surgeon appeared. He smiled at Fiona and checked the monitors.

"Good. He seems to be doing fine," he said. "Vitals are normal. He just needs rest. Older bodies take time to recover."

"Thank you, Dr. Scanlan. You saved his life." Her voice was shaky.

Scanlan gave Fiona a reassuring look. "As I said after surgery, he was lucky the bullet glanced off a rib. There was minimal tissue damage. He'll be fine. For someone of his age, your father's as tough as boot leather."

She nodded.

As if on cue, she felt her father's hand move in hers. The long thin fingers curled around hers.

"Dad?"

Though his eyes remained closed, his lips twitched.

Dr. Scanlan examined his patient.

Thomas slowly opened his eyes. "Good God, my side hurts," he said.

Fiona beamed. Her vision blurred and she dragged the back of her hand across her eyes.

"I got one of them, you know," he said to Scanlan. "Fuckers."

Stress and worry poured out of Fiona in a burst of laughter.

"You should be hidden away with the cops," said her father.

"We both have round-the-clock protection now. But they reckon that we'll be safer since the thieves got what they wanted. Dad, I – I'm so sorry. This is all my fault."

Thomas shook his head. A mischievious smile appeared on his face for a moment. "I'll tell you later." He closed his eyes and let out a long breath.

"He's right," said Scanlan. "You should go home and rest."

"I suppose you're right."

She kissed her father's cheek, grabbed her coat and walked out past the garda sitting in the corridor reading the Sunday papers. Outside, she waved to the officers in the squad car parked beside her own vehicle. They followed her home and parked in their spot outside her front door.

Chapter 22

The next morning Fiona woke to knocking at the door. She pulled on a long dressing gown and stumbled through the house. "Nice start to a Monday," she muttered, yawning.

Opening the door, she saw a garda brandishing several letters. "The postman came," said the fresh-faced young officer. "But I wouldn't let him near the house. Oh, and Sergeant O'Dowd expects you to go to your father's house today, after you visit the hospital. There's some stuff there he wants to go through with you."

Fiona's mind was still climbing into full consciousness. She smiled, nodded and closed the door.

She made a coffee and sat at the table. The first envelope contained a bill from the undertakers. Holy shite, it was expensive to bury someone these days. She made a mental note to make a will requesting that she be cremated when the time came. Two letters from the insurance company: one agreeing to a payout, the other requesting a meeting the following week to sign documents and finalise everything.

The last envelope was brown and Fiona braced herself for another bill. It took her a moment to comprehend the document she held in her hands. After last night's events, she'd completely forgotten about Johnny's death certificate. Yet here it was.

She turned on her laptop, connected it to the printer/scanner in the corner and scanned the certificate. Attached the scan to an email and sent it to Johnny's account. Then she traipsed back to the bedroom and retrieved his laptop from her bedside table. While that was booting up, she poured another coffee and considered the plan of action. She was going to have to break the rules and O'Dowd would be upset to say the least, but there was no other way around it. She didn't want him to see whatever Johnny was hiding, not yet anyway. Not until she knew what it was. She sighed. More paranoid secrets. Maybe this was Johnny's joke on her: to make her more like him. She bet he was grinning in his grave. Her gaze wandered to the painting of him on Bronx Spirit. Looking back, that had been his happiest moment. Probably Pat McCormack's crowning achievement too. Fiona found herself thinking about who could've bailed Johnny out and paid for this house. It occurred to her that she'd never really thought about the matter properly. In the beginning, Johnny was so happy she gave up pressing him for details, afraid to jinx his happiness. Suddenly, she wondered if the answer hadn't been right in front of her the whole time.

Johnny's computer chimed its readiness. Fiona opened the email and forwarded the death certificate along with a brief explanation to Brendan Tynan. Hoping he would reply promptly.

She changed into sweatpants, stretched and hit the treadmill.

An hour later, she checked the email.

Dear Dr. Buckley,

Many thanks for your understanding and for the death certificate. I would be happy to meet you any time at your convenience. My place of business is Toughers Industrial Estate, on the old Naas Road. I'm there during business hours, but I can stay later this evening if it helps.

Yours,

Brendan Tynan.

P.S. If you have the keys, please bring them as your husband installed his own locks. Please find my number below.

Fiona punched the numbers and found her heart thumping as she waited for Tynan to pick up.

"Hello?"

"Hello. It's Fiona Buckley. I just got your mail."

She made an appointment to meet him at lunchtime and said she'd look for the keys.

After that, she emptied Johnny's nightstand. Nothing. Then she tried the gym. The locker there was full of bodybuilding supplements. Jars and jars of pills and powders. Bowel-regulator medicines and two types of antibiotics. But no keys.

Then it struck her. She grabbed his van key from a low hook by the front door and went outside. She pressed the fob and the vehicle clicked, indicators flashed. The guards put down their newspapers to observe her.

Fiona was taken aback as she opened the driver's door: there was no seat. She'd forgotten that. In fact, she couldn't remember the last time she had sat in this van.

She looked at the system of rails and hydraulics that enabled him to get into the minivan and drive it without moving from his chair. There was even a modified seatbelt system that held him in place once his wheelchair was locked into position.

She threw her eyes around the immaculately valeted interior – no surprise there – before opening the glovebox. No keys. She checked the centre console and found spare change and a protein bar.

Under the passenger seat, she found two thermos flasks. Weird. Curious, she opened one. Empty, but the lid was crusted with a rust-coloured powder and a smell like dried beef hit her. "Jesus, Johnny, what the hell?" She screwed the lid back in place.

About to give up, she checked the sun visor. There, secured behind two elastic bands, was his driver's licence in a clear plastic cover along with a single key.

"Thanks, Johnny," she muttered, taking it down.

She pocketed the key and got out, making a show of waving the driver's licence at the guards. She locked the van, went inside and readied herself for the hospital.

In her father's hospital room, Fiona set all the day's newspapers on his bed.

"Am I a celebrity?" said Thomas, picking up the *Irish Times*.

"The shooting's mentioned alright. So's your name, but fortunately nobody's made the connection to me."

"Yet."

Fiona pursed her lips and opened the *Racing Post* on the table. "There's also one of your pedigree-assessment articles in it."

Thomas went to pull the table towards him, but he winced. "*Ooh* ... still a bit tender." He put a hand to his side. "That reminds me – see that little jar on the bedside locker?"

Fiona picked up the clear plastic container. There was a small piece of metal inside which looked like it used to be a cylinder, but was squashed, distorted.

"Dr. Scanlan gave me that this morning. Asked if I wanted to keep it."

A shiver shot through her. "Look, Dad. I never would've left those things with you if I'd known what would happen. I'm so sorry."

He put his hand on hers. "Don't you give it another thought. You put those things in the right place. Don't blame yourself – you're not the one who did this to me." He flapped his hand at her. "Sure, I'm fine." There was a mischievous glint in his eye. "Best fun I've had in years."

"Dad!"

"It was. I tell you, the adrenalin was flying through me when I had that fella in my sights. His friend got some shock and all. Took off like a scalded cat."

Fiona fiddled with the newspaper. "He got what he came for anyway."

"He didn't get what he thought he got."

"What?"

Thomas inspected his daughter, and threw a glance at the open door. "Shut that, will you?" he said, winking.

Half an hour later, Fiona left her father and walked down the corridor to the toilet. She paused with her hand on the door. Shot a look at the guard outside her father's room engrossed in his phone. She backed up a few paces and dashed up the stairwell. On the next floor, she walked through two wards and descended in a lift at the other end of the hospital. Back on the ground floor, she crossed the Accident and Emergency wing and exited into the car park. Donning a baseball cap and winding a thick scarf round her neck and chin, she crossed the road to the taxi rank. She'd be at Toughers Industrial Estate in ten minutes and back at the hospital before anyone missed her.

After her father had filled her in on a couple of things, she told him the full story, including Johnny's warnings and the suspicions she had. He'd grunted as if it was no surprise to him, but said he'd keep it to himself and cover for her while she slipped out. As she left his bedside, he couldn't help but make a snide remark about "that little fucker". She had a feeling that whatever she found today would be the key to what her husband had been up to. She stared out the taxi's window. *Husband*. God, she hadn't thought of him as that in a long time. He had simply become an obsessive-compulsive lunatic she shared a house with.

Pieter sat under a tree, just a few yards from his motorbike. There she was. Trying to look different with a cap and scarf, but Pieter had spent too many hours watching her. He knew her mannerisms. Her long legs and cat-like stride stuck out a foken mile. He pulled on his helmet and swung a leg over the bike. He'd have to be very careful. His orders were clear this time.

Chapter 23

Marcus's head throbbed as he climbed back to consciousness. Felt like the worst hangover of all time. He opened his eyes, blinding light cut into his brain. He was hot. Grimy with sweat. Thick, stale air. He jammed his lids shut again and tried to move a hand up to rub his forehead and wipe dried spittle from the corners of his mouth, but he couldn't. His hands were tied behind his back. And he was seated. On a hard chair. What the hell? He tried his eyes again, squinting against the light. He was still in his racing suit, but it was filthy, creased. The left sleeve was torn, his shirt pushed up, exposing his forearm. Marcus saw a crusty streak of blood on a vein. He'd been injected. Once, he'd seen a film about a policeman who was abducted and turned into a heroin addict. Oh God, not heroin! Panic forced his heart into overdrive. Sweating anew, he craned his neck, but he was surrounded by bright light.

"*Hello?*" he called, his tongue thick.

No answer.

Marcus called again. Nothing. All of a sudden he felt fuzzy and the back of his head pounded harder. Then he smiled. He was dreaming. Any minute now, he'd wake up in the Sheikh's hotel. Or at home next to Fiona. He knew alcohol made him dream like this, it always had.

The fist came out of nowhere. Knuckles slammed into his cheek. He felt a crack and a tooth rattled onto his tongue. He swayed on his chair. Only the restraints kept him from falling off. He spat out the tooth. Managed, "*What the fuck?*" through a throbbing jaw.

A voice bellowed into his ear. "You'll speak only when you're spoken to." The accent was thick and rough. "Now for the tenth time, my stupid little *oke* – what the fuck have you and the Buckley woman been doing to the horses?"

Marcus took a moment to process the words. He had a feeling of déjà vu. Somewhere in the recesses of his mind, floaty images swam around. He couldn't understand it.

"Why am I here?"

A shape moved in front of the lights, giving his eyes partial relief. The man was tall and powerfully built, but Marcus couldn't make out his features.

"You're here because people want answers, my friend. The sooner you start speaking, the sooner you can go home."

Marcus felt his heart jump. Something in that statement

didn't ring true. "I don't get it," he mumbled. "I've kept him informed all along. He knows what I know. There must be some mistake. I did what he wanted, I told him where the research was. Please call him, I can't believe he would've authorised you to do this to me."

The dark shape disappeared. A door slammed shut.

Wikus crossed the corridor to another room. Plonked himself down at the table opposite Danie who was smoking a roll-up and glancing at the door with a longing, sadistic espression. Wikus rubbed his temples. "It's no good. I'll have to call the client. This fucking *oke*'s useless. He thinks he's told us everything already."

Danie flicked the empty phial off the table. "Man, I told you that stuff would fuck him up. Let me go to work on him."

He pulled a too-eager smile that made Wikus regret not tossing him off the team or even a ledge long ago.

Wikus cut him a dark stare. "You'll only make a mess. Now, give me the encrypted phone."

Danie passed it and Wikus punched out a number. The client picked up on the first ring.

The client pressed a button and the car's tinted rear window slid down. Sunlight cut into the car, flashing off his wristwatch. He nodded at the courier, accepted the briefcase and closed the window. The driver started the engine and pulled into traffic without a word. He knew better than to disturb his boss when he was in a bad mood.

Opening the briefcase, the man saw a sheaf of papers

bound together with string. He pulled the sheaf out and put it on the seat beside him. He checked the briefcase again. Nothing. No discs or USB chips. That was unusual for a scientist. He hoped those rent-a-thugs hadn't missed anything.

He put the case in the footwell and tugged the knotted string binding the papers. After two pages he swore and began flicking through the whole document, tossing sheets all around him on the seat and in the footwell. This was not what he was looking for.

He blew out a breath and swore.

The driver flicked him a nervous glance in the mirror.

He pulled out his phone, was about to make a call when it rang in his hand.

He listened.

"You idiots!" he said into the receiver. "*Stop the car.*"

The driver pulled up immediately at a bus stop.

The man got out and stood in the shade.

He turned away from his car and spoke deliberately. "You idiots took the wrong bag from the father's house. There's no genetic information there, only documents about pedigrees and bloodlines."

"How was I supposed to know that?" said Wikus. "You told us to get horse documents. That house was full of the stuff. Pieter said he'd have needed a sodding truck to cart it all out. The old man was guarding that case up in his room. Seemed the logical choice."

"And was it 'logical' that you never checked what was in it?"

"Hey, Pieter didn't exactly have time to sit down and do that!"

The client grunted. "Why did you call me?"

"We've reached a dead end with this Hamilton fella. He's talking rubbish, saying he's already told you everything he knows. Says he wishes he hadn't. He keeps going on about how he loves Fiona Buckley."

"Don't tell me you messed that up too."

"It sometimes happens with sodium pentothal. People can babble, talk shit. It gets difficult to know what's the truth. I told you that before we gave it to him."

"So give him some more."

"I can't give him any more, he passed once out already. It's not a Hollywood spy movie – this stuff isn't guaranteed. And if I OD him, well, that's an expensive mess to clear up. And I don't think people are going to accept that he disappeared into the night straight after his big win, do you?"

Another grunt.

"So what now?" said Wikus.

The client went quiet for a moment. Cleared his throat. "Do you have Hamilton's mobile telephone?"

"It's sitting on the table in front of me. Turned off with the battery removed. Why?"

"Things need to go up a level."

The client relayed his instructions and ended the call just as a bus pulled up and honked at his car.

Chapter 24

"That's great," said Sergeant O'Dowd. "Send it over, will you?" He cradled the receiver and spun his chair round. The fax machine was already spitting paper at him. When the three-page document finished printing, he snatched the papers and spun back to his desk. The office in the station was a constant drone of noises: chattering, ringing phones and smutty jokes. O'Dowd was used to the background noise, it soothed him as he typed reports, but now when he read the fax he couldn't hear a thing. He had a rush of energy and spun back to look at the flow chart he'd pinned to the board behind his desk. Totally focused, he checked the fax again. There was no way it was a coincidence.

He picked up the phone and called the officers guarding Dr. Buckley. "Is she *still* in there?" he said,

172

when he was told they were at the hospital.

"Hasn't moved."

"Get off your holes and check. *Now*. And be on the lookout for mercenary types."

"What?"

"I got an ID on the dead man."

"Jesus, that was quick."

O'Dowd waved a hand as he spoke. "I pulled a few strings. Name's Felix Vander. Age forty-five. South African. Former soldier, now working for a security company based on an island in the Persian Gulf. These types don't mess around."

O'Dowd hung up. He pinned the fax to the board beside the photo of a powerful man. If a rich horse owner was willing to bring mercenaries into the country just to get hold of some kind of genetic information, well ... O'Dowd shook his head incredulously. *Lengths people'll go to, just to win races.*

Toughers was a maze of warehouses. Most had large signs advertising the occupying businesses, but some were adorned with *To Let* placards.

The taxi slowed. "Where to, love?" asked the rotund, smiley driver.

"Could be anywhere." She rang Brendan and said; "I'll give you to the driver," when he picked up.

The driver wedged the phone between his shoulder and ear. "Yeah ... Yep ... Gotcha." He steered them into a long alleyway between two large warehouses and handed the device back to Fiona. They stopped at a small green door, next to a huge roller shutter. Over the door was a small plastic sign that declared it to be *Tynan Storage*.

Fiona got out of the taxi. "I won't be long. Keep the meter running."

"Oh, don't worry, love," he grinned. "Take your time."

She looked left and right down the alley. On one side, there were rows of doors and roller shutters of varying sizes. In between them, cars were parked against the structure. Opposite there was an aluminium window factory. A van laden with windows pulled out and passed Fiona. Its driver eyed her up and down. At the other end, a motorbike shot past the alley. The sound of its exhaust bounced off the corrugated steel sidings, amplifying the noise. Fiona opened the door under the *Tynan Storage* sign and found herself in a tidy reception area that smelled of fresh paint. There was an uncluttered, unmanned desk and several chairs for waiting clients. Behind the desk was an open door leading to the warehouse.

Fiona waited for a minute. She heard footsteps: heavy shoes on bare concrete.

"Hello?" she called, stepping around the desk.

No reply. Footsteps getting closer.

Fiona peered into the warehouse just as a man strode to the doorway, head buried in a file in his hands. He bumped into her and their heads clacked together.

"*Ow!*" said Fiona, reeling.

The man looked up, stunned. He was deathly pale and thin. "Oh, I'm so sorry. I didn't see you there."

Fiona rubbed her head. "Brendan Tynan?"

"That's me. You must be Dr. Buckley." He dropped

the file on the desk and offered her a hand. She shook it. "Again, I'm very sorry. I was engrossed."

"It's OK. Anyway, I found the key at home. I take it my husband rented a storage facility from you?"

"He did, he did."

"How long for?"

"Oh, from year to year."

"No, I mean, when did he first rent the unit?"

"I'd have to look that up," he said, sitting at the desk and shifting the computer mouse. "One minute now."

A couple of clicks later: "January 2010. Huh, time flies."

Nearly six years. She'd had no idea and she was willing to bet nobody else had either.

"I need to see the unit, please."

"Right you be. Follow me."

Outside, they passed the curious gaze of the taxi driver and walked down the alley.

"Your late husband wanted privacy. He took the unit at the end of the row, farthest from the office and nearest the exit." He pointed to the last green door on the right.

At the end, a motorbike turned into the alley and droned past them. Fiona flicked a glance at the rider's black visor, pulled her bag onto her shoulder and clamped her arm over it. Wondered if Johnny had known his paranoia would be contagious.

They came to Johnny's unit. Fiona looked over her shoulder and beckoned to the driver. He coasted down the alley towards her.

"Here we are," said Brendan.

They stood at a plain steel door, its green paint chipped and weathered. It was bolted and secured with an expensive-looking lock. Beside it was a roller shutter two metres wide and high enough to fit a van, if fully opened.

"Your key should open that padlock," said Brendan. "But the shutter has to be unbolted from the inside."

Fiona pulled out the key and inspected it, glancing at the lock.

"That's your man," said Brendan, pointing at the key. "We recommend that make of lock to our customers. Right, I'll leave you to it, so." He spun on his heel and walked away.

Fiona felt like someone in a Swiss bank, accessing a long-lost safety deposit box. She slid the key into the lock. It clicked and smoothly dropped open. She removed it, opened the latch and pulled the heavy door. A rush of fetid air hit her. Like rotten meat. She gagged. The taxi pulled up beside her.

"Are ya alright there?" called the driver, his window down.

Fiona nodded. No turning back now. She stepped inside and felt the wall for a light switch.

The harsh flourescent tube flickered into life. She stood stock-still. The room was five metres wide and ten deep. The windowless space was stuffy – what the hell was that smell? She opened the security bolts on the shutter and tugged it. It rattled up into its casing and fresh air rushed in.

She spun round and faced what she could only imagine was a base for Johnny. Some kind of improvised work area, almost like a crude lab. She winced.

Along the left-side wall there was a long aluminium table with various objects on it. Opposite was a desk with a TV monitor and several diaries stacked on it. A video camera stood on a tripod beside the desk, wires ruuning from it to the monitor. She approached the desk, saw three DVD discs in clear plastic covers.

She picked up the diary labelled 2015 and flicked through pages and pages of handwritten notes. There were dates, times, quantities and ingredients, but no names. Some photocopied pages fell out of the diary. They were lists of the end-of-season racing statistics for owners, trainers and stallions in Britain and Ireland: 2010 to 2014.

She put the book down and followed her nose to two stacks of black binliners piled in the corner. She gingerly opened the top bag of a stack. It was full of empty plastic water bottles. She frowned and rummaged about. Only water bottles. No Coke or Sprite or anything. And all empty. She picked holes in the other bags in the stack. More bottles. The next pile stank of rotten meat. Fiona held her breath and opened the top bag. It contained animal bones. Butcher's waste, like her mother used to get for the dog. Fiona shook her head. She was about to turn back to the workstation, when something in the corner caught her eye. A large white container with a green lid, perhaps thirty-litre capacity. She turned the heavy container away from the wall to read the label. It was a popular make of garden pesticide, useful for killing ants and fruit flies.

Johnny, Johnny, Johnny. What the hell?

She went to the table and looked at the industrial-strength food processor. It was standing next to a small hydraulic press, a power drill and large granite mortar and pestle. On the floor under the desk there were three metal flasks. Just like the ones in Johnny's van. She picked one up and prised the lid off. Empty, except for a fine dusting of rust-coloured powder inside the lid. Fiona spun round and spread the diaries out on the desk – six of them. She decided to start at the beginning and opened the 2010 book. A photograph was glued inside the front cover. Fiona studied it and she couldn't help but think of the book Johnny kept in the gym. Was Johnny doing all this for *him*? Then that meant that he had ... Johnny, were you his servant? Was that where the money came from? So if Johnny was working for him, then that meant ... She put her hand to her mouth. Inhaled sharply.

She looked around the unit for a chair. A smile cracked her face: of course there was nowhere to sit. She glanced at her watch, sat on the desk and began skimming through the diaries. Johnny's spidery writing was difficult to read – Fiona remembered mocking him about it when they were dating. "Mister tidy-freak has the messiest handwriting," she used to say to people in bars, when they went drinking after racing. Johnny loved the slagging: he was proud of his obsessive organising and didn't give a shite about his handwriting.

The diary revealed Johnny's passion for his project. She vaguely remembered him trying to broach the subject with her several times over the years. She had never really listened to him – he wasn't a qualified scientist.

By the time she'd skimmed the last diary, Fiona was torn between excitement and dread. She wished she'd listened – maybe she could have stopped him before it was too late. She would need to crunch the numbers and do a lot of research. It might be years before she could announce anything, but surely there were other scientists in the world with the same ideas? She'd make inquiries.

She wished Johnny was still alive. There were so many things to ask him. For all his meticulous notetaking, there were no names that she could find in any of the diaries. Neither horse, nor human. Maybe that was another paranoid tactic.

One DVD cover was marked *Endgame* with a black pen in Johnny's scrawl. The other discs were unmarked. Fiona considered opening the camera and playing *Endgame*, but she heard the parp of a car horn outside. The driver's boredom was probably starting to outweigh his running meter. She made for the door to tell him she'd be out in a minute, but her phone chimed, stopping her in mid-stride.

She saw Marcus's name on the screen. Grinning, she swiped the device and put it to her ear. "Hiya! Great win!" she said, smiling. "Too much brandy last night?"

Silence.

"Marcus?"

Chapter 25

Fiona staggered and fell against the workstation, knocking the mortar and pestle onto the ground with a loud clatter.

"*Marcus?*" she repeated, her heart pounding. A shiver ran over her scalp.

Eventually a harsh voice responded. "Please hold the line, Dr. Buckley."

"Where's Marcus?"

Then she heard his voice. Broken, distressed. Pleading.

"Fiona, they want you to tell them what you did to the horses."

"Where are you? Are you OK?"

"Please, Fiona. They want you to fix the problems with the horses."

"Fix what?"

"What you and Johnny did to the horses."

"What the –"

"Fiona," said Marcus, "they know you still have all the latest research. They want you to bring it to a back road that goes behind the runway at Dublin Airport. There's a lay-by where people often pull in to watch planes."

Fiona searched her mind. "I'll find it," she said.

"Be there in two hours. Bring everything. We –"

"And no foken cops, understand?" another voice growled into the phone. "Not if you want to see your lover again."

"Wait, I –"

The line went dead.

Fiona checked her watch. Nearly five. She scooped up the diaries and *Endgame* DVD, slammed the shutter down and locked up.

Pieter stood at the far end of the alleyway. He put his earpiece in and dialled the client.

"I'm watching the Buckley woman. She's at a storage-unit facility. She's removed a pile of books from it. Seems to be closing up. I'll stay on her."

"What a great stroke of luck!"

"I'll stay on her," said Pieter.

"*No. Grab her. Now. The books too.*"

Pieter's eyes bulged. "Grab her? It's broad daylight, and I'm on a motorbike. That's a bad idea."

"I do not pay you to question my orders. Improvise." He hung up.

Pieter swung a leg over his bike just as the taxi turned

out of the alley and disappeared. He swore and gunned the engine.

Fiona's phone rang again. Her stomach flipped when she saw the number. She let it ring through to voicemail. A second later it rang again.

"You going to answer that?" said the driver, pulling out of the alleyway. A biker overtook him, roaring towards the exit. "Bloody idiot! Youngfellas these days."

Fiona watched the phone, hoping it would stop ringing. Eventually it went through to voicemail again. Then it rang a third time.

"Sounds important," said the driver, flicking her a glance in the mirror.

"*Shit.*" She stabbed a finger at the screen.

"Dr. Buckley, where are you?" said O'Dowd.

"What? Oh, I'm still with my father."

"We know that is not the case. Dr. Buckley, I would caution you that it is an offence to lie to a police officer."

Fiona searched for a lie. "I needed some time to myself," she said. "I went for a walk around Naas." It was all she could think of.

"I need you come to the station right now. I believe I know who hired those men to burn down your lab and steal your research."

Funny, thought Fiona, she'd a fair idea herself now.

"OK. It'll take me a while to walk. I'll be there in an hour or so."

"I'll send a car to pick you up. Where are you?"

"Oh, *erm*, that's OK. I could do with the walk. Look, I'll have to let you go, my battery's dying ..." She ended the call.

The taxi eased down the access road, flanked on either side by massive warehouses. Ahead, the biker had stopped. He got off his motor and made as if to lower the kick-stand, but the heavy bike overbalanced and fell over, hitting the road with a clang.

"Ah Jaysus," said the taxi driver, "what kind of a feckin' clown is this lad?"

Fiona saw the man wave, flagging down the taxi. Strangely, he had not removed his helmet.

The car slowed as the driver hit the window button. He pulled up beside the biker. "What're you playing at there? Get your bike out of the road."

The biker shrugged, his visor was tight shut.

Fiona's heart thumped. She tapped the driver on the shoulder. "Drive on. I'm in a hurry."

The driver sighed and felt for the door handle. "I'd better help this clown pick up his bike."

Out of the corner of her eye, Fiona saw the biker reach inside his leather jacket.

"*No! Drive, now!*" she yelled. Snaking her arm past the driver's shoulder, she hit the door lock. "*Drive!*"

The cabbie's jaw dropped open as he saw the biker whip a small black pistol out of his jacket.

"*Drive!*" roared Fiona in his ear and ducked low in the seat.

The driver threw the car in gear and slammed his right foot down. The heavy saloon lurched forward, running over the guy's foot and hitting his bike. There was a crunching sound as the taxi crushed the chrome exhaust and ran over the back wheel.

They screamed towards the industrial estate's exit in

first gear. Fiona risked a glance out the rear window. The biker was down, clutching his foot.

"Holy shite, love. What was that all about? We'd best go straight to the Garda station." He pulled onto the road, headed for Naas.

Fiona saw the motorway sign ahead. "Take the motorway."

"But there's a station in Naas!"

"Please!" She tossed a fifty onto his lap.

The driver swung onto the motorway for Dublin.

Fiona stared out the rear window and drummed her fingers on the diaries.

She needed a plan.

If she told O'Dowd about Marcus, he would probably detain her in the station and send cops to the airport lay-by. She would lose all the evidence she had in her hands and probably Marcus too.

Since her father's winking confession in his hospital bed, she knew her research was still safely hidden under reams of pedigree papers in his house, but suddenly she began to wonder if her recent discoveries were a step too far. She had successfully mapped the genes for the performance-impairing, inherited lung condition Exercise Induced Pulmonary Haemorrhage and the debilitating bone-weakening disease Osteochondritis Dissecans. She had thought if breeders could predict the incidence of these problems, they could sell horses they believed to be deficient. Likewise, people at horse sales could swab DNA from prospective purchases using saliva-testing units she had found in America. She could have offices at every horse sale and could interpret the results for her clients. The idea was to weed deficient stock out of the gene pool, thus making the breed stronger and healthier. She supposed the sales companies wouldn't see it that way, as clearance rates would fall: nobody wanted to buy deficient horses. Sellers would have mixed feelings and bloodstock agents would be out almost of a job. She winced. Too far?

Then it hit her: *that's why somebody wants to control the technology*. If you were the only one with the information, you'd be invincible. But how could anyone outside Equigenes have known what she'd been working on?

As the car sailed towards the Dublin Ring Road, Fiona scribbled notes inside the front cover of the 2010 diary. The photograph glued inside the cover stared back at her. Johnny on Bronx Spirit, with Pat and her in the winner's circle at Churchill Downs.

She chewed her lip. Perhaps her research should be destroyed. Perhaps it would all be irrelevant anyway after what Johnny had done. She needed time to put the pieces together.

Darkness closed around the car. Fiona stared at the river of headlights on the ring road. The airport was five junctions away. She needed help to find Marcus and a place to do her research. She checked her watch. Just under an hour till rendezvous. That was enough time.

She swiped at her phone and made the call. It rang for an eternity before it was answered.

Chapter 26

10 November 2012

Johnny hung from the ceiling rings. He had the house to himself for the next week. Fiona had gone to attend a conference in Australia. Alone. Part of him hoped she'd find an Aussie surfer dude, fall in love, ditch Hamilton and move down under. She'd be happier. After all, she could find a lab anywhere and she wouldn't have to cope with Irish gossip. Australian breeders would queue up to invest in her – hell, some already had.

He turned his mind to exercise. Flexed his back and launched into his final set of pull-ups.

Later, after a shower and a protein shake, he parked himself at the table and inserted a DVD into his laptop. The system whirred as it loaded the disc. An image of Fiona appeared on-screen. A couple of years ago, Johnny had filmed her giving her standard introductory talk on genetics. He kept the footage and watched it every now and then. She stood behind the lectern, hiding really, talking about her passion to an audience who rarely understood much of what she said. Wow, she looked beautiful, even onscreen. Her hair flashed under the lights. Deep, rich tones of red. Johnny felt regret tip over him, something wet dropped onto the touchpad. For a moment, he thought the roof was leaking, until he realised. "Fuckin' eejit," he muttered, wiping another tear away. "What's done is done."

He opened his notepad and concentrated on Fiona's words. Watching her deliver her speech helped him to refine his theories and document his research.

She started with her usual introduction to genetics and the equine DNA code. This led into her own research and the collection of samples from Trelawn Park and just about every other big farm in Ireland, so she could compile a database. Then she got to the bit Johnny found fascinating.

"We then started investigating the gene Myostatin," said her voice onscreen, *"which is a negative regulator of muscle development. In early 2005 we made a breakthough and discovered that when Myostatin was inherited from both parents, the offspring had abnormal muscle mass. We saw examples of this in cattle, greyhounds and even humans."*

Fiona smiled and flashed two slides onto the screen behind her. The first was of a greyhound that looked like it had been pumped full of growth hormones and steroids. The second was of a toddler with bulky muscle mass on her arms and legs. On the recording, Johnny could hear a collective gasp shoot around the room.

187

"This is the child of a pair of Olympic weightlifters from the 1980s. As you can see the effect is dramatic, but as in the case of the greyhound, abnormal muscle mass can be detrimental to performance. The dog's body was effectively too heavy for its fragile limbs to carry it and it snapped a tendon in training. And as far as I'm aware this child has not won an Olympic medal."

A wave of murmuring swept through the crowd. Johnny always got upset during this bit. Upset with Fiona and the narrow-minded people in the crowd.

"But why?" Johnny roared at the screen. "Nobody ever thinks to ask *why* the offspring of those weightlifters had that muscle problem! Was it pure genetics, or were there other factors involved?"

Johnny composed himself and stopped the DVD before she mentioned her tests and the crowd started shouting inane questions at her.

He found his mind filling with images of the famous American sprinter Florence Griffith Joyner. If truth be told, Johnny's interest in athletic performance had started as a schoolboy when he had watched her win all those medals in Seoul in 1988. He had realised that modern jockeys would have to act more like professional athletes and less like gentleman riders or pissheads. It was a work ethic Johnny swore helped him to become so successful so quickly. He had still enjoyed life though. On the surface he behaved like a rockstar jockey, but he never drank before racing, and very little after. Johnny was the master at making one vodka tonic last all night, but naturally a legend grew that he was a hardened party animal. A legend he was only too happy to accept. Which was why everyone found it so easy to believe he'd been at the nose candy before Elegant Flaw's Derby.

Johnny had given it little consideration when he saw the news reports of Flo-Jo's death in 1998. It was only when he started lifting weights and forming his plan that he gave the matter deep thought. How does the fastest woman in the world die of a seizure barely ten years after she set all those world records on the track? Her family announced that she had some kind of congenital brain condition that gave her epileptic seizures. Still, Johnny wondered if she'd simply spent too much of her life running her body to extremes. Or was it something subtler and more consistent? Where she lived, how she lived? Or what she ate? Was she given any drugs? She never tested positive, but hell, most of her records still stood today – twenty-five years later. Was it a lethal cocktail of genetic predisposition, lifestyle and life circumstance? Johnny shuddered as he remembered how steriods had made him feel and how addictive it had been. He was glad he'd kicked the habit after only a few months.

He ejected the DVD and opened a web browser to access the latest racing statistics. The flat-racing season had finished in Ireland and Britain last weekend. He scanned the leading owners list. He was sure he could see a pattern, especially if he compared the list to last year's stats.

Pat McCormack had a very quiet season with his fleet of homebreds. He had a runner in nearly every top race, but they usually fell short and many were plagued with injury. He had still won a few big races, but a quick check revealed that these horses were ones he had bought as yearlings, either privately or at the sales.

Marcus Hamilton had finished the 2012 season as champion trainer on both sides of the Irish Sea again, which also made him champion owner. Everyone was talking about his genius with a horse and several other owners approached him to train horses for them. Interestingly Marcus had announced that he was only interested in training horses he bred himself at Trelawn Park. That got tongues wagging.

Sheikh Abdul's predicament was more interesting. He had had a disappointing year with his homebreds and his private trainers, his second in a row. Even his expensive sale purchases had been disappointing on the track. To top it all off, he had lost a horse in the Epsom Oaks. The poor filly shattered a hock two furlongs from the line and had to be euthanised on the track. Of course, the gossip-mongers were saying the Sheikh was piggy-backing on Hamilton's championship, having quietly bought an interest in Trelawn Park. Even so, for a man whose word was law in his homeland, the relative failure of his stud farm and trainers was a serious loss of face.

Johnny sighed. Feed wouldn't make a difference if everything else was wrong. Still, it was surely only a matter of time before the accumulative effect kicked in. Of course, he had to keep up the pace. These statistics were the first ripples on the pond. If he was to make waves, there could be no letting up.

He briefly wondered whether he should point Fiona

in the right direction. Ask her to test the horses. Her findings would take the mystery out of it, even at this early stage. No, that might make it too obvious. He didn't want the cat out of the bag. Not yet.

Chapter 27

19 October, 2015

Maura cupped her hands around a large mug of tea and threw a disapproving eye around the clutter. She had turned her dining room into a makeshift office since the fire, but she was tired of working from home. She loved driving from Leixlip to Kildare and back every working day. It was a reverse commute so she rarely had to sit in traffic and her lunchtime walks on the Curragh plains were a tonic.

But Maura wished her boss would make up her mind. Dr. Buckley was slow to make a straightforward practical decision – as usual. Still, Maura didn't want to hassle the poor woman. It had been one thing after another for Dr. Buckley lately.

Somewhere in the house, a phone rang. Maura cocked an ear. She'd left the thing in the kitchen. She placed her mug carefully on a coaster and left the room.

The screen told her it was Fiona's mobile calling. Maura smiled and crossed her fingers – surely, the good doctor had decided by now.

"Hello," she said, chirpily.

"Maura, hi. Look, this is going to sound a bit weird, but I don't have time to explain."

Maura's brow creased. "Go on."

"I'll be in Lexlip in about fifteen minutes. Can you meet me at the post office?"

"I can, of course. But you'll have to hurry, it'll close soon."

"And bring an empty shopping bag with you."

"What for?"

"Things of Johnny's. Hurry." She hung up.

Fiona hung up. "Take the next junction. We're going to Lexlip first."

The cabbie threw a satisfied glance at his meter. "Not a bother."

Fiona pulled her purse out of her handbag. She would need to get cash in Leixlip. She'd given him her last fifty to get away from Toughers. The meter read 140 euro so far, and she really couldn't see the man accepting a cheque.

Her phone rang again: **Private number**. She snatched it to her ear.

"Marcus?"

"No, no, Mrs. Buckley. This is Sheikh Abdul Khaledam."

Her stomach knotted. "Oh. How did you get this number?"

"It was not difficult. I am calling because I would like to meet with you to discuss the future of Equigenes."

Fiona opened her mouth, but words failed her.

"I am in London on business for the next day or two, but I could fly to Ireland to meet you. Or alternatively, I could send a plane to collect you."

"Look, now's not really a good time. Perhaps you heard – my father's house was broken into and he was shot."

"That is terrible. I'm sorry to hear that. Was he killed?"

There was a tone to his voice that made Fiona shiver. Detached and authoritative, almost demanding.

"No, he's in hospital – he'll be OK," she felt obliged to say.

"Who would do such a thing? What did they steal?" Abrupt, clipped words.

Fiona froze, her mind a mess of thoughts.

She heard him take a deep breath.

"Mrs. Buckley, is there anything I can do to help? Anything at all?"

"No, thank you."

"Really, it is no trouble. Where are you?"

She wasn't going to tell him that. "Sheikh Abdul, do you know where Marcus is? Have you heard or seen him since the race?"

"Is he not with you?"

"No."

"Then he must be back at Trelawn."

She hesitated. Chose her words. "His phone is turned off. That never happens."

"Perhaps he stayed in London to celebrate? That is quite possible, don't you think?"

"He told me he would come home that night."

"Men change their minds, Mrs. Buckley. Where are you? I can send someone to help you look for him?"

"That won't be necessary. I have to go now."

She ended the call and stared at the phone. It stuck to her clammy palm. That was weird. In all the years the Sheikh had been a stakeholder in Equigenes, he had never called her in person. She had always dealt with some sort of assistant or secretary.

Abdul tossed the phone on the bed and drained his tea glass. Natalya crossed the room just as she'd pranced down the catwalk at her last lingerie show.

He looked out the window. Mrs. Buckley was a problem. He could see the whole situation getting out of hand. She was her own worst enemy. And as for Hamilton, well, he was a good little servant. Always had been.

Abdul swiped at his phone, intending to make another call, but was robbed of thought. Natalya draped herself over the sofa. Ran a hand down her stomach and played with the jewel in her navel. Diamonds. She was ravenous for them. And other things.

His call could wait for a few minutes.

Fiona tugged on a handful of her hair, twisting it through her fingers until her scalp hurt. She'd have to throw O'Dowd a bone, just to keep the cops on her side, but she wasn't at all sure they could help her get Marcus back. She needed refuge, but who could she trust? Who would help her? Probably the same man who had helped Johnny – she'd figured that out at last. Funny, it was staring her in the face all this time. How could she not have guessed? Maybe she hadn't wanted to. Of course, she'd have to offer him something in return.

She was about to make the call when the car stopped.

"Here you are, love, Leixlip post office," said the cabbie.

"*Huh?* Oh right. Thanks." The place was closed. "Shit, too late," she muttered.

Maura walked round the corner, saw the cab and approached. She carried her handbag and a large shopping bag.

Fiona pulled her cap down to her eyebrows. Wound her scarf round her chin and climbed out of the car. Diaries and disc tucked under her arm, she glanced up and down the darkened street. Pedestrians bustled along through the streetlights' amber glow. Busy, places to go. No men in hoodies, but shadows everywhere. Plenty of hiding places.

Maura's eyes shone with excitement. "This is all very cloak-and-dagger."

Fiona shot her a look. "Hold the shopping bag open."

Maura opened it. Fiona stuffed the DVD and diaries in.

"Right. We've missed the post office, so you'll have to dash to the courier down the street. Get everything posted," she said.

"OK. Where to?"

Fiona handed her a slip of paper.

Maura frowned at the address. "I don't get it. Sure, I could drop these over for you."

"No. Courier them. I don't want you holding on to them."

"But –"

Fiona held up her hand. "I don't want you to end up like my father."

"These diaries aren't yours. What's in them?"

"What everyone's been looking for. It's why the lab was burned down, I'm sure of it."

Maura arched her brow, her jaw fell open a fraction.

"Go, quickly," said Fiona. "I'll call you later."

"Where are you off to?"

"To meet the only man who ever helped Johnny when he was down."

Maura stared at her boss.

"Go, Maura."

Maura shouldered the bag and strode away.

Fiona dashed across the road to an ATM and withdrew some money. Then she ran back to the car, stuffing a wad of notes into her pocket.

"The airport,"she said.

At least the proof of Johnny's deeds was safe. She wouldn't need his notes to conduct her own research. All the relevant points were in her head and everything else she could find out for herself.

Maura stacked the diaries on the counter and handed the address to the clerk. She couldn't take her eyes off the strawberry-blonde, blue-eyed young man as he typed the details. He was like a young Robert Redford.

"It'll be there first thing in the morning," he said, sealing the books into a padded plastic sleeve. "That'll be forty-six euro, please."

"What? Oh, yes." Her cheeks reddened as she fumbled in her handbag.

She paid cash, folded the receipt neatly and put it in her handbag. She hung the shopping bag in the crook of her other arm as the clerk tossed the package into a large sorting bin. *If I was twenty years younger*, she mused, also wishing she hadn't been afflicted with crippling shyness when it came to such matters.

Outside, it was starting to pelt with rain. Maura trotted down the street, rounded the corner and headed for her road, regretting not bringing an umbrella.

Ten minutes later, she opened her front door.

She dropped her handbag and the shopping bag on the mat. Peeled off her sodden raincoat, hung it on a chair and put the shopping bag beside it. She felt something rattle in the bag, reached in and closed her in hand around a DVD cover.

"*Oh feck it*," she said, mad with herself for not checking the bag at the courier's. Behaving like a silly young one, distracted by Robert Redford.

She looked at her dripping coat, heard the rain hammering on the roof tiles and decided against running back to the courier's. "Sure, it'll be closed anyway," she muttered, justifying her decision.

She placed the DVD on the kitchen table and went upstairs to run a bath.

Chapter 28

Fiona twirled her phone in her hand. One more call to make.

Pat McCormack picked up on the first ring. "Fiona Buckley. What a pleasant surprise. How are things progressing with Equigenes? Do you have a timeframe for getting back on track?"

Questions, questions. Everybody was so bloody curious. Still, she couldn't blame Pat. For the first time ever, she understood why he was so persistent.

"Yes and no," she said. "I'm calling about another matter."

"Go on," he said, after a beat.

"Look, I know it was you who bailed out Johnny all those years ago, and I'm pretty sure you set him up with his job at the feed company."

"Why are you calling me?" said Pat in a measured tone.

Headlights flashed past on the Dublin Ring Road. They would be at the meeting point in twenty minutes, but she didn't want to end up there. Not at all. Trouble was, she also didn't want to lose Marcus.

"I need your help, Pat. I'm hoping you can bail me out like you did Johnny."

A pause. "Go on."

"This is going to sound crazy: Marcus has been kidnapped and I have to meet someone in a lay-by near Dublin airport in twenty minutes. They want my research, but I don't have it. I've been told not to involve the police and, to be honest, I'm not so sure they'd be able to catch these guys. I need your help. I know you're a powerful man. *Please!*" Her voice cracked.

"You've got yourself into quite a pickle. Why do people want this research of yours?"

"It's groundbreaking stuff, a game-changer. Look, I can give you first access to it if you help me get Marcus back."

Silence.

Fiona watched the driver indicate and sluice off the ring road, headed for the airport. They'd be at the lay-by in a few minutes.

"Pat, please. I also have information about what Johnny was up to when he worked – for you – at Winline Feeds, and why Tony Carey's in such a tizzy about feed analysis."

"What are you talking about?"

The same sharp tones as Sheikh Abdul had used.

What was it about horse owners? Passion for their horses, or the desire to win at all costs?

"Johnny was doing something to certain batches of feed. It was like a personal project of his."

"What was he doing?"

"I can't say for sure yet. I need a lab to figure it all out, but it could be something big. Bigger than a few genetic tests."

More silence.

The taxi turned left, avoiding the airport's main entrance. They passed long-term car parks. Fleets of hire cars parked in massive lots. They stopped at the lights. Up ahead, behind a high chain-link fence Fiona could see the dark hole in the city night. Her heart began to pound.

"Meet these people," he said. "Set up a time and place to exchange the research for Marcus Hamilton. Remember the licence plate of their car. Call me back and I'll get people onto it. We'll get Marcus back for you and you won't have to give anything in return."

"Are you sure?"

"Positive."

"*Um*, OK. Great. Is that it?"

"No, Dr. Buckley, I'm afraid it isn't. I will take you up on your offer of first access. I'll even give you a lab to set up in. If I like what you've discovered, I might even buy it from you and take over your company."

She didn't know what to say to that. The car pulled into the inky blackness of the lay-by. A heavy shower rattled on the roof, making Fiona flinch. There was no time to discuss details.

"*Sure! Fine!*" she shouted over the rain.

"I'm also interested to know what your late husband was up to. I didn't think jockeys were academically minded."

"Yeah. Look, I'm there now, Pat. The other car's here too."

"Call me back when you've done the deal."

The line went dead.

Fiona's armpits and palms were clammy. The rain eased off.

"That was some shower," said the driver.

"Wait here," said Fiona.

"Oh, not a bother." The meter read 190 euro.

Fiona stood in the sodden darkness, staring at the other car. Two people. The faint glow of a screen pressed to the driver's cheekbone. Another glow appeared and went up against the face of the passenger.

Fiona inched towards the car, knowing she was silhouetted against the floodlights of the massive car park behind the hedgerow. Traffic splashed by, spraying water on her feet. A few steps closer. The shapes in the car seemed oblivious to her. She got close enough to knock on the driver's window.

The man flinched, dropped his phone. Peered at her.

There was a skid and splash behind her. She whipped round. A van had veered off the road, squelched to a halt between her and the taxi. The side door slid open.

"*Dr. Buckley, come here,*" said the voice.

She stepped around a puddle. Passing headlights threw grotesque shadows on the van. Fiona squinted, but she was at the wrong angle to read the plate. Across the road, a jet filled the air with thunder as it streaked up the runway. Fiona felt vibrations as it roared skyward.

"*Did you bring the papers?*" shouted the man in the back of the van.

"Not here. I need more time." She took a step closer to the van.

"That's not what you were told." The man leaned back and said something to the driver, who spoke into his phone.

Fiona took another step closer. She was trying to place the man's accent, but with all the ambient noise, she was struggling. It wasn't Dublin anyway.

The man leaned forward again. "You have twenty-four hours. We'll call you with a location. Simple exchange: papers for boyfriend. And no cops, or it's goodnight and good luck." He slid the door shut. The van circled round her and shot onto the road, narrowly missing an oncoming car. Fiona glimpsed the number plate in the headlight of the car and repeated it over and over. She typed it into her phone and made for the taxi.

Before she got in she made the call.

"Pat, I have twenty-four hours." She read him the licence number.

"Good. I'll get people on it. You will go to Weston Aerodrome in Lucan. My plane is waiting. Get on it. I'll have your name added to the manifest. You're lucky – if you'd called an hour later, it would've been over the Atlantic."

"What? Where am I going? This wasn't part of the deal."

"Dr. Buckley – Fiona – you asked for my help, and

203

this it it. I have offices and a small pharmaceutical facility in the Bronx, New York. You will be provided with space there and my people will see to it that you have access to whatever you need. You will go to work while I rescue Marcus Hamilton."

"But –"

"You'll be out of harm's way in New York. Leave it to me, Fiona. I have sufficient resources. I'll get Marcus back – however, I will need access to your research papers in case we have to pay the ransom."

"Oh, yes, of course."

"Where are they?"

"They're at my father's house. Hidden amongst all his pedigree notes."

"I'll send someone to get them."

"He's in the hospital, but there's a spare key hidden in a fake rock at the edge of the grass of the garden, to the right of the front door. Your people will need to go into his office. Look for a box file hidden underneath piles of papers and books. It's purple and marked *Foundation Mares in the 1800s*. Tell your people to be careful – my dad was shot by these lunatics."

"Don't worry yourself. Trust me, it'll all work out. Just get on that plane."

"OK." A thought hit her. "*Oh no!*"

"What is it?"

"I have only a driver's licence on me. No passport."

"*Hmm* ... It won't matter leaving Ireland, but it might pose a problem in America. Where is it?"

"At home."

"The plane cannot wait. It's taking an employee of

mine to an oncology clinic in Manhattan, but I can smooth it over with the authorities."

"I don't get it – how can I board a plane without a passport?"

"Private air travel is different to flying economy with a public company."

She got in the taxi, told the driver where to go and thirty minutes later they pulled up by the aerodrome's small terminal building. Fiona counted out the notes as the driver rubbed his hands. "Thanks for your patience," she said.

"Oh, not a bother," he chuckled, folding the notes.

She entered the building and put her bag through an X-ray machine. A ruddy-cheeked uniformed man behind a desk welcomed her with a smile.

"I'm a passenger on one of the jets," she said.

"Right you be, madam," he tapped a keyboard. "Which one?"

"Pat McCormack's plane. It's bound for New York."

"Oh, I know the one. Prevenalux Incorporated. Begod, that's been on the go the last few days. Your name, please?"

"Fiona Buckley. It might not be on the list, I'm a last-minute traveller," she said, mustering a sort of smile.

"Identification, please."

She handed him her driver's licence.

"Have you no passport?"

She made a face.

He sucked air between his teeth. "No skin off my nose, but I'd say the Americans'll give you a hard time." He checked the list. "You're on it alright." He looked her up and down as he handed her back her licence. "You look like you need a cup of tea and a sleep."

"It's been a long day."

"Out through those doors, turn left and someone'll direct you. Have a nice flight."

A minute later she trotted up the steps and into the soothing golden light of the cabin.

"*Wow!*" she said, taking in the wood panelling, huge leather seats and thick carpeting.

"Welcome aboard, Dr. Buckley," said a sharp-featured and suited woman serving water to two seated people. "I'm Catriona, Mr. McCormack's assistant. This is Mr. Regan and his son Cathal."

Fiona smiled through her tiredness and offered her hand to a craggy man who looked like he had spent his life working the land. He held her hand in a vice-like grip.

"Eddie Regan," he said in a meek voice.

The young man beside him looked pale and gaunt. He smiled thinly and offered Fiona a weak hand.

"Wheels up in ten," said the pilot, bounding into the cab, hauling up the steps and sealing the door.

"Yes, Captain," said Catriona.

Fiona turned off her phone, sank into a seat and melted with exhaustion. As the plane taxied onto the runway, she vaguely heard Eddie asking her what kind of doctor she was. Sleep was wonderful and welcome.

Nearly two hours had passed since Pieter dragged his bike to the side of the road and called for help. He huddled under an awning as rods of rain rattled down around him. "Foken Irish weather," he muttered. He'd be glad when this contract was over and he could windsurf and bask in the Persian Gulf sun.

Cars leaving the industrial estate caught the wounded machine in their headlights. Drivers rubbernecked. Pieter glared. At least nobody stopped.

Eventually, a van pulled up and the side door slid open. "Need a ride, *oke*?" said Vaughn.

Pieter grimaced. "What about the bike?"

"We'll put it in the back."

Mike flicked the hazard lights on and joined them. The three brawny men loaded the bike.

"Right," said Vaughn, slamming the door. "We've got to search that unit the Buckley woman was in today. Where is it?"

Pieter directed them. They backed the van up against the shutter. Vaughn snapped the lock with a bolt cutters and they were about to go inside when a voice called out in the darkness.

"Excuse me, what're you doing there?" A tall thin man hustled towards them, cowering under an umbrella.

"What's it to you, mate?" said Vaughn.

"I'm the owner of this facility. What do you think you're doing?"

"Oh, we're with Mrs. Buckley. She sent us to clear the place out."

Vaughn saw the man glance from the boltcutters to the cut lock on the ground, then take a small backward step. Vaughn lunged. Swung the boltcutters. Missed. The man let out a cry, dropped his umbrella and ran. Vaughn sprang after him. It only took him two strides.

He pushed the man to the tarmac with a splash and a squawk. Limbs thrashing wildly. Vaughn dodged an arm and delivered a kick to the man's temple. The thrashing stopped.

"*Fuck*," said Vaughn, hooking his hands in the man's armpits. He dragged him back to the unit. "Open the shutter."

Pieter disappeared inside and in a second, the shutter rattled open. Vaughn pulled the man over the threshold and dropped him with a sodden thud.

Pieter flicked on the lights and the three mercenaries took in the scene.

"What the fuck?" said Pieter.

"We load everything."

When the romantic comedy finished, Maura dabbed her eyes with a tissue and went to make another cup of tea. While the kettle boiled, she noticed the DVD on the table. Picking it up, she read the word *Endgame* scrawled in untidy letters. Endgame. That didn't sound positive. She wondered what Dr. Buckley was up to. It wasn't her handwriting, but what if she was planning to sell the business? Where would that leave Maura, Cathy and Denise? Surely not. Dr. Buckley would've told her. But then, why all the secrecy?

Maura drummed her fingers on the DVD. It wouldn't hurt to have a little sneak peak.

She made her tea and brought the DVD through to her cosy sitting room. Loaded the disc, hit play and sat back to spy on the future of Equigenes.

The image that appeared onscreen made her jump,

knocking her tea off the arm of the chair. Johnny Buckley's pallid features stared back at her. His eyes dark with rage. He rasped a gutteral cough and spat bloody phlegm into a tissue.

Rooted to the spot, Maura blessed herself. Tea soaked into the carpet as she watched every second of Johnny's video.

Even when the disc finished, Maura couldn't move. She'd forgotten all about the spilled tea. Eventually she snapped out of it and called Fiona, but failed to connect.

She paced round her dining table. Tomorrow, she'd have to go and follow those couriered papers to their destination.

Chapter 29

O'Dowd stood at the lectern in the briefing room. The air was thick and stale like someone had smoked a crafty cigarette. Behind him on the whiteboard were handwritten notes and photos of Fiona Buckley, her father, Felix Vander and Sheikh Abdul Bin Omar Khaledam. Lines were drawn, connecting the images. More notes and documents were held to the board with small magnets.

"Of course," he said, "we need evidence. But, above all, we need to locate Dr. Buckley."

In front of him, four officers slouched in their seats, nodded unenthusiastically and sipped tea from large mugs.

"Kenny and McMahon, you'll relieve the lads at the hospital. I'll be over later today to interview the man again. Carroll and Jones, you get back to Dr. Buckley's house and let me know if she turns up."

More nodding.

"I'll put out an APB for Dr. Buckley. I'm waiting from a reply from the company that Felix Vander worked for. I've asked them for information on clients and who was working with Mr. Vander."

"*Huh*, good luck with that," said Jones, cocking his chin and letting out a cackle.

O'Dowd gave him a shrug of resignation. "I'm sure you're right for once, but if they want the body released, they'd better help me out on this one."

The duty officer knocked on the open door and entered carrying a package. "Sergeant, this came for you. I signed for it."

"Thank you, Karen," said O'Dowd, accepting the heavy parcel. He stared at it for a second, frowning as he read the delivery receipt. He looked up at the others. "That's all. Go on."

They ambled out of the room. O'Dowd set the packet on the lectern and pulled on latex gloves. He fished a penknife out of his pocket and carefully cut along the side of the packet. Gingerly pulled out six black A4-sized books and a folded sheet of paper. One by one he set the books down on chairs and checked the package was empty. Inspecting the books, he saw they were day-per-page desk diaries. Consecutive years. 2010 to 2015.

Pinching the corner of the cover between his thumb and forefinger, he slowly unfolded the sheet of paper. His brow shot up.

Sergeant O'Dowd,
I'm sorry I lied to you yesterday. I discovered these last

night in a storage unit belonging to my late husband. I believe THIS is what everyone is looking for, not my research. I was followed there and nearly attacked. I am now with the man who helped my husband, in the hope he will give me the means to figure out the implications of this whole mess. These diaries and the DVD are evidence. I'll be in touch in a few days. Don't worry about me, but please keep my father protected.

I'll call you soon.

Fiona Buckley

"Bloody cheek of the woman! Who does she think she is?" He checked the packaging again. "What DVD?" He swore, grabbed the diaries and packaging and marched out of the room. In the corridor, he collared a young recruit. "You. Pull any prints you can off these and send them off for processing."

The young guard looked at him like he'd just been told to shoot someone.

"It's not brain surgery. Take the prints and send them to the lab at Phoenix Park HQ."

"Yes, sir."

O'Dowd made a beeline for the Superintendent's office and brought his commanding officer up to speed.

The Super rubbed his face and let out a long slow breath.

"Jesus Christ! And do we have *any* idea where she is?"

"I tracked her phone to up near Weston Aerodrome yesterday evening, then it was turned off."

"So she's out of the bloody country?"

"Looks like it."

"Right, go back and give her father the third degree – the auld bollix must know where she's gone. And get someone to start going through the diaries. *Immediately*."

On his back way through reception, O'Dowd noticed a woman patiently waiting for Karen to get off the phone. He thought he'd seen her before, maybe a week or so ago. He grabbed his coat and keys and hustled for his car.

As he started the engine, Karen dashed across the tarmac, frantically waving. She was a keen young recruit with severe black hair and no sense of humour, but O'Dowd liked her. He slid down his window. "What is it, Karen?"

"Sergeant, I've just taken a call from an Alfie Connors. He said he's the head man at ..." she looked at the note in her hand, "Trelawn Park Stud ..."

O'Dowd nodded. An image of Marcus waving a bottle of wine flashed through his mind.

"He says that he hasn't seen or heard from his boss, a Marcus Hamilton, since Saturday evening. Mr. Hamilton's phone is turned off and apparently that's highly unusual for a racehorse trainer."

O'Dowd killed the engine and pulled out his notepad.

"Mr. Connors says that he tried to reach Mr. Hamilton's girlfriend, Dr. Fiona Buckley, but he can't get hold of her either. He's coming to fill out a missing persons report, but I thought you'd want to know about it ASAP."

"You did well, Karen."

O'Dowd screwed his wide face into a thoughtful grimace, tore a page off his pad and handed it to Karen. "That's Fiona Buckley's number. Keep trying it for me

213

until the end of your shift. If you get through, be nice and polite, but find out where she is – no matter what."

Karen nodded, her face full of purpose.

"And when Connors turns up keep him here till I get back from Naas hospital. I'll need to ask him a few things about his boss. Right, you'd better get back to reception."

Twenty minutes later, O'Dowd pulled into the hospital car park, squinting in the low October sun. Sunshine after the rain for once, he thought, as the electric doors parted letting him into the lobby. He made his way up to Thomas Riley's floor and strode down the corridor. Officers Kenny and McMahon stood when they saw him, folding their newspapers.

"Is he alone?" asked O'Dowd.

"Yes. No visitors or doctors," said Kenny.

O'Dowd entered the ward and closed the door behind him. Thomas Riley was standing at the window, sunning his thin face. A faint smell of urine hung in the air.

"How are you feeling, Mr. Riley?"

Thomas turned slowly. "Not a bother, Sergeant. Isn't that a grand bit of sunshine? The ground must be wicked soft after all that rain last night."

"*Hmm.* Are you well enough for a little chat ?"

He nodded. "I am indeed. The doctor says I can go home tomorrow."

"That's good news, but I'm afraid we'll need to keep officers at your house until ..."

Thomas shuffled gingerly over to his bed and got in. "Until what?"

O'Dowd sat on a chair. Pulled out his notepad. Fixed his eyes on the older man. "Your daughter has gone missing. Do you have any idea where she is?"

Thomas's mouth fell open. "I – I don't."

"Mr. Riley, it is imperative that you tell me anything you know, or I will not hesitate to prosecute you for obstruction of justice. I've had quite enough of you and your daughter telling me half the story."

Thomas's eyes widened.

O'Dowd held him in a searching gaze.

The words fell out in a torrent: "Fiona came to see me yesterday morning, she told me she needed to get away from your men for a couple of hours so she could check out a storage unit that her husband had rented. I suppose she went there, but I haven't heard from her since." He raised his hand. Palm flat. "Swear to God."

O'Dowd saw panic in his eyes. If he was lying, he was good at it. "Where is this storage unit?"

"Oh, er, that place between here and Newbridge."

"Toughers Industrial Estate?"

"That's the one."

O'Dowd pulled his lapel radio to his ear and barked an order, keeping his eyes fixed on Thomas. A squad car would be dispatched immediately.

Thomas looked nervous. He bit his lip and stared at the floor.

"Now then, Mr. Riley. What else should I know?"

"Well, erm, those papers that were stolen from my house ..." he said slowly, like a schoolboy in the headmaster's office.

"Go on."

"They weren't the important ones – the ones that they're looking for are still in my house."

O'Dowd clenched his jaw. He'd had enough of Buckley and her father thinking they were smarter than the gardaí. "*Tell me where.*"

He told him everything.

"You know, you'd have saved me a great deal of trouble and perhaps your daughter would not currently be unaccounted for if both of you had been straight with me from the beginning."

Thomas nodded. Worry furrowed his brow.

"One more thing, Mr. Riley. How does your son-in-law fit in to all this? I thought he had nothing to do with Equigenes?"

Thomas shuddered. "Son-in-law, *huh!* Little fucker did nothing but upset my daughter and now she's on about him doping horses or something." He flapped a hand dismissively. "I don't know any more than that – she wouldn't go into details."

"Thank you for coming to your senses, Mr. Riley. I'll go to your home now and you will inform me if you hear from your daughter."

Thomas nodded.

O'Dowd stood and left.

Chapter 30

New York City
Monday night, 19 October
9 p.m. local time

Fiona stared out the vehicle's window as they crossed the Hudson river into Manhattan, the island a shock of lights under a black sky. Larger than life. Unreal.

Two weeks ago, Fiona had been happily working away on her latest tests. Her mind had been full of arrogant amusement at how those in the business of racing and breeding would react to her forthcoming saliva-analysis device and her tests. She had imagined herself as a revolutionary, a visionary to be lauded. Now her life was unrecognisable. She felt hunted – and Marcus ... well, she didn't want to thnk about what they'd do to him if Pat and all his resources failed to find him. How long till the deadline? What time was it here?

Fiona fondled her phone – she should turn it on and call her father, tell him she was fine, but that'd probably mean having to deal with the police. Besides, something nagged at her but she couldn't grasp it. Her brain was like a room full of people all trying to get out the door at the same time. She badly needed a computer and a lab.

At least she felt rested. Catriona had woken her with a hot meal twenty minutes before the plane touched down at Teterboro Airport in New Jersey. They disembarked the private jet straight into this luxury minivan. Oh, how the other half travel! No wonder Pat had been so relaxed about passports.

Cathal's eyes were glued to the window too. So were his father's. Fiona hoped the brave young man's battle would be more successful that Johnny's.

After a slow shuffle through New York traffic and another bridge-crossing, the van pulled into an underground car park.

"We get out here, Dr. Buckley," said Catriona.

Then she told the driver to take Cathal and Eddie to the Times Square Marriot.

"Cathal, it's only nine so you've time to go out and have a look about before bed," she said in homely tones with a warm smile. "It's a mad place! Put whatever you want on the room bill and I'll be there at nine in the morning to take you to the clinic."

Eddie's eyes welled up. "God, but you're very good and Pat's a saint altogether."

"Mr. McCormack is very loyal to his people. He never forgets anyone."

"Thanks a million." Cathal's eyes sparkled. "C'mon, Dad, let's have a look about."

218

Catriona slid the door closed and the van streaked away up the ramp to street level.

The air was warm and dirty in the underground garage. City air. Fiona wrinkled her nose. Catriona approached a pair of elevators while rummaging through her bag. She produced an ID card with a flourish, swiped it at a sensor and the doors slid open. Inside, she pressed the top number and the shiny doors slid closed.

Fiona inspected her dishevelled reflection on the polished steel. "Where are we?" she asked.

"South Bronx, just across the Harlem river from Manhattan. Close to Yankee stadium."

Fiona shrugged.

"It's one of Mr. McCormack's smaller facilities. I've arranged for you to have an office and there'll be someone to help you out. The lab floors are closed now, but there's a small apartment on the top floor for visiting consultants, which I suppose is what you are." She grinned. "There's always a bottle or two of wine in the fridge, so don't be afraid to have a drop. If you need food, you can order up and the security guard in the lobby will have it brought up to you."

The elevator stopped and opened out onto a small area with two doors and a guard slumped in a chair, switching his gaze between a monitor and an iPad propped beside it showing a football game.

"Evening, ma'am – ma'am." He nodded twice, stood and swiped a card, opening the door to the apartment.

"How are you, Ted?"

"I'm good, ma'am," he replied, flashing a movie-star smile.

Catriona grinned back as she swept through the doorway.

She gave Fiona a quick tour of the comfortable but impersonal two-bedroom unit. The open-plan lounge /kitchen had a south-facing, full-length glass window displaying the city in all its flickering neon glory.

"*Wow!*"

"We're only twelve floors up, so you can't see that much."

Fiona laughed. "It's so exciting. I think I'll have a quick walk about in a while. Clear my head."

Catriona looked embarrassed. "Oh, I'm sorry. The boss said that you're to stay in tonight. He said you'd understand – that it's safer that way?"

"Oh yeah, right. I suppose."

Catriona put a hand on Fiona's arm. "I'll let you in on a little secret," she said with a wink. "If you ask Ted nicely, he'll let you up to the roof through that other door." She flapped a hand towards the entrance. "There's a helipad up there. Great spot for a glass of wine at sunset – or a nighttime drink." She wiggled her eyebrows.

Fiona smiled. "Thanks."

"OK, grand. I'll be off then," Catriona said. "Night."

As Catriona strode to the door Fiona considered asking her for news of Marcus, but something stopped her. She wasn't sure how much Catriona knew and, anyway, it wasn't something she wanted gossiped about amongst Pat's employees. It'd be better to talk to him directly.

"Is there a phone here?" she called after Catriona.

"No landline, I'm afraid. The boss'll call you in the morning."

"OK – see you then."

"Oh, I have to go to our main production facility upstate in Albany tomorow. This place is only a small research and 'face' building where deals get done. After that, I'll be busy helping the Regans. So you won't see me again." She opened the door. "Try to get some sleep."

The door closed softly.

Fiona stared out the window at the madness of New York. Below people scuttled like ants and she felt odd. Almost trapped. She couldn't wait to get started in the morning and shed some light on this whole mess.

O'Dowd swore repeatedly. He'd gone through Thomas Riley's reams of paperwork, files and books twice. He had even checked the other rooms in the house and the garden shed. There was no purple box file marked *Foundation Mares of the 1800s*. He went to his squad car and called Kenny, who questioned Mr. Riley again in his hospital bed. According to Kenny, the old man was telling the truth.

So where was this famous genetic research?

Bill Harris sat at his desk in the Balmain Stud offices. It was nearly lunchtime and his stomach rumbled. He phoned reception, asking for a someone to get him a roll from the village shop. He'd been there since before dawn, foregoing his usual rounds of the farm to read through the purple box that had been hand-delivered to him. Pat had called him late last night to say that Dr. Buckley was on her way to New York to use the Prevenalux labs to finish her research. Said he'd done a deal with her. Bill had to smile at that: Pat loved to stay ahead of the game.

Bill had been ordered to read through the papers and see what he thought. So he'd hopped out of bed and dashed to the office to learn what secret advantage Pat had purchased.

Some of the scientific jargon was a bit heavy, but overall Bill was disappointed. It was hardly lightning in a bottle. On the other hand he could see an opportunity for Balmain Stud. He ate his lunch when it arrived and scribbled a few notes before he called his boss.

"What's your take on all this?" Pat barked into the phone, without even saying hello.

"Well, I don't really see what all the fuss is about. I mean, genetic tests for Osteochondritis Dissecans and Exercise Induced Pulmonary Haemorrhage? Hardly a magic bullet for winning races, but the portable saliva-testing device is a good one. You said you've done a deal? Does that mean her findings are ours and ours alone?"

"It does."

Bill grinned. "So we'll test our own stock and sell the ones that don't measure up. Like Shine On and her foals, for instance. We'd also be able to test any animals we want to buy at the sales. It'd give us a massive advantage. Sure, nobody'd have a clue what we're at. Be years before anyone figured it out. You'd make a fortune, streamline your breeding operation *and* refine your bloodlines." The thought of it filled him with excitement. A return to the glory days.

"It's an interesting concept, Bill, and I'll probably go down that road as soon as Dr. Buckley's ready, but you're missing the big picture. There's something wrong with my horses. Something deeper than OCD, EIPH or pedigrees. I know it, even if you're too stupid to see it. I don't accept that I'm just in a slump."

Bill was lost for words.

Chapter 31

February 2013

Johnny ate tofu, steamed brocolli and baked potatoes and revelled in his post-workout muscle burn. He sat at home on a dark Friday evening and congratulated himself on another good week's work. Fiona was working late, or with Hamilton. Or both.

He thought about the coming racing season and how it would hopefully confirm his suspicions. Upon careful reflection, he decided that he'd need to wait at least another two – maybe three – years before he presented his findings to Fiona. And if she displayed lack of interest again, well, he'd just have to convince her. He'd dangle a divorce and fill her mind with the money and fame she'd get from the discoveries.

A sad smile cracked his face. Despite everything, he still felt something for her. He might even call it love, as much he could love any more. If he hadn't taken that ride on Elegant Flaw, life might've been very different.

Darkness misted over him. No regrets. He had become something greater than he was. *Fate*.

His laptop screensaver flickered. Johnny fingered the touchpad and went through the website of an international news magazine, soaking up all the latest gory details. After that, he opened his file of saved articles and read through his favourite piece again. At this stage, he almost knew it by heart, but the impact of the piece stayed with him.

The piece had been published in 2010 and started by referring to a 1986 *The Lancet* article. In the mid-eighties, two groundbreaking papers had been published showing the correlation between a pregnant woman's nutrition and her child's higher-than-average risk of cardiovascular disease as an adult. At the time, it had seemed an outlandish idea. The effects of nuture (our environment) on a species' nature (genes) weren't supposed to happen so quickly.

Johnny grinned. Tip-of-the-iceberg stuff. Move over, Darwin. Johnny read on. He never tired of reading about Dr. Bygren's work.

In Sweden in the 1980s, preventative health specialist Dr. Lars Olov Bygren began studying people living in the 19th century in Norrbotten County in Sweden's isolated north. A place so isolated that in the 19th century, if the harvest was bad, people starved. Johnny let out a whistle every time he read this, while trying to imagine being completely at the mercy of the elements.

In Norrbotten, it seemed the harvest had been

savagely unpredictable. In 1800, 1812, 1821, 1836 and 1856 crops failed totally and people starved. In 1801, 1822, 1828, 1844 and 1863, the harvest was so abundant that the same people gorged themselves for months. Bygren drew a random sample of a hundred people born in 1905 and used historical records to trace their parents and grandparents back to birth. Norrbotten county kept meticulous agricultural records and Bygren was able to take advantage of these records to determine the food available – and its extreme fluctuations in quantity – to the test subjects' parents and grandparents when *they* were young.

Bygren was fascinated with research showing that conditions in the womb could affect health not only when one was a foetus, but on into adulthood.

When Johnny had first read this, a notion had hit him like a steamroller. If for humans, then why not for horses?

Bygren wondered if that effect could start even before pregnancy. Could someone's early life experience somehow change the traits they passed on to their *own* offspring? Apparently, few took Bygren seriously at the time. Too radical an idea. Johnny swore – *stupid people!*

Established wisdom told us that no matter what choices we made during our lives that might ruin our short-term memory or shorten our lives, when we had kids of our own the genetic slate was wiped clean. Because we could never change our genes – our actual DNA.

But then Bygren's research showed that Norrbotten boys who enjoyed those rare overabundant winters – kids who went from normal eating to gluttony in a single season – produced sons and grandsons who lived shorter lives. In a 2001 paper, Bygren showed that the grandsons of Norrbotten boys who had overeaten died an average of six years earlier than the grandsons of those who had endured only poor harvests.

Bygren then adjusted for socioeconomic factors and variations. The difference in longevity jumped to an astonishing thirty-two years.

That really blew Johnny's mind.

Later papers using different Norrbotten test groups confirmed these drops in lifespan and also revealed that they applied along the female line. So daughters and granddaughters of girls who had gone from normal to gluttonous diets also lived shorter lives.

In other words, thought Johnny, the data suggested that a single winter of overeating as a youngster could initiate a biological chain of events that would lead someone's grandchildren to die decades earlier than their peers did.

Incredible stuff, thought Johnny. He rubbed his hands together and almost smiled.

He felt a sudden cramp in his guts and wheeled himself to the bathroom.

Chapter 32

The Bronx
New York City
Tuesday, 20 October 2015
9 a.m. local time

Fiona slept fitfully, her night punctuated by nightmares of Marcus being walloped by those thugs. God, she hoped Pat was as good as his word.

She showered, sniffed at her stale clothes and reluctantly put them back on. She ordered coffee and a bagel from the deli menu pinned to the fridge and an overweight security guard brought it up. Shortly after that, there was a knock at the door. She opened up to find a pale, precise man wearing a khaki lab coat. Pens clipped to his breast pocket like military medals.

"I'm Ronald," he said in an almost cartoony nasal voice. "Manager of Product Development."

"Fiona Buckley."

"I've been assigned by the general manager to escort you to my office and help you in any way I can."

Fiona shook his clammy hand. As they descended in the elevator, Ronald blabbered nervously while eyeing Fiona up and down in the door's reflection.

"I suppose you know what we do here. Since Prevenalux was set up by Mr. McCormack and his late partner, we have patented ninteen products. It started making cholesterol meds, then branched out into other preventative medicine technologies. You'll be using my office on the fifth floor. I understand your area is genetics? Me, I'm interested in cancer. Got a few things in the pipeline. Oh yes, *veerrry interesting*." He nodded contentedly and glanced at Fiona's breasts.

Guys like Ronald were the reason she preferred female assistants.

"So," he continued, "I gather you're working to a deadline and you lost most of your research in a fire?"

Fiona cut him a sideways look.

"*Gee*, that's too bad. But don't worry – whatever you need, I'm your man." He cocked a thumb at this chest.

Mercifully, the doors opened onto a bright reception area. Pastel colours and abstract art on the walls gave the place a 1980s feel.

A head-setted girl sat behind a large desk answering a torrent of calls. "Good morning – Prevenalux – Michelle speaking. How may I help you? Certainly, please hold." Her fingers flowed over the switchboard. Behind her was a frosted glass door.

Ronald approached the desk.

Michelle flicked a glance, snaked a hand from the keyboard and picked up a plastic card on a cord.

"Thanks, Michelle." Ronald turned to Fiona. "Keep

this access card round your neck at all times. It'll get you in and out of the office and elevator. Security carry out regular checks and you don't want to be found without it."

Fiona inspected the card. It had her name and even a photograph lifted from her website. Pat was certainly efficient. She hoped he was as good at locating Marcus.

Ronald swiped his card and the door opened with a suck of air. Fiona followed him into the carpeted quiet of the offices. He went down the corridor, throwing furtive glances into any open doors. People hunched over their desks, staring into multiple screens. The rattle of keyboards fluttered into the corridor.

At the final door he swiped his card again and opened the office. "You can have this place to yourself. I'll be down the corridor if you need me. You can call cells from the switchboard." He indicated the elaborate phone. There was an A4 sheet of numbers taped to the desk beside it. "My PC is good to go." He tapped the keyboard and the unit hummed into life. "I've set up a new username so you can surf the net, email and create files, but you can't access company files or research data. If you need any genetic information, call me. I'll see what I can do."

Fiona arched a brow. "You have equine genetic information here?"

Ronald squinted at her, drew breath as if to speak, but then didn't.

"Never mind," she said, sliding behind the desk. "Thanks very much, Ronald."

He took his cue and shut the door behind him.

Fiona snatched the handset and wedged it on her shoulder. She ran a finger down the number sheet. The boss was not listed. Hardly surprising. She pulled out her own mobile, turned it on and scrolled through her contacts.

Pat answered on the first ring.

"Who's this?" he demanded. There was a dull whine in the background and the signal was scratchy.

"Pat, it's Fiona Buckley. Can you hear me?"

"Oh, yes, yes. I hope my people are looking after you."

"Yes, thank you. Look, what about Marcus? The twenty-four hours'll be up soon."

"Try not to worry about it, Dr. Buckley. I have people on the job. Private investigators. Expensive, but efficient. They'll get a result. And, if we run out of time, I can always hand over your OCD and EIPH research in exchange. Don't you worry. God help us, there's been enough trouble over this already."

"OK. Thank you."

"However, if the agency can return Marcus without having to hand over the ransom, I will keep the research. It will become my private property, as it were."

She slouched in the chair. Closed her eyes. If Johnny's theories proved right, then that research would be almost useless. Anyway, the patent on the saliva-test kit was owned by another company, so unless Pat bought it from them he couldn't own that. She reckoned Equigenes could do without the OCD and EIPH tests after all. It was a pity that she had to give them exclusively to Pat who would just use them to his advantage for the next couple of years. But, strangely, Fiona felt that she owed Pat for helping Johnny. And she was glad that creepy Sheikh

Abdul wouldn't have access to it through Equigenes. That was a bonus. When she got Marcus back, she'd tell him to get out of business with that man.

"Fiona," Pat said in her ear, "are you there?"

"Oh yes, right. I suppose that's fair. You're sure you'll get him back?"

"Positive. One way or another." He cleared his throat. "So what the hell was your husband up to?"

She sucked air between her teeth. "It's too early to say. Give me some time."

"But you can surely give me some idea? After all I'm doing for you."

She frowned. So, Pat put Johnny in the feed company to pay him back – to look after him – but didn't known about his side project?

"Sorry, Pat, I have to get to work."

She hung up, pulled a legal pad off a shelf and tapped the mouse, waking the computer into life. She wrote out charts on several sheets of paper and made a list of questions. Then she searched the net. Eventually she found a number for Dr. Christian Neumeyer at Massachusetts Institute of Technology. They'd collaborated weekly when Fiona was starting Equigenes and he was the top man at the Horse Genome Sequencing Project. Christian would help her fill in the gaps. After that, she'd call her father.

Sheikh Abdul's phone rang in his hand.

"Good afternoon, Vlad, I hope it is good news."

"You're not going to believe where the Buckley woman's phone signal has popped up."

"Where?"

He told him.

"Stupid woman. Find her. Get her. Immediately. Use whatever resources you need."

"Yes, sir." Vlad hung up.

Abdul banged his fist on the mahogany table. He knew he should have stayed longer at the funeral that day, had a proper talk with Mrs. Buckley. Forced her to come with him. It was too late for that now.

"Christian, how are you?"

"Hey, Fiona Buckley! Blast from the past. How're you doing?"

"Well, to be honest, life's a mess."

She told him about Johnny's death, Marcus being kidnapped and her papers being lost.

"You're kidding? I'm so sorry to hear that," he drawled. "You got the cops on the job?"

"Yeah, thanks. But that's not why I called. I wanted to pick your brains and get access to any information you might have on a certain subject."

"Sure thing. Door's always open for you, Fiona."

"Great, but before I tell you anything I want to ask you a question. Give me a top-of-your-head answer first. Then we'll discuss the case."

"Cool! Fire away."

"Why would anyone put powdered plastics, crushed bone marrow and pesticide into food?"

"Say that again?"

Chapter 33

Marcus walked another lap of the room. His sweat dripped onto the concrete floor. The useless air-conditioning vent in the ceiling wasn't even the type people in movies crawled to safety through. He'd lost a tooth and his gum was swollen. His nerves jangled at the thought of torture. They'd mentioned it a couple of times when they brought him food and water. So he waited for it.

To occupy his mind, he tried to work out where he was. The room was six metres by six, windowless. There was a second chair against the wall and no other furniture. The only exit was a steel door, and a single fluorescent light flickered overhead. They had removed the blinding interrogation lights after he'd spoken to Fiona – however long ago that was. At least the drugs had worn off. There was a clean bathroom across the corridor where they'd watched him relieve himself. No windows there either. On his last trip to the toilet, he had seen several other doors leading to God knows where and steel sliding doors at the end which could only be an elevator.

He was obviously in a basement, but where? In one of the Sheikh's many dwellings? Or in the bowels of some some skyscraper in a desert city-state?

Marcus was appalled that the man saw fit to abduct him.

And why ...

Because he could ...

Marcus had co-operated, so what was all this shit for? He wondered if anyone at Trelawn had reported him missing yet. God, he hoped Fiona was alright. If the man laid a finger on her ... Marcus didn't care if he was a crown prince or a ruler, he would ... actually, he didn't know what he'd do. First thing was to get out of here and contact Fiona. Then, he'd go public about the Sheikh's little games. After that, he would simply walk away from Trelawn. Let the man have it. The staff would follow him out the door, so he'd set up shop somewhere else and continue breeding and training champions. Maybe even for Pat McCormack. Pat could do with the help.

He paced his cell and laughed at the ridiculousness of his plans.

He froze. Voices outside. He'd ask the thugs for the toilet again and then he'd see if he could ... could ... maybe overpower them? Another laugh.

Then the door opened.

The taut-faced man again. He offered Marcus a bottle

of water and a limp sandwich. Marcus drank and devoured.

"Listen, *oke*. Time's running out." He checked his watch in a way that Marcus could not see the hour. "Why don't you make this easy on yourself? I mean, one way or another, it'll all be over soon, but you can choose the easy option. You know? Why don't you be honest with us, my friend?"

Marcus tried to stare calmly at the wall. Inside he was screaming.

The man's phone chimed. He made for the door and locked it behind him. Marcus dashed over and pressed his ear to the steel. He heard a muffled voice and heavy footsteps, as the man paced the corridor while he spoke.

Fiona swivelled in the chair and stared out at the afternoon sun. Thoughts and ideas flashed about, her synapses fired, giving her a kind of adrenalin rush that could easily erupt into a meltdown.

During their first date, she had known that Johnny was smart guy. Probably too clever for his own good. That should be his epitaph really: *Too Clever by Half*. Still, she should have listened to him. Now that she thought about it, he'd tried to broach the subject a number of times, but she'd had tunnel vision for her own work. I mean, what would an obsessive-compulsive lunatic know about this?

She wiped her cheek, realised that she'd probably let go of her marriage too easily. But at the time fixing a fractured relationship and a damaged spouse had seemed like a distraction from her work and Johnny had got so ... weird.

236

She'd make sure Marcus understood that no matter what the work pressure, they had to keep their relationship healthy. Life was too short.

She sighed and spun back to the desk. She scanned the pages in front of her: nearly two legal pads worth of notes, and another file on the computer. Pat had her where he wanted her now. What would he do with all this? Probably insist on buying out all her other investors. Would that be so bad? After all, he had the money to fund whatever research she – or he – felt like doing.

A wasp buzzed past her ear and hit the window. Fiona flinched. Bloody thing, how did that get in here? She watched the flying insect charge the glass several times, then apparently giving up it landed on the filing cabinet by the wall. It moved scratchily on the smooth surface, as punch-drunk insects do in the late autumn.

"Dopey thing," she muttered, picking up a legal pad to deliver the death blow. Her hand stopped in mid-air. She stared at the black and yellow abdomen.

Holy shit.

She fell back into the chair, sending it into a spin. Swivelling back to the desk, she grabbed the mouse, clicked a search engine and typed two words: **histone code**.

The results appeared in a flurry before her. Scrolling down the list she stopped at an article and commentary on a science website, quoting Dr. Paul Hurd of Queen Mary University of London and other researchers at the Australian National University.

The article was all about research in the honey bee and its histone code. Bascially a series of marks on the histone proteins that are wrapped around DNA, letting it fit into the nucleus of a cell. Fiona knew it existed in humans and other complex organisms to control changes in cell development. But now it seemed it had been discovered in bees.

Fiona chewed her lip. Bees all shared a common DNA but later developed into queens, female workers or drones, that was known. So it looked like this finding would help to explain how eating royal jelly ensures honeybee larvae turn into queens and not workers. If a bee larvae was going to be a queen, it was fed only royal jelly, while workers/drones were fed pollen or nectar. It was about turning genes on or off during development to make a worker or a queen, which would be a pretty clear example of epigenetics in action. The honey bee's histone code might also help to explain why bees are so sensitive to environmental change. If bee histone code worked as it did in other organisms, then marks on the histone proteins might act as one of the switches that control how the larvae develop.

Fiona blew out a breath. So, Johnny thought the concept would work on horses? And what about people?

An image of Johnny on his deathbed popped into her mind. Then she remembered half-conversations over the dinner table when Johnny had regaled her with his father's bee fascination. Ger Buckley had been convinced there was something in royal jelly even before it became a fashionable dietary supplement for rich people but, being a simple beekeeper, nobody had listened to him. Fiona shuddered. She hadn't listened to Johnny either. Perhaps if she had, Johnny wouldn't have

... No. It would do no good to torture herself about the past. She was lucky enough to have been given a second chance with Marcus. Oh God, *Marcus.* Checking her watch – still on Irish time – she put a hand to her mouth. The deadline was nearly up.

Her hand was hovering over the receiver when the computer screen flashed and pinged melodically. The Skype icon opened and she saw an image of herself in the corner of the monitor. She clicked the mouse, answering the call.

A grainy image of Pat popped into view. He seemed larger than life on the widescreen monitor. He sat in a wing-backed chair, leaning on a desk. Behind him was a huge painting of a horse.

"That's good timing," she said. "I was just about to call you. What's your progress? Where is Marcus?"

"It's all in hand, Fiona. Is your phone on? Charged up?"

She checked the device. Nodded.

"Good. They'll call you to make the exchange and, when they do, agree to everything then call me straight back. My people and I will get Marcus back for you."

"Just like that? You really think it'll be that easy?"

"Of course it will. My people will exchange the papers for Marcus, then once we have him safe and sound, my investigators will close the trap on the kidnappers."

"You can really hire people to do that?"

"Money can buy anything in this world, Fiona. It is easy to purchase efficient services." He sighed and clasped his hands on the desk. "Loyalty, however, is another matter."

"What do you mean?"

"Oh, never mind. Look, I –"

Fiona's phone buzzed, shuffled towards her on the desk. She stared at it like it was a bomb. "*Um*, it –"

"Answer the bloody thing!"

Fiona pulled a legal pad towards her and swiped the phone.

"Dr. Buckley," said the rough voice, "why are you not in Ireland waiting to make the exchange?"

"What? How do you –"

"If you want to see Marcus Hamilton alive again, you will get the research papers to a meeting point in five hours. We'll call you with a place. No games, Dr. Buckley, or it's good night and good luck."

The line went dead.

"Well?" said Pat.

"They know I'm not in Ireland. Oh God, I should never have listened to you! I should be there waiting with my research."

Pat raised his hands. "Relax, relax. I was informed that this was a possible scenario. Now we wait again. That's standard kidnappers tactics, or so I'm told. *Erm*, I don't suppose a number came up on your phone?"

Fiona shook her head.

"Never mind, I've been told that we can locate the caller using the phone company. That'll be happening as we speak." A ringing sound overshadowed Pat's voice. He picked up his phone. "Fiona, I'll call you back. This is the vet calling me with news of Atavistic. His leg's healing well."

"OK, but –"

The picture went black.

She felt in limbo, like a relative waiting for news of a missing airliner. Something niggled at her, scratched the back of her mind. Made the hairs on her neck prickle.

She looked back at her notes and read the histone-code article again. Something didn't quite fit.

The computer screen went dark and again the Skype icon appeared melodically.

Pat looked agitated.

Fiona drained a glass of water.

"Right, where were we?" he said. "Oh yes, about the feed company and your husband's side project. Tell me everything."

She didn't know where to start.

Chapter 34

Wikus tipped his chair back against the wall by the exit. Rested his head on the concrete and wiped the sweat from his eyes. The bloody air-con was pathetic in this shithole. Some jobs were just a pain in the ass. He couldn't wait to finish with the horse trainer, collect his money and piss off home. After that, he'd quit and buy that kitesurf school in Cape Town that he'd had his eye on since last year. He sipped tepid water from a bottle and wiped his brow on his sleeve.

His phone chimed. The client.

Wikus answered on the speaker, fed up with pressing the thing to his ear and sweating all over it. "Yes?" he growled.

"Take care of him like we discussed. It's getting close, I want him out of there as soon as possible. And remember: an accident."

"When?"

A pause. "In a few hours when the place is busy. You'll be able to slip out quietly."

Wikus made a face. "I'm on my own right now. I'd rather wait until Danie comes back tonight. It's safer that way."

"You're a soldier. I pay you a fortune. Don't whine to me about being alone. Danie is bringing the transport and Oscar's waiting to receive you, so you won't be alone for long. Get it done."

The line went dead.

"Charming."

What was it about rich cunts who'd never experienced danger – let alone a firefight – that made them such an authority on how soldiers should act? Wikus had left the army because he got tired of taking shit from dickhead officers. He dragged himself to his feet and went to the elevator. He'd go get some cold water and maybe another bottle for the trainer. Come to think of it, he'd slip him a sedative. Make it easier to move him alone.

Sheikh Abdul paced the carpet barefoot. He had just finished praying when the call came and since then he'd forgotten all about putting his shoes back on.

The Buckley woman was stupid. Like so many academics, she lived in her own world. But the time had come to atone for that. We must all atone for our sins, he thought. It is the path to Allah.

Abdul heard a cough, whipped his head around. An assistant was standing in the doorway, head lowered, offering a gold-plated phone on a tray. Abdul strode over and snatched the device.

"Hello."

"It's Vlad."

"Where are you? I need her taken care of before this goes any further."

Vlad gave his report.

A slow grin spread across Abdul's face. "Excellent."

Chapter 35

Fiona tapped her pen on the desk.

"Basically, Pat, without getting into specifics in this fledgling science, from Johnny's observations it seems that both you and Sheikh Abdul Khaledam –"

Onscreen, Pat bristled and she paused.

"Have what could be major flaws in your horse management, which may have influenced their genetic make-up and thus their performance."

Pat stared hard. Fiona felt as if he was in the room, sitting across the desk from her.

"What exactly *was* Johnny doing?" he said eventually. "He was supposed to be making high-tech horse feed. *You're* the one supposed to be dabbling in genetics."

"Oh, he *was* making good feed and that's the point. He was obsessed with nutrition, but his little side project took that obsession a step further ..."

She reached for a bottle of water and gulped it down. Thought of her home gym and Johnny's book.

Holy shit. How had this never occurred to her? Suddenly, she wished she'd brought Johnny's diaries with her, or read them more thoroughly. He'd been careful not to write names down, but she felt certain that the answer was there. The *Endgame* DVD. Why hadn't she watched it? At least it was with the guards now. Trouble was, it'd be more use to her here and now.

She reconnected her mind to the screen.

Pat pulled a smile over his anger. "Fiona, I'm not a fool. I can see that my homebreds – and bloody Abdul's – are underperforming. The racing gossips are having a field day about it. Marcus Hamilton's horses, by contrast, are tough, consistent performers."

The words hung.

Fiona had a feeling this was going in the wrong direction.

"As a businessman," continued Pat, "I've got to say that when I look at your company and I see that only one of your big three investors is successful on the racetrack, it looks a bit strange. Don't you think?"

"You think *I'm* doing something to Marcus's horses?" She threw herself back in the chair, scoffing. "That's ridiculous!"

Pat clenched his jaw, sharp breaths flared his nostrils. Then his face relaxed and he flicked a hand across his chest. Fiona could've sworn he blessed himself.

"Fiona, I'm going to come clean with you," he said calmly. "Ronald will be up to collect you shortly. He'll take you down a few floors to a lab where you'll be able to access genetic data on all my horses. I've been keeping my own data bank, you see."

Her mouth fell open. None of her other clients had ever done this, despite her suggestions that it was a good idea. Kind of like keeping a blood-serum bank from all horses as a historical aid in case of disease outbreak.

"OK."

"I want you to look through the data and tell me what is wrong with my horses."

"It's not quite as simple as that."

"Well, you'd better find a way to make it simple, because I'll expect you to come up with a solution to the problem."

"How on earth?"

"You're the geneticist. *You* figure it out! I'll call you again tomorrow. By which time I'll have Marcus safe and sound. And Fiona?"

Her face was pale. "Yes."

"Believe me, if you can fix my problem, losing your OCD and EIPH research to a bunch of inept kidnappers won't matter in the slightest. You'll become famous. *And* rich."

She nodded at the screen. Not that she believed him. He'd just make her sell the whole company to him. She couldn't help but wonder though what impact Johnny's diaries would have on the field of epigenetics.

There was a knock at her door.

Vlad Glazov gazed out of the chopper's window at the teeming Manhattan streets below. They thumped through the air over Central Park. Brightly coloured people ran the laneways like lab rats on a treadmill. The chopper headed north, towards Harlem and the Bronx.

When he'd left the Spetsnaz and entered the world of private security, Vlad immediately enjoyed the novelty of using air transport without having to parachute out of it with heavy things strapped to him. Things that exploded if you dropped them.

Brutally and all of a sudden, Vlad had become disillusioned with the Russian military and his pitiful salary. Still, it took him several years to actually request discharge, and a couple more to receive his papers. After the army, Vlad had spent a few years working for his country's oligarchs. On one trip to the Persian Gulf, he had calmly diffused an incident between his cocaine-addled employer and a young Sheikh. The Sheikh had been impressed and immediately made Vlad a lavish offer of employment. Initally Vlad's job had been to discreetly shepherd about the shiny girls imported to amuse rich young men. When he'd proved his loyalty and efficiency, Sheikh Abdul Khaledam put Vlad in charge of his personal security. That was eight years ago. It was nice having only one boss and even nicer that he was a reliable person. Even if Vlad hardly ever got to fire a weapon in action. A small price to pay for high living and a far cry from his parent's village on Russia's eastern steppes. They were proud and grateful for the money he sent home every month.

He glanced at the pilot, slid a hand under his jacket, checked the ceramic pistol strapped under his shoulder. When it came to delicate missions like this – and there had been a few of them over the years – the Sheikh preferred Vlad to hire outsiders to work alongside him rather than use the Sheikh's permanent team. It was more discreet and prevented the permanent staff from gossiping amongst themselves, but Vlad hated having to deal with the hired help, issuing terse orders and treating failure harshly. So they never liked him. Today's pilot was no exception.

Vlad pulled on the headset. "You're to set me down on open ground, where Harlem River meets East River. I'll continue on foot. You wait there."

"Are you outta your mind? I have clearance to set you down and return. Nothing else."

"You will do as you're told if you want your paycheck."

Vlad noticed the pilot's neck stiffen.

Filtered air-conditioning hummed in the stark, polished lab. Workstations were covered with state-of-the-art blood-analysers, centrifuges and other machines Fiona had never seen before. The back wall was lined with glass cages. Dozens of white rats shuffled about in their homes. Some segregated, some in small groups. Noses twitched, eyes glowed red.

Ronald sat in a corner fiddling with his phone and glancing far too often at Fiona.

She perched on a stool, absorbing DNA readouts plotting damaged genes. Trouble was, she couldn't tell if the subjects had been born that way or not. A few times, she crossed the room to the touch-screen computer and tried to locate more horse information. It turned out there was very little on this computer that she could access without the right codes. Ronald told her she was only authorised to assess information already printed and on the desk.

She needed case histories and new samples and said as much to Ronald. He left the room and returned, offering her a negative shrug. Later on, possibly out of sheer boredom, he asked if there was anything else he could do. Short of a plane back to Ireland, Marcus and her own lab, nothing Ronald could get her was going to help.

Frazzled, she yawned. The wall clock said ten after five. It'd be night now in Ireland. Tuesday night? Time was a blur. Marcus must be with Pat's men by now. Why hadn't she heard anything? She turned her back on Ronald and tried Pat. Left a voice message. What was the hold-up?

Chapter 36

The briefing room was nearly as dark as the night outside. Only the flickering glow of the TV screen threw blue-ish light on the six officers glued to the bizarre recording.

On the first viewing, O'Dowd had been convinced that the man was, at best, talking rubbish. At worst, ranting like a paranoid fool. But this time, he wasn't so sure.

O'Dowd yawned. He'd get no sleep tonight. He stopped the DVD, turned on the lights and returned to the lectern.

The officers facing him were dumbstruck. Johnny Buckley's *Endgame* had made quite an impression.

"Right, lads!" He clapped his hands together. "As you know, the Buckley woman's secretary brought this to me this morning, though I only got a chance to view it a few hours ago. Apparently it should've been sent

251

with the diaries. So. We're all working tonight. Nobody clocks off without reporting to me." He held up a hand. "And before I hear any complaints, the Super has approved overtime for all of you."

There was a murmur of approval.

"First up, still no word from Fiona Buckley or Marcus Hamilton. So, Karen, chase up Weston Aerodrome, find out if Bickley really did get on a plane there. Second; Kenny and McMahon, go to that fella's stud farm. I don't suppose for a second he'll actually be there, but find the farm manager. Question people, see if they can help us locate the man. The office'll probably be closed, but there has to be someone on a stud farm at all times. And, for God's sake, be nice. Apologetic even."

Kenny's features reddened. "What are we supposed to do so? Bend over for the man? Fuck that shite. If he is actually there and I get one sign from him that he's being difficult, it's cuffs on and jail for the night. I don't give a shite."

O'Dowd had to stifle a smile. In an ideal world, Kenny was right of course, but politics were a shadow that remained even on cloudy days. "Go easy, Kenny. You're not Dirty Harry. We don't want to rub them up the wrong way. A man that rich can vanish and take his investments with him. Jobs get lost and it'll be us catching the fall-out. So nothing heavy-handed until we're sure. Or until we get proof." He cocked a finger at the TV. "Bad as it seems, that shite's purely circumstantial. It's only a video confession of motive and crime by a bitter paraplegic."

Kenny slapped his partner on the gut. "C'mon, so!"

They hauled themselves out of their chairs.

"Oh, one more thing," called O'Dowd.

They stopped at the door.

"If you get to speak to him, ask him if he knows where Marcus Hamilton is."

They nodded and left.

"Karen, while you're at it, issue an APB for Buckley and Hamilton and send it to all air and sea ports. Better contact the British too."

She hustled out of the room.

O'Dowd turned looked at the others. "Jones and Carroll. You take over the night shift at the hospital. And be vigilant."

A few hours later, O'Dowd was stuck to his desk. Johnny's diaries were spread out in chronologial order but not making any sense. There was an unfortunate lack of names connected to the quantities, formulas and theories. He rubbed his eyes and sipped cold coffee.

Karen appeared in the doorway, her eyes wide with optimism. "*Erm*, Sergeant."

"Yes, Karen?"

"The secretary," she glanced at her notes, "Maura Delany, said Dr. Buckley told her she'd gone to see the only man who ever helped her husband."

"Correct."

"So in light of what we saw on that DVD, I broadened my request from Weston Aerodrome."

"And?"

"Fiona Buckley *was* a last-minute addition to the manifest on a private jet belongong to Prevenalux, the pharmaceuticals company owned by Pat McCormack.

253

Flew out Monday evening. Bound for Teterboro in New York. According to Weston tower logs, that Prevenalux plane has been on the move a lot lately. So has the plane registered to a corporation, owned by an investment company, that originates from the Emirate ruled by Sheikh Khaledam's father."

"Good job, Karen."

"Thanks. So, then I got the airport people to send me through the names on those flight manifests. I've spent the last hour going through it carefully. Another name cropped up, one that changes the picture considerably."

She handed him the list. His jaw dropped open.

"Holy Mother of God! How the feck are we only finding out about this now?"

Karen shrugged. "Private air travel. Separate set of rules for the rich."

"Call Kenny now, fill him in. Tell him he's welcome to drag the fucker back here against his will."

She nodded.

"Oh, and what time is it in New York? And, more importantly, who the hell can I call there and get them to take me seriously?"

Karen looked blank. First time O'Dowd had seen her look like that.

"Karen, get a call through to Kenny or McMahon. Immediately."

She darted out of the room.

O'Dowd sighed and picked up the telephone. He'd have to wake the Super and involve Garda Headquarters. He'd need clout from Phoenix Park if he was going to get anywhere with the Americans.

Chapter 37

New York

Fiona's stomach growled. Part of her wished she could eat, curl up into a ball and sleep until this whole nightmare passed her by. She stood and stretched.

"OK, Ronald. I'm done for now. It's all a mess, I'll need to discuss it with Pat and continue analysis back in Ireland."

Ronald hopped to his feet, shrugging. "Whatever."

Fiona left everything as it was. The door shut behind them with a whump and a click.

She summoned one of the twin elevators and found herself wondering if there was a specific ratio between the number of floors in a building and the number of elevators required. Even at twelve floors, she'd rather not take the stairs.

There was a ping and the shiny doors slid open. She

bid Ronald goodbye and stepped in. He opened his mouth as if to speak, then closed it again, then opened it as the doors slid shut. Fiona stared at her reflection as she ascended to the apartment. Her hair was matted and she couldn't remember what had happened to the baseball cap she'd pulled on when she left the hospital. Seemed like a lifetime ago. She needed a shower, fresh pair of jeans and a top. And underwear. God, she was dying for clean underwear. She'd have to go shopping. Surely there was somewhere nearby she could get clothes? When the elevator stopped at the top and opened to reveal Ted the security guard, she smiled, said sorry and pushed the lobby button. On the way back down, she pulled her wallet from her pocket, counted 200 euro in cash and checked she had her credit and ATM cards and driver's licence. It occurred to her that leaving America on a commercial airliner might just be impossible without her passport. Anyway, first things first: she'd buy new clothes and try to make the time pass until Pat called her with news of Marcus. Maybe she'd even have a glass of wine to calm her nerves. Help the afternoon slip into evening. She wondered what O'Dowd was up to. Hopefully Johnny's diaries and DVDs would keep him placated.

Vlad leaned against a streetlight and studied the glass-fronted building. Not a skyscraper, but taller than the old brownstones flanking it. There was some kind of repair crew working at the corner of the building, dismantling a grill in the street. Steam billowed out at them. He prowled across the road, scanning traffic and dodging cars. Flung the lobby door open and flicked his eyes from a styrofoam coffee cup and half-eaten doughnut on the counter, to the flabby man behind the desk, to the swipe-card security at the elevator doors, to the list of companies displayed on the wall.

The building was a multi-let. By the look of it, Prevenalux had several floors. The other companies had the kind of names he regularly saw outside offices in the Gulf states. They could be doing any kind of business – or none at all. Still, Vlad wondered how the multi-let worked. Surely Prevenalux owned the whole building? What if they had a lab accident? Or what about sabotage? Squeezing his left arm against his side, he felt the weapon nestled in its place.

"Goddamn," he said, smiling and forcing some American into his accent, "am I glad to be here," he read the man's nametag, "Bennie."

Bennie mopped sweat from his brow, pulled on a duty face and stood.

Vlad leaned on the counter. "I got a delivery for Prevenalux." He pulled a plastic pouch from his jacket pocket and waved it. "Took me ages to find the place."

Bennie grinned. "You're not the first, buddy, and you won't be the last. It's some kinda hike from Downtown, eh?"

Vlad grinned and cocked a finger at Bennie. "Now you said it. Say, you got a parking garage here?"

"Yeah, basement levels one and two." The meaty face frowned. "No, wait. They converted basement two into storage, couple months back." He sighed and fanned himself.

There was a ping and a set of chrome elevator doors eased open. Vlad did a double-take and snaked a hand to his pistol. Christmas had come early.

Fiona looked up and saw a man standing at the desk manned by a fat security guard. She'd seen the guy before: his cold blue-eyed look and military haircut. It had been raining on him. Now the guy darted a hand under his jacket and grinned at her. Of course – he'd held the car door for Sheikh Abdul at Johnny's funeral.

The hand appeared from under his jacket, gripping a small black pistol. Fiona sucked in air and everything seemed to slow down. The guard saw the gun and fumbled on his belt. The guy scythed his arm at the guard, slamming the pistol's butt into the fat man's cheek. He dropped like a stone. Fiona flung herself back into the elevator and jabbed at buttons. A hand sluiced between the closing doors. She kept a finger on a button, bared her teeth and bit the hand. She tasted blood and wanted to retch, but jammed her jaws together and ground her teeth.

"You fucking stupid bitch!" growled the man. *"Let go of me!"*

Fiona tore her mouth away. The hand retreated and the door closed.

Desperately, Fiona punched buttons. Heading back up to the apartment, she shook with adrenalin and realized there was something in her mouth. Disgusted, she half-spat, half-vomited. And stared at the bloody fingernail by her feet as the elevator climbed to the top floor.

258

***

A searing pain shot up Vlad's arm. He pocketed his pistol and gripped his damaged finger. Blood flowed from the wound and down his wrist. He watched the floor numbers ascend on the display. The red numbers stopped flashing at twelve. Top Floor, had to be. Blood dripped onto the floor. He dashed behind the desk, stepped over the fallen Bennie and looked for something, anything to wrap around his hand. Paper napkins, tucked under an empty burger carton would have to do. He dabbed his finger, saw the nail was missing and wrapped the wound, balling his hand into a fist to hold the dressing in place.

Underneath him, Bennie groaned.

"*Stay down, you fat fuck!*"

A swipe card dangled from the man's belt. Vlad ripped it free and dashed. He swiped it through the sensor and summoned an elevator, repeatedly jamming the heel of his hand against the button. The bloody stupid Buckley woman had fallen into his lap and he'd wasted the opportunity. It wouldn't be long before the whole building would be on alert. Still if that guard was what passed for security here, it should present no serious problem. But he needed to get that stupid woman. Behind the doors, he could hear mechanisms rumbling in the shaft.

Fiona fell out of the elevator and babbled at Ted. He made placating gestures with his hands.

"Ma'am, calm down. Take it easy."

"*Call back-up, call the cops – there's a man in the lobby with a gun – he attacked me.*"

"Is that your blood?"

"What?"

Ted raised a hand to his own lips. "There, on your mouth. Your blood?"

Fiona felt queasy again. That metallic taste. "No. It's his. I bit him."

He gave her a funny look. "Ma'am –" His radio crackled.

"*You ready?*" it asked.

"Ma'am, I'm gonna have to ask you to go into the apartment." He swiped his card at the door. "I got a chopper coming in on the roof. Need this area empty. I'll call Bennie in the lobby, see if he's seen your guy."

A chopper? Fiona's mouth fell open. She wondered if it was Pat. Or maybe Marcus arriving. Was that possible? She checked her watch – what was the time difference again?

She looked at the elevators. The numbers on one were rising, on the other falling.

She pointed, her eyes glued to the rising numbers.

"He's coming up to get me. Can't you just call the cops and lock him in the lift?"

"The what?"

"Oh bloody hell, *elevator*! Stop the elevators. *Now*. Or I'll call your boss."

He looked at her like she was crazy. Looked from her to the elevators and back. "Like I say, ma'am, you gotta go inside."

Marcus flinched when he heard the door clang open. He had dozed off slumped on the table, head rested on an arm. He tried to stand, but he was wobbly and his arm was tingling. The thug came in again. This time he had two bottles of water and a pair of handcuffs. A black cloth was hanging out of his back pocket. Just like the one he'd had put over his head when they took him. So, they were going to move him or ...

The thug sat on the table and handed Marcus a bottle. "Drink, you must be thirsty," he growled, cracking the seal on the second bottle. He took a long slow drink.

The bottle in Marcus's hand was ice-cold. He smacked his lips and opened it, but there was no crack. Hadn't been sealed. He stared at it for a moment then glanced at the thug.

He stared back, stonyfaced.

Shite, were they trying to drug him again? That couldn't be a good sign. His heart rate rocketed. He started sweating again. There was no way he was going to end up in a hole in the desert. He needed to do something. Anything. But if he got out, what then? Hell, he didn't even know where he was. One step at a time. He put the bottle down.

"Drink."

"I'm not thirsty."

"Don't give me that shit, *oke*. You're dehydrated. I can see it in your face." He finished his own bottle, exhaled contentedly and tossed the empty plastic vessel into the corner. Checked his watch. "Listen, I don't have all day. Drink the foken thing or I'll pour it down your throat."

Reluctantly, Marcus took a sip. Winced. Filthy chlorinated crap. God, he'd love a bit of fresh Irish spring water!

"And again," said the man.

Another sip.

"More."

He gulped a mouthful. His thirst told him to finish the bottle, but his mind made him stop after one swallow. As Marcus put the bottle back on the table, the thug grabbed his wrist, held it like a vise and snapped a handcuff onto it.

"Give me your other hand."

Marcus offered it and felt the cold steel bracelet enclose his wrist.

"Good boy. That wasn't so hard, was it? Right, off we go." The thug stood and tugged on the cuffs.

Marcus stood. The steel bit into his skin as the thug pulled him across the corridor and into the toilet. There he relieved himself and told Marcus to do the same. Then he pushed Marcus out of the toilet again. Ahead of them the windowless corridor led towards doors that could only belong to an elevator. Harsh flourescent light made Marcus squint. He wondered how he'd react to the dazzling desert sun when he got outside.

At the elevator doors, the thug halted and swiped a finger on his phone. His speaker-phone filled the air with a crackly ringing.

When the call was picked up, Marcus could hear a man's voice over whining noises. Traffic. The other guy was in traffic.

"What's the status, Wikus?" said the tinny voice.

"Good, Danie. I'm on the move. Where are you?"

"En route. Be with you in two. Don't forget to hood him before you get outside. And fo ... sa ... be ... to ..."

"You're breaking up. I'll see you outside."

The call ended and the thug pressed the elevator button.

Marcus began to feel a bit off. Foggy. God, he'd only had two sips. If he was going to do something, it had to be now. At least get away from this guy and then ... And then? Well, one step at a time. If Danie was still in traffic, then he wasn't here yet. Wherever here was. So, maybe he would have time to make a break for it before the transport arrived. The lift doors opened in front of him.

He felt Wikus push him. He stepped into the elevator, screwed up his eyes and wished for luck. He turned and saw Wikus, inches from his face, pulling the black hood out of his pocket. Wikus' phone rang again – he swore and fumbled for it. Behind him, the doors began to slide together.

It was now or never. Marcus clasped his hands and rammed them into Wikus' throat. Pushed hard. Wikus gurgled, tipped off-balance. Marcus kept pushing and Wikus toppled backwards, dropping his phone, falling through the closing doors. But his foot caught between them. Marcus stared in horror as the doors opened again and Wikus, coughing, rolled onto his front. Marcus shunted the foot with his own, shoving it out into the corridor. Wikus tried to get up.

Marcus turned and frantically pushed a button. Sweat in his eyes. His heart thumped. "*Come on, come on! Bloody thing!"* Mercifully, the doors slid closed and the elevator began moving. What now? Was he going up or down? How could you tell in an elevator? Was it going fast or slow? He wiped sweat from his eyes with his sleeve.

The elevator stopped and the doors slid open with a flourish. Marcus looked up. Went cold and pale. His stomach churned.

No way. That was impossible.

He'd drunk too much of the tainted water. Now he was starting to hallucinate and he'd never make it out of this damn place.

Chapter 38

Johnny glided out of his office. His hard rubber wheels streaked silently across the factory floor. Underneath the extrusion machine, he spun a full circle on the spot, checking he was alone. Then he flicked the brake on and tightened his leg-straps. The aluminium flask nestled in a pouch on his belt. Johnny's meaty arms reached for the support column. Huge shoulders flexed as they hauled him out of the chair and up to the first crossbeam. From there it was an easy climb to the walkway running alongside the extruder and dryer. He reached the dryer and slid under the intake pipe. Took a multi-tool from a pouch on his belt and deftly unscrewed the large jubilee clip that secured the air pipe over the intake. At this stage, he could almost do it with his eyes closed. Again he checked the production floor was empty. Checking, always checking. Johnny didn't believe in paranoia; he believed in being meticulous.

When the clip was loose, he eased the pipe off the intake. The opening was large enough for him to look into the dryer. He could just make out the conveyor belt. At shortly after seven tomorrow morning the first batch of the day would be down there being air-dried. Johnny pulled out the flask, screwed off the top and tipped the fine brown dust onto the small ledge of pipe in the intake hole. A quick tap of the flask and the last of the powder fell out, leaving a fine cloud of dust in the air. He flapped a hand and exhaled, dispersing the dust, but was careful not to disturb the pile of powder. He used to be so worried about this small exposure to his mixture that he'd considered using a mask, but it would've raised too many eyebrows if he'd been caught wearing it down below. As time went on he stopped worrying and, after five and a half years of work, he hardly ever gave it a thought. He wasn't stupid though, he still took every precaution in his lair when he was making the stuff. Gloves, a dust mask and a plastic smock covering him and his chair.

He replaced the pipe and patted the dryer for luck.

Tomorrow, when the feed was on the belt, the heater would force hot air through the pipe and over the feed. Johnny's powder would bind itself to the cooling product and any excess would be sucked through the outlet at the other end and up the waste chimney.

He bounded back to his chair. Before he made for his office, he paused, examining the machine. He wondered how much of the residue actually remained inside the

266

dryer? He could always have the next batch analysed, but he didn't want the cat out of the bag. Not yet anyway. Switching all the batch samples with clean ones from Hamilton's feed had definitely been the safest course of action. He had been able to organise the production schedule so that Hamilton's feed was produced every fortnight, just before the tainted batch. And Hamilton's results on the racecourse meant that Johnny could fairly easily deduce that any excess residue was well gone from the drier by then. Even without having the analysis done. Off course, there might be some remaining residue in a batch or two made directly after Pat's tainted one. But he thought the traces, and therefore the effect, would be negligible. And he alway alternated the order of clients whose feed he prepared straight after Pat's, doing Sheikh Adbul's just before Hamilton's.

It was the Sheikh's horses that troubled Johnny. But perhaps that was all down to inept management and a yes-man culture within his organisation. As for today's headline revelations, they had hit Johnny hard. He never thought the Sheikh could be so stupid. Or arrogant. Then again, thought Johnny, as he wheeled back to his office, I was that stupid once upon a time.

There on Johnny's desk was the *Racing Post*. The front page blared its headline: *Sheikh Abdul Khaledam Steroids Scandal*.

Johnny was due to meet Alan De Courtney tomorrow at the Sheikh's stud. More discussions about feed. Alan had apparently done some thinking and wanted to tweak the ration to better suit the individual horses. Over the years, Johnny had had many conversations

267

with the man, but he just never seemed to understand what the real problem was on the Sheikh's farm. Alan's lack of understanding depressed Johnny and made him feel as if he was wasting his time.

Apparently the Sheikh was in town too. That could be interesting; if it turned out to be a three-way meeting. Johnny chewed his lip and realized that he'd probably have to break the golden rule tomorrow.

The following morning, heavy electric gates opened and Johnny eased his van slowly down the winding tree-lined avenue. Immaculate grass verges flanked the driveway, but the paddocks behind them looked worn, rough and unhealthy. He pushed the brake lever and disengaged the automatic gearbox, stopping the van with a jolt. Tut-tutting and shaking his head, he counted twenty yearlings crammed into the area. It wasn't like the Sheikh was short of land – or money. He just had too many horses. He was notorious all over the world for offering people huge sums of money for their horses. When he just had to have one, he gave little thought to where and how he would keep them. They just got sent to his farm and then to his trainer. There was a hayrack in the middle of the paddock and Johnny watched a dominant colt pin his ears back and drive several others away from their meal. Then the horse pranced around the rack, before settling into an unhurried meal, all the while keeping his ears back and flicking his head from side to side. The rest of the herd formed an orderly queue behind the leader. If there were another couple of racks or fewer horses in the paddock and even better land management, this kind of dominant behaviour wouldn't be a problem.

At what point does love of racehorses become overdone and abusive? Alan De Courtney certainly wasn't much of a manager if he could neither see this nor advise the Sheikh what a mess he was making. I mean, Abdul was easy to talk to – Johnny knew that.

He continued down the drive and pulled in at the office. As his chair was lowered to the ground, Johnny felt a twinge of pain across his shoulders. He'd been feeling unsually stiff and sore lately, but chalked it down to age, stress and possibly over-training. He knew he should probably see a physiotherapist, but kept putting it off. After all, he could still bench-press nearly 150 kilos, so how serious could it be?

Johnny coasted up the ramp, spun his chair and backed into the swing doors, pushing them open with a flourish. He spun again and glided into reception, halting silently beside the desk. Flashed a winning smile at the girl taking precise notes with a phone clutched to her ear.

She hung up. Grinned. "How're you, Johnny? It's pure madness around here. Between reporters, crank callers and animal-rights organisations, the phone hasn't stopped."

Johnny winked. "No better woman to handle it, Sarah."

"Oh, I'm not so sure." Sarah leaned over her desk. "It's a total embarrasment altogether. The Sheikh acts like it's not a problem. Like it'll all just go away. And Alan ..." she rolled her eyes, "you know the story there." She picked up the phone. "I'd better let them know you're here." She hung up and cocked her head towards the huge mahoghany doors. "He's in the conference room."

Johnny had to push hard to propel his chair through

the plush carpeting. Most stud-farm offices were bare lino or wooden flooring. This place looked deeper underfoot than the paddocks outside. Again he felt a twinge in his trapezius muscles.

He was about to reach for the door handle when it burst open, hitting the footrest on his chair. Alan De Courtney nearly fell into his lap. He was crimson with rage rather than embarrassment as he picked himself up and strode across the hall to his office.

"Mind yourself there, Alan!" Johnny called.

The room was a shrine to over-polished wood and gold fittings sparkling under a barrage of halogen lights set in the ceiling. Abdul sat the end of the plate-glass gold-legged table. Eyes closed, his hands palm up in front of him, his lips moved silently.

After a minute, Johnny wheeled round the table and parked beside the Sheikh.

The man blinked, rubbed his hands down his face and smiled warmly at Johnny. They shook hands like old friends.

"How are you, Johnny?"

"I'm good, Abdul. I'm good, but ..." His stomach growled. It had been doing that a lot lately. He pulled an antacid from the pouch on his chair.

"You have stomach trouble?"

"Ulcers, I'd say. From the stress."

"You look pale, Johnny."

Johnny shot the Sheikh a deadpan look. "It is any wonder I've ulcers?"

"Perhaps you are eating the wrong foods. Stomach acid is not to be ignored. My uncle has been plagued with such troubles all his life. He cannot so much as look at fruit or tomatoes without feeling sick."

"I didn't come here to talk about my diet. Horse feed, Abdul. Horse feed. I've made the best in Europe. Nobody's doing what we're doing at Winline, but it's tough, you know? I'm trying to drag stud-farm feeding into the 21st century, but it's not going to work if big owners keep treating their horses like chickens or commodities." He cocked a thumb over his shoulder. "I got an eyeful of your paddocks on the way in. Nothing's changed, has it?"

The steely gaze of the Bedouin hardened.

Johnny sucked air through his teeth. Abdul wasn't going to like this, but he couldn't hold it in any longer. "And, as for steroids? Are you thick or what?"

The Sheikh's dark skin glowed crimson.

"Look," continued Johnny. "I know how seductive steroids can be. Miracle drugs and all that shite. Back a few years ago I was hooked on them for a while."

"You call me stupid, but why did you take them?"

"Thought they'd help me train and build my crumpled body and life. Get me out of a hole. And they did for a while. Until they dug me a deeper one. And anyway, nobody was testing me. I wasn't a competitive athlete. Your horses, on the other hand? I mean, what possessed you?"

The Sheikh glowed red again. He wasn't used to being spoken to like this.

Johnny didn't care. He was angry and he felt like he'd been wasting the last years.

"Why would you bother?" he continued. "I mean, what I'm doing would've been enough to get you an unassailable advantage, but not only do you squander that by mismanagement, or misunderstanding, or whatever, but then you go and get caught doing this?"

"You assume that I had knowledge of the drugs being administered?

Johnny cut him a deadpan look.

"I am a busy man. In addition to my racing interests, I have affairs of state to attend to and a successful polo team. If my trainer decides to flaunt the law to gain an advantage, that is his stupidity. Not mine. He will be punished for it. I fail to see how it is my fault."

Johnny snorted. "The disciplinary authorities are going to throw the book at you and your operation."

Half-smiling, Abdul waved a hand dismissively. "I will get myself a little slap on the wrist. Nobody will ban me or warn me off. Leaving aside the fact that my country supplies energy to many different places, I own too many horses, farms, training centres and people. I have expanded my business interests quietly and steadily during the last ten years. My money trickles into every corner of this business. You of all people should know that. What is it they say about the banks? Too big to fail. For appearances' sake, I'll find a few heads to roll for this scandal, but otherwise I'll continue as before. Anyway, Johnny, you must know I'm not the only one cheating. Look at Marcus Hamilton. What is your wife doing for him? Many things, I suspect."

Johnny ignored the dig. "Look, the only things Hamilton's doing differently are feeding his horses with my product and treating them like athletes as they grow up. It's how he raises them to be tough, hardy horses that run their hearts out."

The Sheikh laughed and fiddled with his watch, but there was uncertainly in his eyes. "Do you expect me to believe that?"

Johnny was astounded. "Believe it? I thought you *understood* it. That's been my whole point all this time. But you don't get it, do you? Or maybe you don't want to get it? But you know he does something, don't you? I mean, why else would you buy into his horses. And quite often Hamilton's horses are your best performers."

The Sheikh looked out the window. "More rain. It's supposed to be summer." He paused. "Where was I? Oh yes, I bought Trelawn Park Stud because Marcus Hamilton gets results. I really don't care how he gets them, and if he ever gets caught doing something illegal it will not reflect on me."

"Hold on a second – you *bought* Marcus's stud? Like, *the whole place*?"

The Sheikh swiped a finger across his phone, smiled, then stood abruptly. "We have nothing more to discuss." He left the room.

Johnny slumped in his chair. He used to think he was special, more than just an employee, but now he realised that he'd been blind. Abdul just didn't get it. When it came to his horses, he knew Abdul's heart was in the right place, but he seemed to think he knew better than everyone else.

Johnny wheeled himself to his van. Depressed, just like he had been all those years ago. The soreness in his neck stabbed at him and his stomach kept growling. He'd go to the doctor if it didn't get better in a few days. Just in case he was coming down with an infection.

273

Chapter 39

New York
October 2015

Wikus scrambled to his feet, coughing and rubbing his throat. He cursed himself for agreeing to move a prisoner alone and reached for his phone, but it wasn't there. He must've dropped it in the elevator. He jabbed the call buttons. There was no bloody way Hamilton would make it out of the building looking like he did. Hell, he might've even passed out in the elevator. Still, the whole thing had been a clusterfuck from day one. The client thought he was some kind of all-powerful God who knew better than the professionals he'd hired. Wikus was going to let him have it when he saw him. Something else occurred to Wikus. He'd better get paid before this whole thing went tits-up and the client ended up in trouble. It was always a nightmare to get the money when that happened.

The doors opened and Wikus stepped in and pressed the top-floor button. Then he saw his phone in the corner. "Result." Another cough. Speech was tough. That bloody Hamilton would pay for punching him in the throat.

Wikus dialled Danie, but there was no reception in the elevator shaft. The doors slid open on the top floor and there he was hunched over a security guard. The roof door was open and the roar of the chopper filled the air.

"What the fuck, man?" said Danie. "Where's the prisoner? We're supposed to be at the plane in ten minutes."

"He's fucking gone. Must be in the building somewhere," Wikus said, grabbing the guard's radio. "*Calling all units!*" he shouted over the swirling noise. "*Security breach and biohazard accident – close the lobby – nobody in or out!*"

"*Uh*, say again? You're breaking up."

"*Security breach and biohazard accident – close the lobby – nobody in or out!*" Wikus repeated.

"*Uh*, this is Baker on Lab floor. Nothing here. What's that background noise?"

"Whoever's in the lobby, come in, please," said Wikus.

"Hey, who is this?" said a new voice.

"Who's in the fucking lobby?" said Wikus. "Close it up. *Now.* That's an order from the boss of this company, Pat McCormack."

"*Holy shit!*" said the voice. "Bennie, you there? Wake the fuck up! Close the lobby!"

Wikus, made for the still-open elevator. "Danie – tell the chopper to wait. We're going to the lobby to fetch Hamilton."

As the elevator doors slid open, Fiona screamed at the security guard. "*Jesus, Ted! Do something!*"

She considered reaching for Ted's gun because she'd be damned if she was going to let that thug grab her. In America, you could shoot someone in self-defence, right?

A shadow stumbled out of the elevator.

She didn't understand.

Marcus looked dazed. And filthy. His face was bruised and swollen. Hands cuffed.

At first she couldn't figure it out, then it dawned on her. Everything fell into place. The world went quiet as answers rained down on her. *Oh my God. What have I done?* Once again, she thought of the gym and Johnny's book. And then she knew. It wasn't about who had helped Johnny. It was about who *hadn't* helped him. *That* was why Pat didn't know about Johnny's project.

"*Sir, identify yourself!*" said Ted.

Marcus shuffled towards her. She caught him in her arms. Hugged him tight.

A loud thumping filled the small area. The roof vibrated.

Ted's radio blared. "*Rooftop sector, come in, please. We have touchdown. Motors will stay running. Where are our passengers?*"

Ted pressed the respond button and opened his mouth. The other elevator pinged.

The doors opened and the man from the lobby stepped out, a pistol in his hand. Fiona yelped. Marcus turned to look. Everyone froze, looking at each other like a film stuck on pause. A violent thumping filled the air. The ceiling tiles rattled.

Ted spoke into his radio and fumbled the strap on his holster. The man lunged at him, delivering a sharp punch to the stomach. Ted buckled, the man changed his footing and brought his knee up to Ted's nose. Blood gushed from the damaged orifice, spraying the guy's jeans. Ted fell backward into a heap. Fiona watched in horror. Marcus looked slightly unaware.

The man faced Fiona, softened his features. Smiled. She gripped Marcus and shuffled backwards towards the apartment doors. Ted's radio blared. The chopper pilot was getting impatient.

The guy raised his hands, palms facing her. "Dr. Buckley, I'm sorry I startled you down in the lobby. My orders were to take you away from here with the minimum of fuss and explanation. My employer wanted to explain things to you himself."

Her eyes went wide as saucers.

"My name is Vladmir Glasov – you can call me Vlad. I work for Sheikh Abdul Bin Omar Khaledam. I am here to help you – and Mr. Hamilton, but I had no idea he was here."

She couldn't believe it and yet she could. And she just wanted to get out of this building, city. "One of the elevators has gone back down," she said.

Vlad whipped his head around. The LCD numbers descended quickly. The second set of doors began to close. Vlad dashed and stuck an arm between them. They jerked open and he wedged his back against one and his foot against the other, holding them open.

"Dr. Buckley. The helicopter on the roof has nothing to do with me. We need to get back to the streets to get you to safety."

Marcus shook his head groggily. "No."

"It's OK. We have to go with this man." Fiona gripped him by the shoulders and guided him towards Vlad.

Vlad glanced up at the numbers. "Quickly. We'll have company soon." He grabbed Marcus and flung him against the back of the small elevator.

"Hey," said Fiona, "watch it!"

Vlad ignored her and pressed the ground-floor button. The doors closed and the elevator moved.

Marcus rubbed his eyes. "They gave me something. Put it in water, I only took a sip, but ... feel foggy. Is all this real?" He looked at Fiona. "Thought I'd never see you again. Where am I?"

Fiona opened her mouth, but Vlad cut in.

"*Focus*. Listen to me very carefully. You're in Pat McCormack's Prevenalux building in New York City. How did you get here?"

Marcus looked stunned. "What? Where?" He blinked several times. "I remember being at Dublin Airport. Then in a hot dark room. They beat me and asked about Fiona's research, about what I'd been doing to the horses. I never could understand why the Sheikh would've done that to me. I've always been honest with him. Told him everything he wanted to know." He looked sheepishly at Fiona. "I'm sorry, I had no choice."

"The Sheikh didn't take you," said Vlad. "McCormack did." He looked at Fiona. "You, he managed to get here willingly. How could you be so stupid?"

"I thought he was Johnny's saviour."

"You know your late husband was working for the Sheikh, right?"

"It only just dawned on me."

Vlad holstered his weapon underarm and slid his bloodied hand round to his back pocket. "Got to get those cuffs off." He produced a small leather pouch. Flipped it open.

Fiona stared at the set of lock picks. It only took Vlad a second. The cuffs tumbled to the floor.

They felt the elevator slow down.

"Right. We're going to dash outside and run a block or two, then we'll get a cab. Dr. Buckley, we'll help Hamilton between us, OK?"

They got into position either side of Marcus, his arms over their shoulders.

Fiona noticed the caked blood on Vlad's fingers. "Sorry I bit you."

"Shit happens. Don't worry about it."

The elevator pinged and the doors eased open.

They moved in unison for the front doors and the street. Behind them, the other elevator pinged.

Outside, people bustled along in the evening rush hour. Everyone had somewhere to be, nobody gave them a second look.

"I love New York," muttered Vlad.

Marcus's head lolled forward. Vlad slapped his cheek.

"Fight it, man! We're nearly home and dry."

They managed to cross the road at a corner, disrupting traffic. Horns honked, drivers shouted abuse. They turned up a cross street. Quieter. Fewer people.

"We'll hail a cab at the other end of the block," said Vlad.

"Can we slow down?" said Fiona, breathless.

Vlad checked behind them. "OK."

They slowed a fraction and let Marcus find his feet. He wobbled between them as they got to the far corner of the block and the bustle of a north-south artery. Vlad raised his arm and a yellow cab snaked towards them, sliding to a halt inches from the kerb. Fiona got in first, slid across the seat. She gripped Marcus's arm as Vlad fed him into the vehicle.

"*Yo, yo, yo!*" said the cabbie. "He ain't gonna vomit in the car, is he?"

"He's not drunk," said Fiona. "Just sleepy."

"Whatever. Hun'red dollar surcharge if he vomits."

Vlad checked the street behind them again. A man was sprinting towards him. Had to be one of McCormack's mercenaries. He hit Vlad full-on, slamming them both onto the cab. They pivoted and rolled off the back end, landing in a tangled knot on the tarmac. Pinned on the road, Vlad targeted the man's eyes. Drove his thumbs in beside the eyeballs and forced his index fingers into the man's ears. The mercenary grimaced, roared, let go of Vlad. Without relaxing his grip, Vlad rolled over, got himself on top. He smashed the mercenary's head off the tarmac until he went limp. Like a panther looking for fresh prey, Vlad sprang up, checked the street again. Another man ran towards him, but he slowed, looked from Vlad to the body on the ground.

Vlad flung himself into the cab, locked the door and growled at the dumbstruck cabbie. "*Teterboro Airport. Now!*"

The second man reached the cab and drew a gun level with the window.

"*Shiiiiiiitt!*" said the cabbie. The tyres screeched as he barged into traffic, U-turned in front of four lanes of cars waiting at a red light and dashed away up the street.

"Man, now I've seen everything," said the cabbie. He looked at Vlad in the mirror. "What the hell you do?"

Danie mouthed the licence number over and over as the cab sped off and pulled across several cars. For a moment he considered running after it, but stopped to check Wikus. He pulled him up onto the kerb and checked his pulse. Still going. Danie slapped him.

"*Wikus! Man, what the fok?*"

A motorcycle courier pulled up, threw out his kickstand and dashed into the building beside them.

Wikus put his hands to his eyes. "Can't see out of my left side. That *oke*'s a savage. Which way d'they go?"

Danie looked up after the cab. "North, I can just make them out a couple of blocks away."

"Leave me. Follow them and keep in touch. *Now!*"

Danie sprang up. The courier hurried out of the building, strapping a bag to his back. Danie drove a foot onto the man's kneecap, downing him instantly.

"*Aaah, what the fuck?*"

In one swift movement, Danie kicked the guy in the balls, ripped his helmet off and threw a leg over the bike. The engine started with a growl and he took off, suddenly realising the street was a sea of yellow. Repeating the plate number over and over, he broke two sets of lights. He zipped past cabs, checking rear windows for three heads. Most cabs carried one or two occupants. More red lights ahead. Traffic bustled across the junction. He'd have to stop. He squeezed the bike between two SUVs and ended up at the front line next to a school bus and another cab. He shot a glance inside it. *Bingo*. The woman was in tears, looking out the window at him. Danie was glad he'd taken the helmet. Hamilton was in the middle and the guy who'd fucked Wikus up was at the other side. Danie fought the urge to whip out his gun and finish the fucker off there and then. No, he'd do as Wikus wanted and tail them, report back and wait for orders from the client. Danie shrugged – whatever happened from now on, it was far from the original plan. Wikus had never wanted to take this job. Maybe he'd been right, but the money had been too good to refuse.

The lights changed and the cab set off. They turned onto Webster Avenue, passed Claremont Park and hung a left, before sluicing onto Interstate 95. Danie kept back about six cars from his target, but they weren't looking for a biker. When they crossed the Hudson River on the George Washington Bridge, he could guess where they were headed.

Barely able to breathe, Fiona stared out the window at the river. Tears and sweat caked her face. Beside her, Marcus rubbed his eyes and appeared to be perking up.

Vlad scanned traffic. "I don't see anyone tailing us."

Fiona still couldn't quite believe that Marcus had literally appeared from nowhere and that she'd made it out of Pat's office block. She couldn't get Marcus's words out of her head. *I'm sorry, Fiona, I had no choice.* What did that mean?

She put a hand on his chin and brought it towards her, raising his face so their eyes met. He was sheepish and missing a tooth, like a little schoolboy. She kissed his filthy cheek and slipped an arm around him. He rested his head on her shoulder.

"Don't get too comfortable," said Vlad. "We're nearly there."

"I thought I was going to end up in a hole in the desert," Marcus said to Fiona.

"Why the desert? And what did you mean when you said you had no choice?"

"I thought the Sheikh took me to find out more information. He made me tell him that your research was at your dad's house."

Fiona pulled away from him, looking wounded.

"What?" he asked.

"He sent men there. One of them shot Dad."

"Oh my God! Is he ..."

"He's OK."

"That wasn't the Sheikh," Vlad cut in. "I'm in charge of his security. I went to your father's house that night, but my mission was to take those papers for safekeeping. The Sheikh didn't want them destroyed."

Fiona and Marcus stared at him.

"Only problem, I got there too late. Heard gunshots and had to abort. Must have been that bulldog McCormack. Like all the rest of this shit."

Fiona blinked, her mouth fell open.

Marcus sat up, his eyes wide now. "How's he managing that?"

Vlad shrugged. "If I had to guess, I'd say he's been following both of you since he had the lab burned down. Hired those goons. *Hmm.* That reminds me."

He checked the cabbie had his eyes on the road, then unstrapped the holster under his jacket and pulled it off. Using the end of his shirt, he carefully wiped the gun and holster. Then he stuffed the bundle under the front seat. Fiona and Marcus stared. Vlad returned the gaze in a way that said: *say nothing, forget it.*

"So your father's alright?" said Marcus.

"He'll be fine. The bullet got him in his side – glanced off a rib. He's actually quite proud."

"Tough old fella."

She cut him a lopsided smile, then her features hardened. "What did you mean you had no choice but to tell the Sheikh?"

Even through the dirt, Marcus looked pale. Shame lowered his eyes and voice. "Basically, the Sheikh owns my stud. Lock, stock, the lot."

"But how? You've been so successful."

"When I started winning, I bought too many mares, bred too many horses. Hell, I even dabbled in property – like pretty much everyone else during the Celtic Tiger. Then it all went belly-up. I still had good horses, won big races, but not enough to keep the bank off my back. The Sheikh had always bought a few half-shares from me, so I asked – no begged – him to bail me out. His price was Trelawn Park Stud. After the lab burned down, he kept on and on at me. Wanted to know what you'd discovered, was convinced you'd made some major breakthrough. All along, he'd been sure that you and I were giving the horses some kind of magic bullet. No matter how much I tried to explain it to him, he never could understand that I was just raising them to be tough. Only using your tests to plan matings. So, when I was taken, I thought he'd just lost patience and wanted to interrogate me for answers so he could have the same success with his private trainers."

"Why didn't you tell me you'd lost the stud?"

"How could I? You'd think I was just another Celtic Tiger clown. Which I suppose I was. Besides, as long as I never told you, I could convince myself it wasn't real. My father would've whipped me for being so stupid." He rubbed his temple. "'*You're good with horses, but useless in the real world*' was what he used to say to me. Said our generation needed to get our hands dirty in a war. Make us tougher."

"He might've been right about that," said Vlad.

Fiona held Marcus's face in her hands. "Promise you'll never keep anything from me again? No matter what?"

He nodded feebly. She kissed him.

The cab nosed off the highway and made for the airport entrance.

"Hell, I'd love to take me a ride on a private plane," said the cabbie. A short cackle escaped through his teeth.

Vlad pulled a billfold out of his pocket and offered the cabbie four crisp hundreds. The man's eyes lit up.

Vlad snatched the bills away. "This is amnesia money. You forget us, right?"

285

"Oh hell, I brought two rich old ladies here from the Upper East Side this morning," he said with a dazzling grin. Vlad thrust the money at him and he palmed it into a pocket. "Have a nice day now."

Marcus now steady on his feet, they walked across the tarmac to the building which served as departure terminal. Beyond it, on the tarmac, Vlad could see the black, red and gold livery of Sheikh Abdul's plane. About a two hundred metres further away, there was another, smaller jet bearing the Prevenalux logo.

Inside, the terminal was all plush carpeting and chrome fittings, but strangely empty except for a glowing, smiling woman behind the counter. She asked them for destination and passports in a chirpy voice.

Vlad handed over his diplomatic credentials. "These two are with me. Official state guests of the Emirate of Wakfal. They travel under my documents."

The woman checked Vlad's passport. Took a long look at Marcus. Kept smiling. Picked up the phone.

Fiona thought she was forcing it now. Something was up. They should've stopped to get Marcus cleaned up. Still, at least he was alert now.

The woman said, "I need a supervisor," and hung up.

A squad car and SWAT truck pulled up outside the glass doors. Two uniformed police officers ambled into the building. Behind the counter a door opened and a senior-looking customs officer appeared. Vlad sucked air between his teeth.

***

Dusk was closing in as they walked across to the plane.

Floodlights flickered on and the red glow of New York shone like a fire across the Hudson.

To Vlad's relief, the cops in the terminal had just asked the senior customs guy about the Prevelalux plane. Said their chief got a call from the Irish Police Commisioner. The desk clerk had misunderstood and they were free to board the Emirate plane under supervision.

Out of the corner of his eye, Vlad saw movement. Six SWAT officers in formation, skirting the building, clinging to shadows until they'd have to dart across the open ground to the Prevenalux plane.

Vlad grinned. The customs officer cut him a glare.

They got to the steps. Vlad stuck out his hand. "Thank you very much for your help, officer."

The man ignored it, nodded at each of them and spun on his heel.

Vlad ushered Fiona and Marcus into the plane, threw a last look over at the agents dashing through stark white beams of light to the Prevenalux plane. Satisfied, he mounted and drew up the steps behind him.

Danie had stopped the bike in the car park and watched them disappear into the building.

A while later he'd seen them appear from the rear of the terminal. An official escorted them to a gaudy red, gold and black jet with Arabic script running up the side and Emirate of Wakfal printed underneath it.

"*Fok*," he muttered.

He pulled off his helmet, swiped his phone.

Wikus picked up immediately. "Where the fuck are you? I've been trying to get you."

"Couldn't hear the phone. I'm on a bike, remember? Anyway, I'm at Teterboro. Is Oscar still on our plane?"

"Yes. I've just spoken to him. He's arranging a little surprise for our runaways."

"He'd better foken hurry – they're boarding the Sheikh's plane."

"Don't worry. Back off and drive away. Get yourself to JFK and on the first plane back to base. You mission is done."

Chapter 40

The bedside phone jangled. Pat woke with a jolt. Turned on the light, checked the time and picked up.

"*Erm*, Mr. McCormack, sorry to wake you, but there're two gardaí here at the main gate. Say they need to have a chat with you. Urgent, like."

"Bring them up the the house."

His wife rolled over and opened an eye.

He patted her thigh. "It's alright, Nobuku. Just business."

She smiled and turned over again.

Pat wrapped his bulk with a dressing gown and went down to his office. He plonked himself in his chair and made a call.

Wikus picked up on the first ring.

"Is Hamilton on my plane yet?"

Wikus gave him the bad news.

"*Jesus, Mary and Joseph!* And the Buckley woman too? Can't you idiots get anything right?"

"I told you I didn't want to move him alone, but you couldn't wait. And how was I to know you had the Buckley woman in the same fucking building? That's hardly the smartest move ever, is it?"

Pat banged his fist on the table. "*Don't comment on matters that you don't fully understand!* Who was the man with them?"

"Big guy. Maybe Russian."

Pat closed his eyes. Pursed his lips. He knew who the Russian was. "They'll have gone to Teterboro, you can bet your life Abdul's Khaledam's plane is there. They cannot get on that plane, do you understand?" He tossed the phone on his desk and said a little prayer.

Even if Buckley made it to safety, what could she say? What could she do? She'd been given nothing but help by him. Hamilton was a problem though, one that needed a permanent solution. It'd be easier if he could just be bought off. Silence money. Pat winced – he couldn't see that happening.

The doorbell buzzed.

The gardaí must suspect something, he thought, otherwise this could've waited till the morning.

Pat walked through the house to the front hall. Unlocked the door and greeted the two officers with a warm smile.

"Come in, lads, come in. Blustery night."

"'Tis that," said one, wiping his feet on the mat.

Pat led them back to his office. Rounding his desk, he stopped at the whiskey decanter on the sideboard.

"Sit down, lads," he said, indicating two chairs at his desk. He poured generous measures into three cutglass tumblers. "I could do with a drink at this hour, anyway."

He went and offered them the drinks and a smile.

They stared at the amber nectar.

One of them said, "No thanks," half-heartedly.

"Go on. It'll do you good."

"Mr. McCormack, you realise it's illegal for an officer to drink on duty?" said the taller one.

Pat winked. "I won't tell if you won't."

Both of them bristled at that.

Pat returned their glasses to the sideboard, sat at his desk and took an urgent gulp of whiskey. Composed, he shot a warm smile at their humourless faces.

"So what can I do for you gentlemen at this hour?"

"We'd like you to accompany us to the station, to answer a few questions."

"And that couldn't wait till the morning?"

"No. I'm afraid not. We'd like to go through the passenger manifest of your company's plane."

"Oh, is that all? Sure, I'll have my secretary send the documents over in the morning."

The guards shook their heads in unison.

"I'm afraid we need you to come down all the same," said the taller one.

The sleek phone on Pat's desk buzzed. The guards craned their necks, trying to read the screen.

Pat snapped it up. "Well, hello there. Fancy calling at this hour. How're things?"

"Oscar's on the job," said Wikus. "But it's a risky move at an airport – even a private one. He might end up in jail. That'll cost you more."

Pat's eyes widened.

The gardaí stared.

"Oh, that's perfectly alright. Whatever you need. Not a problem. Bye now." He pocketed the phone and stifled a smile. "Research director in my New York facility. Needs to go over-budget."

"That right?"

"Yes." Pat frowned, cocked his head to one side. "You know I have a pharmaceutical company?"

"Oh, we do indeed." The garda looked at the wall clock. "You'll have to come with us now."

"Let me throw on some clothes and I'll be right down."

He stormed out of the room before they could react. They sprang to their feet and followed him up the stairs.

At his bedroom door, Pat raised a palm. "Lads, my wife's asleep in here. "I'll be out in a sec."

Kenny and McMahon exchanged helpless glances as the door closed.

"You listen at the door," said Kenny. "If he's not out in three minutes, we're going in."

Chapter 41

Vlad closed and armed the door. "Wheels up," he said, cocking his head into the flight deck. No pilots. He whipped around. Found himself staring at the barrell of a small black pistol, not unlike the ceramic one he favoured. Not the first time he'd had a gun to his head either.

The man holding it looked ex-military too, but younger. He had that spoiled look of those mercs who did dirty private jobs for huge sums of money and blew their pay on hookers, cocaine and shiny trinkets. Scumbags, scavengers. He knew how to talk them down. He'd done it before, in the Emirate for the Sheikh. This genius still had the safety on. Which meant he wasn't going to use it in the plane. Just scare them all so he could hijack.

Vlad raised his hands, softened his features and

looked past the man. He saw the pilots, Fiona and Hamilton sitting on the floor, legs crossed, hands on heads. All uninjured.

Vlad switched his gaze back the the guy. "What do you want from us?"

"Like you said: wheels up." With his free hand, the guy beckoned behind him. "*Pilot. Up, start the engines. Radio the tower. We're leaving this shithole.*"

Vlad seized the opportunity. "Hell, you're right there. I don't much like this place either."

The guy's eyes narrowed. Corner of his mouth twitched. "Things we do for a buck, eh?"

"You know, I was just thinking the same thing."

The guy grinned. Vlad pounced. Darted a hand to the gun barrel, forcing it back and down. Twisted, heard the crack as the trigger guard snapped the guy's finger. A scream. Tore the gun loose, further bending the guy's finger. Broken bone slit out through skin. Blood erupted from the wound. The guy sank to his knees, clasping his finger. Blood dripped on the carpet. Vlad checked the gun. Studied the guy's face. Swung his leg and drove the toe of his boot up under the guy's chin. His head snapped backwards. He gurgled, flopped to one side and banged his temple off a table.

"Jesus, you've killed him!" said Fiona.

Vlad shrugged. "Doubt it. Blood's still flowing from his finger."

A red stain grew on the beige carpet.

"You guys OK?" he said to the pilots.

Shocked, they managed nods.

"Then get us airborne."

They went to the flight deck. Vlad helped Fiona and Marcus up. They strapped themselves into the the huge leather seats while Vlad hauled the guy onto the sofa and held him in place with three seatbelts. The engines fired up and the crackle of radio transmissions between plane and tower began.

As they taxied Vlad opened a locker and pulled out a first-aid kit. He doused the guy's wound with iodine and tied a dressing in place. He went to the drinks cabinet and tipped a bottle of soda water on the bloodstained carpet, followed by the contents of a salt shaker.

"That was one of the guys who grabbed me in Dublin," said Marcus.

Vlad shrugged and belted up.

"*Take off positions, please*," said the pilot over the intercom.

Minutes later the plane climbed into the darkening sky. Fiona burst into tears of relief. Marcus threw an arm around her and she buried her head in his chest. When the plane levelled out, Vlad went to the drinks cabinet and came back with a bottle of vodka and three glasses.

Fiona wiped her eyes. "I'd prefer a glass of wine."

Vlad poured three shots. "It's good for you. Calm your nerves."

She took the drink. Vlad threw back the clear nectar with a contented wince. Marcus grimaced and grabbed his jaw. He pulled back his lip and ran a finger over the angry red swelling where his incisor had been.

"Don't worry," said Vlad. "The vodka'll sterilise it." He poured three more doses.

Marcus gulped the second, sank into the chair and

closed his eyes. Nobody said anything for a while. The heavy drone of the engines drowned the silence.

Eventually, Vlad ambled to the rear of the cabin. He opened a door to a dazzling bathroom. Went to a locker. Took out trousers and a T-shirt.

"Might be too big for you," he said, handing them to Marcus.

Marcus took them with a weak smile.

Vlad produced cable ties from another locker, bound the hands of their captive and stuffed a napkin in his mouth.

Pat sat alone in the interview room, throwing looks at the two-way mirror, the breezeblock walls and the chipped paint. Filthy shithole. He was glad he didn't pay tax in this country. Sure, it all got wasted anyway. No such thing as a lick of paint where it was needed. No, no. Waste the money paying these eejits overtime, when they should just be told to work till the work was done. Like the people on his farm. More fuckin' eejits. If *they* worked longer and harder, he'd have less injuries to his horses and better performance on the track, that was for sure.

The door lock snapped him back to reality. The heavy door swung open with a creak. Needed oil on that too. Where was the attention to detail?

A smug-looking cop shuffled in, holding a thick file. Sat opposite Pat and tossed the file on the desk.

Pat stifled a yawn.

The cop's face hardened as he turned on a tape recorder. "Sergeant Gerry O'Dowd. Interview starts at three-ten a.m. Present in the room are Mr. Pat McCormack and myself." He cleared his throat. "Mr. McCormack, do you know racehorse trainer Marcus Hamilton?"

Pat nodded.

"Please respond verbally."

"Oh, right. Yes, I know of him. He's a successful trainer and I breed thoroughbreds too. But I don't know the man personally."

"But you're both investors in a company called Equigenes?"

Pat nodded again. O'Dowd arched his brow.

"Yes, that's right."

"And you never got to know the man personally?"

"Not really, sure business is business. I don't usually get to know every shareholder of every company I invest in."

"We have a missing persons report on Mr. Hamilton, and the last time he was seen was at Dublin Airport, escorting his horse back from the races in England. Then, lo and behold he turns up on a passenger manifest on your plane, departing Ireland for New York early Sunday morning. How do you explain that?"

Pat chuckled. "Oh, that's not possible. There must be some mistake."

O'Dowd casually flipped open the file. Made a theatre of sorting through pages, before selecting one and sliding it across. A name highlighted in bright green: **M. Hamilton**.

Pat ran his eyes over the whole sheet of paper. It was genuine alright. Stupid mercenary fuckers, why did they write his name? Catriona wouldn't have made such a stupid mistake but, then again, she was too straight to be given the details for any delicate tasks. When all this had blown over, he'd hire a new assistant for things like this. Someone who knew the score. Like that guy he'd used all those years ago to arrange the accident in New York.

"Mr. McCormack! Hello?" said O'Dowd, clicking his fingers under Pat's nose.

Rude bastard. "Oh, that's not the trainer Marcus Hamilton," said Pat. "That's a guy who's gone to my factory in Albany, upstate New York." He paused. Rubbed his chin. "Michael, Mark. No ... Mitch – that's it. Mitch Hamilton. Specialist in arterial regeneration. You know I make drugs which lower bad cholesterol? Among other things."

"I do."

Pat needed to stay affable and friendly, but at the crack of dawn he'd ask for his lawyers and concoct the back-up for this story. Shouldn't be too difficult. It never was. As long as palms were crossed.

O'Dowd drummed his fingers on the table, replaced the paper in the file and flipped it closed. He'd love to slap cuffs on the arrogant bastard. Instead he let out a long sigh and left the interview room.

He locked the door and strode along the corridor until he found Karen, feet on a desk, playing with her phone.

She jumped up, reddening.

"Get McMahon to help you process him and put him in a cell. He can sweat for the night. I'm off home."

O'Dowd hustled through reception.

The duty officer was on the phone. He put a hand over the receiver. "Sergeant. It's the Super."

O'Dowd's shoulders slumped. "Grand, I'll take it in there." He walked into the nearest empty room. The desk phone flashed.

"Not only have you ruined my night, but the Comissioner's not happy either. A right eejit you made us look with the Americans. They sent a SWAT team to Teterboro airport and McCormack's plane was empty. NYPD sent a unit to the Prevenalux building, but nothing there either. Oh, apparently a security guard reported that some lunatic – homeless guy, they said – had tried to gain access, and caused a scene in the lobby, but they'd already thrown him out."

"Did they not check the building?"

"They had neither probable cause nor a warrant."

"But –"

"I'm supposed to tell you from on high that you're on thin fucking ice, causing all this fuss in the middle of the night. Except, well, there was one thing. Customs at Teterboro said that people fitting the description of Marcus Hamilton and the Buckley woman boarded a plane under diplomatic coverage from the Emirate of Wakfal. Destination filed on flight plan as Weston Aerodrome."

"What? And why didn't they stop them?"

"Privileged status. I suppose you could call it diplomatic immunity."

O'Dowd swore.

"Ah, come on now, surely you know how much oil and gas the US buys from that place? Ireland too."

"*Hmm.*"

"Ah, quit your whining and make sure there's someone at Weston to meet that plane."

"Yes, sir."

He walked through to the canteen, found Kenny cradling a cup of tea.

"We're off to the airport," he said. "Make a flask of that stuff and meet me in the car. Bring biscuits too. I'll be a long night."

Kenny, grumbling, stuck the kettle on.

Chapter 42

Fiona looked out the window and wondered if Marcus would be the same man after this, but most of all she wondered what would happen to Pat. She stared at the flashing wingtip light and realised she owed it to Johnny to finish what he'd started. Only this time, she'd do it in a lab and ask help from the leaders in the field. She couldn't help but wonder if Johnny'd still be alive if she'd listened to him all those years ago. She gulped back another vodka, deciding it wasn't so bad after all. Thoughts swirled in her head, until fatigue divided and conquered them.

Later she woke with a jolt to Marcus holding her wrist, looking at her watch. She blinked. He looked clean and fresh. Lost in an oversize T-shirt and khakis.

"What day is it?" he asked.

Fiona had no idea any more.

"Tuesday night in New York. Early Wednesday morning Irish time," said Vlad behind closed eyes, his seat fully reclined.

"Last thing I remember clearly was returning to Dublin with the horses Saturday night. What's happened the last few days?"

Fiona filled him in on her discoveries and Johnny's tampering with the feed.

Marcus sat upright. "Wait. If he was doing something to the feed, then my horses should've been affected too, right?"

"No. Johnny wasn't targeting your horses. Besides, he used to keep back-up samples of all the batches produced for a year, in case anyone ever requested a retrospective analysis. Tony Carey told me that he recently had all those samples analysed, and not only were they clean, they were *all* identical to yours. So that means Johnny threw out any tainted samples and replaced them with your clean ones. It was his way of covering his arse in case anyone got suspicious."

Marcus shrugged. "Makes sense, I suppose. But what was he hoping to gain?"

"I think he was trying to prove a point. And get revenge."

Marcus's mouth opened but he said nothing.

Fiona continued. "You said that the Sheikh couldn't understand that your biggest advantage was that you treated your horses naturally. Let them run around in all weathers."

"He never did get it. You've been to his farm, right? You've seen what it's like there?"

"Once, when I took samples for testing."

"He overstocks the place. And De Courtney's either too thick or too weak to do anything about it." Marcus shrugged. "Then again, Abdul's used to his word being law. Probably doesn't give De Courtney a choice in the matter. Bit like he did to me when he wanted information."

"Well, I think Johnny figured that out too."

"Doesn't surprise me. He knew his horses and his nutrition."

"Yes, but it went further than that."

"What do you mean?"

"Turns out Johnny was a student of epigenetics."

"How are our genes are affected by our environment?" Marcus sucked air between his teeth. "I thought you said that was all hype and no proof."

"Looks like I was wrong." She shrugged. "Too focused on my own research. Forgot to look at the big picture."

She told him about Johnny's rented unit and the diaries.

Marcus sat enthralled. "So you're saying that by raising my horses to be strong and tough I'm influencing their genes?" He arched his brow quizzically.

"It's a distinct possibility. It's possible that you're inadvertently enabling certain genes, kind of like switching on the horse's full potential."

Marcus made a face. "While people like Pat and Abdul disable genes. Or switch them off or enable detrimental genes?"

"It looks like Johnny was trying to prove exactly that. He was polluting the feed to enhance the epigenetic effect."

"Like putting epigenetics on steroids," muttered Marcus.

Fiona pursed her lips. They sat in silence for a while before tiredness hit them and, despite lingering stress, they managed to fall asleep in their seats.

The plane thudded onto the tarmac just as the first shades of blue diluted the grey above Dublin. Their captive had regained consciousness, but decided against struggling after Vlad slapped him on the cheek with his own pistol. Checking the window, Vlad saw the police car parked by the hangar even before the plane coasted to a halt. He unstrapped the captive and pulled him upright by his wrists.

"This is where we part company," Vlad said to Fiona. "I don't leave the plane. It's back to Wakfal for me." He jabbed a finger at the window. "There are people here to meet you."

The co-pilot opened the door and let the steps down. Vlad pushed his captive out of the plane. He missed a step and tumbled onto the the tarmac, letting out a muffled squawk through his gag.

Marcus led Fiona down the steps, hand in hand, stepping around the fallen man.

The co-pilot closed the door.

Vlad turned to the pilot. "Request fuel. Get clearance, then take us home." He swiped his phone and called his boss.

"Is she safe?" asked Abdul immediately.

"Yes, and I found Hamilton there too."

"Good. Excellent. Two birds with one stone. You did

well, Vladimir. Now it is time we sat back and let things run their course."

O'Dowd had to squint as sunlight reflected on the wet tarmac. It took him a moment to comprehend that a restrained man was being shoved out of the plane. The man tripped on the steps and landed in a heap.

"Christ, Kenny," he said, "get your hole into gear!"

They burst into a run and, as they closed in on the plane, Dr. Buckley and Marcus Hamilton emerged like a pair of lovers back from honeymoon.

Part of O'Dowd wanted to slap her in handcuffs and charge her for obstruction of justice, but what would that gain? He was just glad the whole thing seemed to be tidying itself up.

The plane's door drew up and snapped shut.

O'Dowd scowled, he would've loved to board that plane and question the occupants, but he hadn't the stomach for a diplomatic incident. He and Kenny grabbed the fallen man by his armpits and hauled him to his feet. Kenny pulled a gag from his mouth and marched him to the car.

"You're a lucky woman, Dr. Buckley," said O'Dowd, stony-faced.

Chapter 43

Nobody said a word on the way back. Marcus was wedged in the back seat between Fiona and the prisoner.

O'Dowd parked right up against the station's front door. Fiona and Marcus were taken to separate rooms. Fiona asked if she could call her father. O'Dowd said she'd have to be interviewed first, but added that he'd let him know she was alright. He slammed the door and left her alone in a small office, staring at filing cabinets and crime-statistic graphs.

Fiona yawned, the room swam around her, the filing cabinets on the far wall seemed to float. Her stomach churned with acid. They should've eaten on the plane instead of downing vodka, but it had been such a welcome sedative. She crossed her arms on the table, rested her head in them and fell instantly asleep.

She awoke with a start to find a severe-looking, black-haired girl sitting opposite her, clutching a laptop to her chest. Two cups of tea and a shrink-wrapped sandwich were on the table, beside an old-fashioned tape recorder.

The girl smiled, warming her features. "I'm Garda Karen Newsom." She cocked her eyebrows at the sandwich. "I thought you might be hungry."

Fiona smiled weakly. "Thanks."

"I'll start recording. You can eat away while you answer my questions."

Fiona ate the foul, soggy sandwich. Johnny wouldn't have approved of her eating such rubbish. Karen opened the laptop on the table and established Fiona's identity for the record before asking her about the last forty-eight hours. Fiona told her everything, from the time she slipped out of Naas hospital, until their arrival this morning. Karen pecked rapidly at the keyboard, shooting Fiona a friendly smile from time to time.

"So, you are familiar with the contents of the diaries you sent us?"

"I had a look through it all, yes."

"And the *Endgame* DVD?"

Fiona shook her head. "Hadn't time."

Karen tapped a note. "Do you know what was on that DVD?"

Another headshake.

"So you believe the diaries and DVD were what Mr. McCormack's men were looking for? As opposed to your own research on, *erm*," she checked her onscreen notes, "Exercise Induced Pulmonary Haemorrhage and Osteochon–chon ..."

"Osteochondritis Dissecans."

"That's the one. Quite a mouthful."

"They didn't really know what they were looking for, I can see that now. I reckon Pat was convinced from day one that Equigenes – my company – was just a front for high-tech doping of racehorses. I guess he thought me, Johnny and Marcus were colluding to damage his horses whilst giving some kind of magic advantage to Marcus."

Karen tapped at the keyboard.

"But, you see, I'm not doing anything to anybody's horses. My tests only tell you what the picture is, they don't alter it in any way or enhance performance. Marcus – and other clients – just use the information to plan their matings on a scientific level: it takes some of the guesswork out of it. The new tests and my hand-held saliva analysis unit will only be more of the same. It'll give people more information. How they use it is up to them."

"So all this is basically just business?"

"Got to make a living somehow."

"So how did your late husband's feed-tampering fit in with all this?"

Fiona thought a moment. Didn't know whether to smile or weep. "Well, that's the thing – nobody knew what he was doing. Not me, not Marcus, not Pat, not Sheikh Abdul."

"Sheikh Abdul?"

"Oh, he was an investor in my company too. I think he was Johnny's ... benefactor."

Karen narrowed her eyes. "So do you have *any* idea why your late husband was doing what he was doing?"

She thought of Johnny's book. "Some kind of weird revenge fantasy – it's clear he was pissed off with Pat. But I don't know the details. I mean, they used to be so close. I always figured it was Pat who'd helped Johnny recover after his fall. Right up until I saw Marcus come out of that elevator in New York." She cradled her chin in her hands. "Now I don't exactly know what happened."

Karen looked like she was wrestling with something. She ended the interview and went to get more tea.

O'Dowd sat with Pat McCormack and his lawyer. On the table was a copy of Marcus Hamilton's statement. Pat's lawyer had requested time alone with his client after he'd read that, but O'Dowd declined, saying he wanted to show them something first.

He had a young officer bring in a laptop. Then he played the *Endgame* DVD for them, barely managing to stifle a smile as Pat boiled and the lawyer squirmed.

"This proves nothing," said the lawyer, attempting bravado.

But O'Dowd knew it made all the pieces fit together. So he left them alone to their discussions and went to his desk.

Karen was waiting for him.

"All done with Dr. Buckley?" he asked.

"I am. She's in the filing room. I was wondering if I could show her the DVD. She hasn't seen it. She still doesn't know exactly *why* her late husband did it."

O'Dowd rubbed his eyes. "Go on then." He ejected the disc and handed it to Karen. "Don't let her make off with it. I'll come and talk to her in a bit."

"What about Hamilton?"

"Doctor's with him now. Kenny can take him home after that. He's been through enough. I'll go to his house if I need anything else."

"And the big man in there?"

O'Dowd winked. A victorious glint in his eye. "This is something Pat Mac won't be able to buy himself out of. He'll stand trial for kidnapping. And we'll have to see what else we can add to that. The rent-a-thug," he glanced at his notepad, "Oscar Ryson, will face charges of abduction and kidnapping – Hamilton can ID him as one of his abductors – but I'll have to consult with the head honchos about him. I'm not sure how we'll handle the ethics of him being restrained for the duration of a trans-Atlantic flight." He shrugged. "I dunno. Anyway, he'll go down. That's for sure. Unless he opens his trap to give us more information on yer man Pat McCormack. We know Oscar Ryson worked for the same security company as that Felix Vander. Hell, he could've been the man's accomplice that night in Thomas Riley's house. Maybe Riley'll be able to identify him. We'll give Ryson a proper grilling after the doctor's looked at his finger." He paused, a grin slipped across his face. "I tell you one thing: the Super doesn't think we're eejits anymore." He yawned. "And I don't care what the Americans think. I'm just glad we got Buckley and Hamilton back."

"Thanks for involving me on this one, Sergeant."

"You're a good garda, Karen. Keep it up."

"What about the men who chased them in New York? There were at least two according to Dr. Buckley's statement."

"Not our problem."

Fiona recognised Johnny's scrawl on the disc Karen inserted in the laptop.

"I thought you might want to see this," Karen said, turning the screen. "Press play whenever you're ready."

Fiona's finger hovered over the mousepad. Part of her never wanted to know what Johnny's endgame was. Eventually she clicked.

Johnny's face appeared. Bald head, sunken eyes. The gaunt mask of a man on the edge of death. His once impressive muscle mass stolen by cancer. He looked so small in his chair. The camera light threw grotesque shadows on the wall behind him. Fiona shivered. She could see the mortar and pestle on the table. Made the place looked like a mad apothecary's den.

"*Right*," said Johnny. A guttural cough rasped through him.

Fiona watched him wipe his mouth on his sleeve, leaving dark smudges on his cuff.

He grunted. "*Won't have to worry about keeping myself clean and tidy for much longer.*" He stared. His eyes a mixture of regret and rage. "*Maybe I never should have … Anyway, back to the clinic tomorrow for another round of chemo. Waste of time … I suppose I should do a disc for each of you, but I've neither the time nor inclination to do three separate farewells. Anyway, Fiona, you'll probably see this first – and the diaries are for you. They contain all my theories and how and when I tampered with the feed. There are no names in the diaries because,*" another cough, "*I – well – just in case … I'd planned to do so much more, you know? You can apply my theories to horses, but I was going to contact that guy Bygren in Stockholm, tell him what I'd done. He's retired now, but I reckon he'd be interested. There's a place in San Diego ... says they've mapped the human epigenome."* He grinned manaically. Rubbed his hands together. *"I was right, Fiona. My dad was right! He always said there was something about the way queen bees were the only ones who ate royal jelly. The drones and workers ate any old pollen, honey, sugar syrup mixture. But not the queens. Not the dominant rulers."* A bizarre grin curled his thin lips, baring his teeth. *"And I also proved that the reverse is true."* He paused to catch his breath. *"Anyway, this next bit is for Abdul. OK, you know I'm grateful for everything you did for me. You're a decent honourable man. I was only having my first ride for you, but you treated me like I'd worked for you for years. Gave me the means to make a new life. Without your money, I could never have got the kind of physical therapy that I needed. And that in turn led me to bodybuilding. And that, to me going to college to study Equine Science and Nutrition. When you bought the feed company and put me in there, I thought we were on the same page. I thought you got it, but you never changed the way you managed your horses and I could never get De Courtney to understand either. Horses aren't chickens. You can't pack them in and let them ruin their paddocks. It's not natural. Come on, it's not like you're short of money. I mean, you're even feeding them right: with proper, untainted Winline feed. All you had to do was treat them like Marcus treats his horses and you'd have been winning. You're trying to breed athletes, aren't you? They have to run around – work out – as they grow, otherwise even the best feed won't give them the advantage. It's that simple. How could you not see that?"* He coughed again. Wiped his mouth. More stains.

Fiona wiped the corners of her eyes.

Onscreen, the ghost continued. *"Abdul, you've got to let your horses be horses."*

Johnny reached behind his chair and produced a water bottle and pillbox. Knocked back his cocktail. Finished the water.

"Now, where was I? Oh, yes. Pat. Pat, Pat, Pat. You pseudo-religious asshole. What better way to fuck you over and dent your massive ego than to tamper with your precious homebred horses? Ha! Seemed such a simple plan at the time. You know, even back in the day, when I rode for you, I could see that something wasn't right on your farm. Not obvious like Abdul's place. I mean, your farm's like Disneyland, but something was off. It only made sense for me when I started studying and took a visit to Trelawn Park one day. Marcus Hamilton, whatever his faults, is a horseman and I respect that. But he also thinks. I mean, he was the first to invest in Fiona's company. Pat, you only got involved because you thought they were doing something dodgy and you wanted a part of it. A little lightning in a bottle, eh?" Johnny shook his head, exhaled a breath of pure contempt. *"Pat, you treat your horses like financial commodities. They're mollycoddled and your staff are too fucking overworked to notice or give a shit. Nobody on the ground level on your farm has time to think – they just do. They follow your orders and keep the horses segregated. Then, when the two-year-olds start training, you expect them to perfom like machines. Well, too late, buddy!"* He paused, grinned. *"So then I discovered epigenetics and nutrigenomics and decided that you, Pat,*

would be my guinea pig. Well, your horses anyway."

Fiona found herself crying uncontrollably. Part of it was like exorcism, getting Johnny out of her system. Part of it was sadness: Johnny had become deranged, she could see that, but she wondered if this was his genetic destiny, or if his life, his environment, his circumstance had made him into the goblin on the screen.

"Would you like to stop?" Karen, offered a tissue.

"No. I need to watch it all ... I didn't grieve much at his funeral."

Johnny leaned closer to the camera. *"I set out to give epigenetics a helping hand. I read a lot, did my research and decided to approach the issue in three ways. I ground up bovine bone marrow and plastic bottles and mixed it with pesticide. The resulting powder was easy to slip into the drying machine the evening before your batches were made. Ironically, Pat, it was your self-importance that made it all possible: insisting that your feed was delivered fresh out of the extruder. First batch of the morning. Like it makes a fucking difference what time of the day your feed is produced when it has a shelf life of nearly a year. Oh, we print a four-month expiry date on the bags to keep people like you happy and ensure a steady turnover, but the stuff's good for nearly a year."* Johnny rubbed his face. Looked at his watch. *"Anyway, every horse on your place was eating this extra shite, baked onto the feed in the dryer. So, your mares were eating it before and during pregnancy. Their foals were raised on it – maybe even picking up residue in their mother's milk – and they stayed on it in training. For me, it was a perfect storm. And the longer I did it, the worse your results got. The way I see it: if a horse started this shite as a two-year-old in training, it might not trigger much of a change, but if its mother had eaten it during pregnancy and then it had been raised on it – coupled with your mollycoddling management system – then the expression of the animal's genetic code would be altered considerably. Not in a way that would damage its health, but certainly in a way that would affect its athletic ability. We all know that athletic ability is a difficult thing to produce, with such a narrow gap between talent and mediocrity. So I figured it'd be easy to tamper with it. And I was right, wasn't I, Pat? And there's not a fucking thing you can do to reverse it. Once you've disrupted the expression of a gene or turned it off, it's off for good. You'll probably call me a lunatic when you see this,"* he shrugged, *"but I don't give a shit, because when the science people actually look at what I did they'll have to admit I was onto something. If for no other reason than the fact that I probably gave myself cancer from inhaling particles of my mixture when I put it in the dryer. It had to have been that. I took precautions when I prepared the stuff, I've been fit all my life and, God knows, I never ate shite. Then again maybe it was the steriods that triggered it? Or maybe it was the combination?"*

He closed his eyes as if in prayer, but Fiona knew he'd had no time for religion.

"Fiona, sorry, but this'll probably make your company irrelevant, at least in its current form. You should work with the human researchers. They're discovering concrete links between pre-pregnancy nutrition of women and the genetic make-up of their kids. That's right: pre-pregnancy."

He slumped in his chair, head down. Apparently out of steam.

Fiona leaned closer to the screen. Was Johnny welling up?

315

His gaze snapped back to the camera, making Fiona jump. Like he knew she'd be staring at him.

"For what it's worth, Fiona, I'm sorry about how things turned out for us. I think if we'd have had a family before the fall, things might've been different. Now I'm dying of a cancer that's probably self-inflicted. I suppose I should've been more of a man and set you free years ago. So you could've married Marcus and had kids. But I was angry, bitter. I felt robbed. When I was riding, I used to joke with the lads in the weighroom: it's not how you fall, it's how you land. Well, I landed in a fucking heap this time."

He was definitely crying now – she could see tears glinting in the light.

The screen went black.

Fiona kept staring at it. Eventually Karen closed the laptop.

Fiona blew her nose, wiped her eyes. "Has Pat seen this?"

She nodded. "Unfortunately it doesn't really prove anything against him though."

"Can I get a copy?"

"I'll have one made."

Fiona nodded. "Thanks." She'd give it to Marcus – he could pass it on to the Sheikh. Seemed like the right thing to do.

Poor Johnny.

Chapter 44

One month later

Fiona paced around the kitchen while Marcus made coffee. She looked at her watch. "He's late."

"Only a few minutes. Probably traffic. Relax. I'm the one who should be nervous."

Fiona drummed her fingers on her thigh. She ran her eyes over the whole room. She'd sell this place. Closure of a chapter in her life. But before she put it on the market, she'd have Johnny's ceiling handles removed. They just looked too weird, even to her.

She heard a large car crunch to a halt on the gravel. She bounced up and opened the door just as Vlad was opening the rear door of the white Rolls Royce. He nodded to her, she grinned. The Sheikh got out, brandishing a warm smile. Gone was the steely gaze of the Bedouin, replaced with a look that could have been paternal affection.

He stuck out a well-manicured hand. "Dr. Buckley. I am so happy to see you."

They shook. He'd called her doctor this time.

The Sheikh stepped inside. Fiona closed the door, casting another glance at Vlad who bowed from the neck and remained by the car, scanning his surroundings.

Inside, Marcus and the Sheikh regarded each other with tight smiles.

"Please, sit down," said Fiona.

The Sheikh installed himself in an armchair, Marcus perched on the sofa.

"Coffee?"

"Thank you, yes."

She brewed a pot, brought a tray and served.

The Sheikh looked at Marcus, but then spoke to Fiona. "Dr. Buckley, I would like to thank you for sending me that DVD. It was most interesting. Educational, even."

"I'm glad. It's what Johnny wanted."

"Marcus," said Abdul, "I take it you have seen the DVD too?"

"Yes."

"And do you agree with Johnny? Are my horses badly managed?"

Marcus cleared his throat. "Simple answer: yes." He put up a hand. "That doesn't justify what Johnny did to Pat's horses, but he did highlight the issue." He pointed to a copy of the *Racing Post* on the table. "Even the press are discussing it now. So are the professional punters."

"I also think that the late Mr. Buckley may have had a point." He sipped his coffee. "So I fired Alan De Courtney this morning."

Marcus and Fiona exchanged glances.

"Now, I have a business proposition for you, Marcus."

Marcus's ears twitched, the hairs on his neck rippled. He'd heard this one before.

"It is very difficult to find good management staff, so I'd like to steal Alfie Connors from you, with immediate effect."

Marcus's eyes bulged. Fiona put her hand on his arm. Squeezed. Marcus blew out a breath. "You know he's in his fifties, right? He'll never move to Tipperary."

"I'm going to – as the saying goes – make him an offer he can't refuse. And you're going to convince him to take the job."

Incredulity arched Marcus's brow but he said nothing.

Abdul smiled. "In return, I will give you back my 90% interest in Trelawn Park Stud."

Fiona gasped and squeezed Marcus's arm again.

"You will once more own your father's land." He raised a finger. "*But* ... I will retain ownership of 50% of each horse. That is non-negotiable. You will proceed as before, and I will pay 50% of the bills *and* I will have the benefit of using your man to improve things on my farm in Tipperary and the one I am buying in England."

"And what'll I do for a head man?"

"You can do it yourself until you can train a replacement for Alfie. After all, you have your own land back."

"Can I get all that in writing?"

"Naturally. The property handover will be handled by my legal team, but our discussion about Mr. Connors is confidential."

"Of course."

"Sheikh Abdul," said Fiona, "I never got to properly thank you for rescuing us. I – I –"

"Please. It seemed the least that I could do. As you say, Johnny would have wanted it that way."

"But how did you know where we were?"

"You don't know? She didn't tell you?"

Fiona looked blank.

"You have your secretary to thank for that," Abdul knitted his brow, stared into his cup. "Maura ... Delany, isn't it? She is a very persistent woman. She managed to contact me at my London hotel to tell me she'd seen a DVD and tried to describe what she'd seen. She wondered if you were with me. She asked me to help you." He smoothed his short beard with his hand. "How did she put it?" He cocked his head to one side, frowning. "I needed to do something, because by the time the cops figured it out, it'd be too late. Yes, that was it. At first, I wasn't sure where you'd gone, so I told Vladimir to locate you. It's his speciality – finding lost women. It was just pure luck that he stumbled across you, Marcus." He shrugged. "I suppose we all need the help of Allah from time to time."

Fiona couldn't believe that Maura hadn't told her. Actually, she could. That was the nature of the woman: slaving away anonymously in the background to make sure everything ran smoothly.

"And now, Dr. Buckley, that brings us to the matter of Equigenes."

Fiona stood, fetched a manila file from her office desk and presented it to Abdul. "It's all in there."

"Good. I will read it on the way to my farm and

telephone you tomorrow," he said, standing. "But do not worry. I promised Johnny I would look after him. When I bought Winline Feeds I put him in there, but I never kept him on a leash. My generosity towards him now extends to you." He sighed. "I must go to Winline Feeds now and introduce myself to Tony Carey. I'll need to replace Johnny and make sure Pat McCormack never tries to go public with what Johnny did." He smirked. "But something tells me he has bigger things to worry about."

Chapter 45

Eight months later

Fiona parked in the visitors' area. Midlands Prison was a newer, lower building than the austere 1830s penitentary looming over it on the outskirts of Portlaoise town.

She'd finally been granted permission for a professional visit to arrange the sale of Pat's shares in Equigenes. Not that his shares really mattered – she was just glad to have a pretext to visit him while he was remanded in custody pending his kidnapping trial. The billionaire had been judged an extreme flight risk and denied bail.

She checked her bag, locked the car and waddled over to the entrance. Showed her ID, was ushered inside and a hardy, teak-skinned female officer searched her.

"When's it due?" said the gravelly-voiced woman, as she ran her hands under and around Fiona's belly.

"Nine weeks."

"Boy or girl?"

"Boy, but we're not telling anyone."

"Bet you're having fun eating for two now, eh?" she said with a wink. "D'you smoke?"

Fiona shook her head.

"Forty a day, me. 'Twas a bitch giving up when I had mine, but you've got to look after yourself for them, don't you?"

"You do indeed." An image of Johnny flashed through her mind, as it did every so often, but she no longer felt sad or guilty when that happened.

She was told to leave her bag in a locker but was allowed to take the documents and the gift into the open visiting room. The cold, stark space reeked of body odour. Twenty tables, each with four chairs. Empty. Professional visits happened outside normal visiting hours. She had wanted this on purpose, in case somebody's relative photographed her sitting with the fallen Pat McCormack. Then she'd be on Page 2 of a Sunday rag. Who was the pregnant woman visiting the rich crook, and why? Or some such rubbish like that.

Fiona wiped crumbs off the hard plastic chair and sat, legs apart, back straight. She put the gift in her coat pocket and laid the documents on the table.

A few minutes later, Pat was brought in. The prison officer locked the door and stood by the wall, eyes on full beam.

Pat had lost weight and looked better for it. He sat opposite her and stared. Fiona felt her heart quicken.

"Congratulations, Mrs. Hamilton," were his first words, thrusting his chin at her belly.

She ignored him, opened the file. "I brought these for you to sign. It's a formality really, but it'll make it easier to sell your share to someone else."

Pat scanned the papers. "Our lawyers could've handled this. That's what they get paid for. Why did you come?"

"I wanted to see you. Ask you things."

Pat signed the documents. "Go on then, I'm going nowhere."

"Why didn't you help Johnny after his fall? Was it the positive drug test? You know he always said they'd mixed up the samples?"

Pat's gaze ate into her for what seemed like an age. Then he just shrugged. "It's funny the way things turn out, isn't it? That's why I always loved racing. You can spend all the money, breed the best to the best and hope for the best and all that, but sometimes you just never know, do you? One little thing can fuck up the whole plan. Waste the entire investment."

On her way here, she had wondered if Pat would tell her anything at all. She supposed that many in his position wouldn't open their mouths, but Pat had such an ego. He loved to control everyone and everything. Now, she hoped, he just wouldn't be able to help himself.

"What little thing?" she prompted.

"You know, all I wanted to do was teach the little shite about loyalty." He leaned in close. His head inches from her nose.

"*Sit back in your chair!*" bawled the officer.

Pat obeyed. His face reddened.

Fiona put a hand to her mouth, covering her smirk.

Ego was a terrible thing. Pat was fuming, dying to spill the beans. She needed to hear him say it.

"That's why I got his sample tampered with," he said, a savage glint in his eye. "Cost me a fortune and it nearly never happened, but thanks to a bit of a distraction in the weighroom and a jockey with a gambling debt, I managed to pull it off."

When she'd realised Pat was behind the kidnappings and all the rest of it, she'd suspected he might have tampered with Johnny's urine sample. But, now, to actually hear him admit it ... She slumped in her chair. Under the table her hands curled into fists. She took a breath to regain her composure.

"Just because Johnny got off your second string to ride for Sheikh Abdul?"

"*Just* because?" Pat gave her an incredulous stare. "It was the principle of the thing." He put his arms out. Palms flat, welcoming, Christ-like. "As you know, I like to look after my people. Provided they stay loyal to me. Derek Jones is fully recovered after that fall, and I paid for everything. And Atavistic's back in training by the way, but maybe you've already heard? And look at young Cathal Regan – you were on the plane with him. There's nothing I wouldn't do for that poor young lad, even while I'm stuck in here. He's getting the best treatment in the world. Pulling through nicely, so I hear. After that, he'll be mine for life – and sure, why not? I mean, he'll owe it to me. But now I'm in here, so he'll probably work for my son and Bill Harris." He scratched his head. "I'd have stood by Johnny too. No matter what. But Johnny had no sense of loyalty, did he?"

Fiona stared at him.

"Just before the Derby, he told me he was going to ride for the Sheikh. I explained that we had an agreement. Not a contract, an agreement, but that it amounted to the same thing in my book." He wagged a finger at her.

"No aggressive gestures," said the officer.

Pat's face became crimson. He clasped his hands on the table. "No way, you don't ride my competitor's horse when I've another in the race. Johnny laughed at me. Imagine that? He fucking laughed at me. Told me that I couldn't own people. I told him that you could – that I buy people every day. Johnny told me he'd do what he wanted, that there was nothing I could do about it. So I thought it was time for a lesson. After the drug positive, he'd have been tainted goods. After he'd served his ban, I'd have welcomed him back and he'd have had no choice but to work for me. And I'd have tied him into a contract then, I can tell you. I just didn't anticipate the horse falling and putting him in a chair. Like I said, you never know in this game, do you?"

Fiona glared. Her breathing quickened.

"After the fall, he asked me for help alright. I came to see him, but you weren't there that day. Were you already fucking Hamilton then?"

She'd never wanted to punch anyone before but the desire took shape inside her. She took a long, deep breath and rubbed her belly.

Pat sat there, smirking. "Of course, I told him to fuck off. Then he got mad, told me he'd tell everyone what I'd done. I said he couldn't prove it, and that no one would listen to him anyway, but that even if he tried to go to the papers, I'd ruin your company just for the hell of it. That gave him pause. He didn't want that. Oh, no."

Under the table, Fiona clenched and unclenched her fists several times, as if she was kneading an imaginary stress ball.

She smirked, pushed the gift across the table at him. "Present from Johnny. You should have plenty of time to read it. It was Johnny's inspiration – his motivation."

Pat opened the crumpled brown paper bag and took out the worn old tome. "*The Count of Monte Cristo*? I don't get it."

"Read it." She calmly replaced the documents in the file. Stood gingerly and steadied herself with a hand on the table. With her free hand, she slapped him in the face and walked away. The prison officer chuckled.

"You know," Pat called after her, "I'll always wonder if poor Cathal Regan got cancer from handling Johnny's polluted feed. What do you think?"

The officer told him to shut up.

Fiona had wondered the same thing. And a few months ago, she might've agreed with Pat, but lately she'd been doing enough research on the global food chain to know that the young lad's cancer could've come from any number of sources. At least Cathal had made a full recovery.

She drove back to Kildare and stopped at the industrial estate to check on her new lab. Construction was nearly finished and equipment would start arriving next week.

Maura called to tell her there were two viewings for her bungalow this afternoon. Apparently the estate agent was optimistic, even in this market. Also, the brass plate had arrived. Maura said she'd take it to the site tomorrow and tell the builders to fix it on the wall by the front door. *The Johnny Buckley Building*. Maura thought it was a nice touch. Fiona smiled into the receiver. It had been the Sheikh's idea – part of his offer to rebuild her business – but she had to admit it was a nice way to remember Johnny.

Sergeant O'Dowd had been kind enough to give her the *Endgame* DVD, saying it wouldn't be needed to prosecute Pat. "This way," O'Dowd had told her, with a wink, "if McCormack's lawyer tries to get hold of it, the gardai can honestly say it's been misplaced."

Fiona had ceremoniously burned it. That way people could remember Johnny for the jockey he was, not the thing he became.

She drove home to Trelawn Park Stud, waddled over to her makeshift desk and looked at the press schedule. She would announce her new tests tomorrow, along with the saliva-reading machine. That would cause a stir and pay the bills while she turned her attention to more important matters.

She stared at the two thick files entitled *Nutrigenomics* and *Epigenetics*. Beside them lay a science journal open at an article about a new gene-editing technology called CRISPR. The future of horses *and* humans. Johnny had been right about that.

Fiona caressed her belly. Felt a stirring. This research would be as much for her child as for her business.

The End

Author's Note

The science of epigenetics (how our environment – through our daily lives – influences our genes) is advancing rapidly. Although the big picture is not yet fully understood, there is mounting evidence which suggests that our genetic code can be influenced far more easily and quickly than previously assumed.

Nutrigenomics is a term used to describe how nutrients interact, directly or indirectly, with a genome to influence how genes are expressed and how those nutrients can impact health, disease, and even athletic performance.

All science-based information in this novel is correct, or was at the time of writing.

However, as far as the author is aware, nobody has tried to study and hasten the epigenetic effect by knowingly polluting a group of horses (or humans).

Acknowledgements

Dr.Ross Williamson BVsc MRCVS for discussion and advice about equine nutrition, epigenetics and raising the equine athlete.

Dawn and Caroline for feedback and reading early rough drafts.

Peter for all his patience and help.

Tara for medical advice.

Michelle for giving me insight into the practicalities of daily life in a wheelchair.

Paula and Gaye and everyone else at Poolbeg for transforming my manuscript into a finished article.

Printed in Great Britain
by Amazon